Data Protection and Data Transfers Law: UK Data Transfer Streams, Laws, and Rules

Data Protection and Data Transfers Law: UK Data Transfer Streams, Laws, and Rules

Dr Paul Lambert

BA, LLB, LLM, TMA, CTMA, Qualified Lawyer, CDPO, PhD, Consultant
Visiting Professor, Manchester Metropolitan University
Visiting Research Fellow, Institute of Advanced Legal Studies, University of London

Bloomsbury Professional

LONDON • DUBLIN • EDINBURGH • NEW YORK • NEW DELHI • SYDNEY

BLOOMSBURY PROFESSIONAL

Bloomsbury Publishing Plc
50 Bedford Square, London, WC1B 3DP, UK
1385 Broadway, New York, NY 10018, USA
29 Earlsfort Terrace, Dublin 2, Ireland

BLOOMSBURY and the Diana logo are trademarks of Bloomsbury Publishing Plc

British Library Cataloguing-in-Publication Data

A catalogue record for this book is available from the British Library.

ISBN:	HB:	978-1-52652-484-3
	ePDF:	978-1-52652-482-9
	ePub:	978-1-52652-483-6

Typeset by Evolution Design & Digital Ltd (Kent)
Printed and bound by CPI Group (UK) Ltd, Croydon, CRO 4YY

To find out more about our authors and books visit www.bloomsburyprofessional.com. Here
you will find extracts, author information, details of forthcoming events and the option to
sign up for our newsletters

Dedication

For Theresa and Walter

Abbreviations

DPP:	data protection and privacy
Personal data:	data relating to an individual, or individual data subject as referred to in data protection laws[1]
Data subject:	the individual the subject of personal data[2]
Controller:	the entity holding (and or collecting, using, processing and storing) personal data relating to a data subject[3]
Processor:	an outsource entity acting for and on behalf of a main controller entity and which may receive or otherwise processor personal data for the controller[4]
GDPR:	General Data Protection Regulation[5]
DPD 95/46:	the data protection law in the EU before the GDPR, namely, the Data Protection Directive 1995.[6] Now replaced by the GDPR.
DPA:	Data Protection Act
DPA 18:	Data Protection Act 2018
EUWA:	European Union (Withdrawal) Act
CCPA:	California Consumer Privacy Act

1 The GDPR contains a definition of 'personal data' which is defined to mean 'any information relating to an identified or identifiable natural person ("data subject"); an identifiable natural person is one who can be identified, directly or indirectly, in particular by reference to an identifier such as a name, an identification number, location data, an online identifier or to one or more factors specific to the physical, physiological, genetic, mental, economic, cultural or social identity of that natural person.' See GDPR, Art 4(1).
2 The GDPR contains a definition of 'data subject' which is defined to mean 'an identified or identifiable natural person ("data subject").' See GDPR, Art 4(1).
3 The GDPR contains a definition of 'controller' which is defined to mean 'the natural or legal person, public authority, agency or other body which, alone or jointly with others, determines the purposes and means of the processing of personal data; where the purposes and means of such processing are determined by Union or Member State law, the controller or the specific criteria for its nomination may be provided for by Union or Member State law.' See GDPR, Art 4(7).
4 The GDPR contains a definition of 'processor' which is defined to mean 'a natural or legal person, public authority, agency or other body which processes personal data on behalf of the controller.' See GDPR, Art 4(8).
5 Regulation (EU) 2016/679 of the European Parliament and of the Council of 27 April 2016 on the protection of natural persons with regard to the processing of personal data and on the free movement of such data, and repealing Directive 95/46/EC (General Data Protection Regulation) (Text with EEA relevance). [2016] OJ L119, 1–88.
6 Directive 95/46/EC of the European Parliament and of the Council of 24 October 1995 on the protection of individuals with regard to the processing of personal data and on the free movement of such data. [1995] OJ L281, 31–50.

ICO:	Information Commissioners Office (the UK data protection supervisory authority)
DPC:	Data Protection Commission; Data Protection Commissioner
Commission:	EU Commission
FTC:	Federal Trade Commission
CJEU:	Court of Justice of the European Union
ECJ:	the previous name for the CJEU
EDPS:	European Data Protection Supervisor
EDPB:	European Data Protection Board
WP29:	Article 29 Working Party (now replaced by the EDPB)

Contents

Part C: Laws

Table of Statutes

Table of Statutory Instruments

Table of European Legislation

PART A

INTRODUCTION

CHAPTER 1

Introduction

INTRODUCTION

1.01   Even small organisations now seek to trade internationally with customers from many different countries. This often involves the collection (and hence transfer) of personal data across borders. Organisations are also under ever increasing pressure to reduce costs. This can sometimes involve consideration of outsourcing to countries outside of the jurisdiction. Any international transfers of personal data, unless specifically exempted, are however regulated.[1] In addition, the global nature of commercial activities means that organisations as part of normal business processes may seek to transfer particular sets of personal data to group entities whom may be located outside of the jurisdiction. Frequently organisations would have transferred personal data to other sections within their international organisation, such as banks. This could be personal data in relation to customers as well as employees (eg, where the personnel or payroll section may be in a different country). There can be similar situations where an organisation wishes to make cross border data flows to agents, partners or outsourced processors.

The data protection regime controls and regulates the transfers of personal data[2] from the UK to jurisdictions outside of the jurisdiction. The transfer of personal data outside of the jurisdiction are variously known as transfers, data transfers, data flows, trans border data flows (TBDFs), and cross border transfers.[3] (The book will, in general, refer to data transfers). There is the default ban on data transfers.

This trend of data transfers across borders has increased, however, as more and more activity is carried out online, such as eCommerce and social media. Personal data is frequently transferred or mirrored on computer servers in more than one country as a matter of apparent technical routine. However, organisations need

---

1   Data transfers within jurisdiction, while not addressed in this publication, are no less important issues to be considered by companies and organisations as they are regulated under the data protection regime.

2   See Nugter, *Transborder Flow of Personal Data within the EC* (Kluwer Law and Taxation Publishers, 1990).

3   Beling, 'Transborder Data Flows: International Privacy Protection and the Free Flow of Information' (1983) 6 *Boston College International and Comparative Law Review* 591–624; 'Declaration on Transborder Data Flows' (1985) 24 *International Legal Materials* 912–913; 'Council Recommendation Concerning Guidelines Governing the Protection of Privacy and Transborder Flows of Personal Data' (1981) 20 *International Legal Materials* 422–450; 'Draft Recommendation of the Council Concerning Guidelines the Protection of Privacy and Transborder Flows of Personal Data' (1980) 19 *International Legal Materials* 318–324.

to be aware that any transfer of personal data of UK and EU citizens needs to be in compliance with the data protection regime. One of the obligations is that transfers of personal data may not occur.[4] At least not automatically. This default position can be derogated from if one of a limited fixed number of channel criteria are satisfied. If none of the channel option criteria apply, the default position in the data protection regime rules govern such that the transfer cannot take place.

Data transfers are a very important area of data protection law and practice. Data transfers are relied on as an essential function of national and international trade, business, and even internet use. It is essential for practitioners to keep abreast of the new data transfer rules and changes for their clients. Yet, data transfers are becoming increasingly complex – especially in the UK. Getting data transfer compliance wrong can be costly in terms of data fines, orders, and even a need to delete certain data.

As a result of Brexit, GDPR, UK GDPR, the Consultation, data law changes, and new UK created model contracts for data transfers, the UK now has to consider the advent of a range of new data transfer streams and lawful transfer channels which apply to the UK. These UK data streams are a multiple of those that applied previously in the EU, and are more complex than the EU-only rules and streams.

UK corporates need to understand the new data streams. Legal professionals need to understand the new data streams as they need to be able to advise their clients who wish to continue using personal data and collecting or transferring such data across international borders. Different data rules will apply depending on which data stream is involved. What the data is, where it flows from, and where it flows to are all critically important aspects.

Such understanding (and practices) will be further complicated as many companies may find themselves in more than one data stream. Separate rules must be complied with.

Data transfers are quite commercial in focus, and as such have generated significant cases and policy changes as regards what data and data protection rules should apply. Added data streams mean that this area of data protection in the UK may become the most complex.

There is significant emphasise on data transfer rules, but also channel tools such as special contracts. There is now research into additional tools at a UN level.

This is an important area for lawyers and companies, but is complex and is also difficult especially when rules change or are invalidated. One theme of modern data transfer rules is that the rules are challenged as being invalid or partially invalid. Yet, they are also extremely necessary to try and give legal and business certainty.

---

4   For one article noting the difficulties that the data protection regime creates in terms of trans border data flows, see Kong, 'Data Protection and Trans Border Data Flow in the European and Global Context' (2010) 21 *European Journal of International Law* 441–456.

The EU just permitted certain EU to UK data transfers via a formal adequacy decision in the summer of 2021. Great debate centres on whether this will be attacked before data regulators and or courts, and also on whether the UK will breach it. The consequences of a breach would be important, as it may call into question whether the transfers from the EU to the UK could continue.

There are proposed new UK created model contracts for companies to follow when dealing with UK-international data transfers. Lawyers and companies, and international companies, need to also be familiar with the new EU Standard Contracts for EU – UK/EU-international data transfers; and the new UK contract aimed at enabling data transfers.

Data transfers are an increasingly complex area of data protection law, and particularly from the UK perspective which has many additional wrinkles separate from the EU. Readers must refer to various issues, such as the *Schrems 1* and *Schrems 2* cases, multinationals, controllers, processors, outsourcing, data contracting process, adequacy, more rules, etc.

The whole area of data transfers (under data protection legal rules) is one of the most discussed areas. It was the area which needed the recent EU adequacy decision.

The UN is also getting involved in data transfer rule research.[5]

Privacy enhancing technologies (PETs) generally refers to privacy enhancing technologies or tools. This is an interesting development which shows that data transfers are recognised as a thorny issue in data protection and have created difficulties for international commercial data transfers, legality, business, policy, and politics, for some time now. There is arguably no greater evidence of this than the changes in the EU-US data transfer space, from the Safe Harbour, to Privacy Shield, and to the new Data Privacy Framework.

Up to now, all professionals had to think of was how to follow EU data transfer rules. Brexit, new adequacy decisions, new standard contracts, forthcoming UK contracts, and now the Consultation on future laws, change all of that. There is now more than one set of transfer rules to comply with. Professionals now have to think about the separate data streams, where the data is coming from, where it is going, and identify the specific rules for that specific stream. The professions need to be on top of the increasingly complex needs of being able to engage in lawful data transfers in the UK given the new distinct data streams and additional related developments. The book addresses a resource gap and brings the different streams of the transfer landscape together and outlines the separate legal rules all in one accessible place. Data transfers is such an important and growing core data protection issue, and Brexit creates more separate data streams and data channels to consider, each with different implications.

---

5   See: 'UN Launches Privacy Lab Pilot to Unlock Cross-Border Data Sharing Benefits' *Information-age.com*, 25 January 2022.

It should also be pointed out as a caveat that this text relates to commercial data protection and data transfer issues, and as such steers away from issues of data retention and law enforcement collection, access and transfers.[6] It may be implied, but it is worth clarifying also that this text refers to international transfers of personal data. There may well be other data protection, legal and compliance issues to consider when one company seeks to transfer personal data to another company within the same jurisdiction. Just because there may be no international cross border element involved, does not in any way mean that data rules do not apply, and which must me complied with.[7]

Examples of some of the recent changes to data protection and data transfer rules include:

* Brexit changes;

* new Data Protection Act;

* new UK GDPR;

* new proposed Data Protection and Digital Information Bill;

* EU new updated standard contracts;

* new proposed UK standard contracts;

* UK data law Consultation;

* UK data law changes;

* EU UK adequacy decision for data transfers to UK;

* EU caselaw changes;

* General Data Protection Regulation (GDPR) changes.

There will be a constant need to pay attention to the ongoing changes in this area of data protection in the UK. The general issue of UK data transfers is timely, very important commercially and legally, and comes at a time of multiple changes.

---

6   There is an extensive separate literature and indeed extensive caselaw dealing with data retention and law enforcement aspects of data. For example, Drechsler, 'European Union EDPB Issues Guidance on Personal Data Transfers Based on Adequacy Decisions in the Context of the Law Enforcement Directive' (2012) 7(2) *European Data Protection Law Review* 221; Rubinstein and Margulies, 'Risk and Rights in Transatlantic Data Transfers: EU Privacy Law, U.S. Surveillance, and the Search for Common Ground' (2022) 54(2) *Connecticut Law Review* 391; Drechsler, 'EDPB Issues Guidance on Personal Data Transfers Based on Adequacy Decisions in the Context of the Law Enforcement Directive' (2022) 7(2) *European Data Protection Law Review* (EDPL) 221; Rubinstein and Margulies, 'EU Privacy Law and U.S. Surveillance: Solving the Problem of Transatlantic Data Transfers' [2020] *Horizons: Journal of International Relations and Sustainable Development* 58.
7   For wider commentary on the data protection regime and its associated processing rules, see Lambert, *A Users Guide to Data Protection* (Bloomsbury, 2023).

PART B

DATA STREAMS

CHAPTER 2

EU-UK Data Transfer Steam

Data Flow Key	
Stream:	Data Stream 1
Data flow:	EU to UK
Origin:	EU
Destination:	UK
Data type:	EU data

DATA STREAM I

2.01   This refers to the data stream of personal data which originates in the EU and is sent to the UK for processing or commercial activities. It proved to be a topical issue in terms of Brexit. The central part of the problem was the question of whether EU data would continue to be permitted to be sent to the UK after Brexit. Part of this related to what overall deal would be agreed between the UK and the EU to facilitate Brexit. While any such deal would naturally be widely encompassing given a monumental variety of issues which would need to be encompassed within it, arguably one of the most important issues for the UK would be that the UK legal environment would be agreed or otherwise deemed sufficient to be a recipient of EU citizens' personal data.

transfer of EU data

Stream 1

This was far from certain. That presented a significant and vexing headache for industry. Industry likes certainty. Companies need to have as much confidence as possible that their current practices are lawful and can continue into the future. The City financial sector, the tech sector, and many other sectors are heavily engaged in providing services and products to the EU market, and which relies on the continued receipt and use of EU personal data being transferred into the UK.

Without getting into the machinations, negotiations, and small texts of Brexit-focused agreements between the UK and EU, the wider UK business sector wished to be assured that Brexit would not present a roadblock to the continuance of the EU to UK data stream it needed for continued business activities.

Unfortunately, without an agreement or some other mechanism, that was a real and present danger. This resulted from the UK automatically becoming a so called outside third country. The new rules would mean that the UK would automatically be deemed as having lessor standards of data protections than applied in the EU as a result of EU data laws. How would UK business and policymakers deal with such a hard stop to the EU-UK data transfers resulting from Brexit? As Brexit came closer and closer, and even as a series of extensions arose, this data transfer conundrum would keep many people awake at night.

Ultimately a solution was reached. But it was not the Plan A solution preferred by the UK, nor the Plan B also pursued by the UK. Plan A was to include a provision in the Brexit agreement that would expressly permit EU-UK data transfers. Plan B was to have in place a decision under the EU's adequacy decision regime to kick in immediately on/after Brexit day (whereby a third-party country located outside of the EU is deemed by an official review process to have laws and standards in place which are equivalent to the EU data protection regime). This did not occur either.

An interesting issue under the EU adequacy decision regime is whether an application by a country to the EU for consideration of being deemed adequate as provided for under EU data laws can commence while still technically being a EU Member State – albeit a leaving one. Plan B above suggests that UK politicians at least hoped that it would be so possible. It did not occur in practice, however.

EU-UK DATA TRANSFER STREAM

2.02   While there is a backdrop of a complicated Brexit process period of negotiations, interim deals, and extensions, UK businesses and advisers must still consider and assess their situation as it may fall under the EU to UK data transfer stream. (There is, however, an extended official literature and wider commentary for those interested in this specific earlier time period).

Post Brexit, many indigenous UK businesses and wider international businesses located in the UK (of which there are many) need to identify if they are or wish to engage with the EU-UK data stream.

If so, it is then necessary to assess whether this is permitted under the relevant data protection rules. Organisations will need to do this to ensure that they are acting lawfully themselves.

Separate to the above, organisations should expect that counterparty entities located in the EU may wish to direct questions to the UK entity to ensure and to satisfy itself that the UK entity to whom it may intend to send EU citizen personal data is data protection complaint (both from a UK and EU perspective) and more specifically that the intended data transfer is legally permissible.

The EU entity may wish to have these assurances from the UK entity, and separately also in terms of making its own assessment, it may need certain information or inputs to come from the UK entity, ie, inputs which would be only within the direct knowledge of the UK entity and not the intended transferring entity in the EU.

ADEQUACY FOR EU-UK DATA STREAM

2.03   The EU agreed to an adequacy decision such as to permit data transfers to continue from the EU to the UK. This occurred on 28 June 2021. This is very important as is applies countrywide and not just to individual companies. It is important for business to assess how to ensure adherence. It will also be necessary for entities to consider how the government may put this adequacy in jeopardy.

The official EU Adequacy Decision[1] for the UK states that the following decision has been made by the Commission, namely:

'For the purposes of Article 45 of Regulation (EU) 2016/679, the United Kingdom ensures an adequate level of protection for personal data transferred within the scope of Regulation (EU) 2016/679 from the European Union to the United Kingdom.'[2]

There is also a provision referring to ongoing monitoring to ensure that the UK maintains compliance. It states that:

'The Commission shall continuously monitor the application of the legal framework upon which this Decision is based, including the conditions under which onward transfers are carried out, individual rights are exercised and United Kingdom public authorities have access to data transferred on the basis of this Decision, with a view to assessing whether the United Kingdom continues to ensure an adequate level of protection within the meaning of Article 1.'[3]

If there is non compliance, the Commission may 'may suspend, repeal or amend this Decision'.[4] In addition, 'The Commission may suspend, repeal or amend this Decision if the lack of cooperation of the United Kingdom government prevents the Commission from determining whether the finding in Article 1(1) is affected.'[5]

---

1   Commission Implementing Decision of 28.6.2021 pursuant to Regulation (EU) 2016/679 of the European Parliament and of the Council on the adequate protection of personal data by the United Kingdom, Brussels, 28.6.2021, C(2021) 4800 final.
2   Ibid, Art 1(1).
3   Ibid, Art 2(1).
4   Ibid, Art 3(4).
5   Ibid, Art 3(5).

The UK adequacy decision also has an expiry date. So, changes can be made in the interim can be reviewed in terms of there being continued compliance and equivalency between UK laws and UK laws. It is provided that:

> 'This Decision shall expire on 27 June 2025, unless extended in accordance with the procedure referred to in Article 93(2) of Regulation (EU) 2016/679.'[6]

DCMS

2.04 The Department for Digital, Culture, Media & Sport (DCMS) issued commentary on and announced the new Adequacy Decision.[7] It stated that the 'European Union (EU) has formally recognised the UK's high data protection standards after more than a year of constructive talks' and that '[t]his will allow the continued seamless flow of personal data from the EU to the UK.'[8]

The Department states that '[p]ersonal data can continue to flow freely between Europe and the UK following agreement by the European Union to adopt 'data adequacy' decisions.'[9]

Officially, the 'government welcomes the move, which rightly recognises the country's high data protection standards. Formal adoption of the decisions under the EU General Data Protection Regulation (GDPR) and Law Enforcement Directive (LED) allows personal data to flow freely from the EU and wider European Economic Area (EEA) to the UK. The decisions mean that UK businesses and organisations can continue to receive personal data from the EU and EEA without having to put additional arrangements in place with European counterparts.'[10]

It is indicated that '[t]his free flow of personal data supports trade, innovation and investment, assists with law enforcement agencies tackling crime, and supports the delivery of critical public services sharing personal data as well as facilitating health and scientific research.'[11]

If examined more critically, the statements following may portent some contention and potential trouble for the just announced adequacy decision. The following statements are made, namely:

> 'The UK, which now operates a *fully independent* data policy, has already recognised the EU and EEA member states as "adequate", as part of its

---

6   Ibid, Art 4.
7   'EU Adopts "Adequacy" Decisions Allowing Data to Continue Flowing Freely to the UK," *Press Release*, Department for Digital, Culture, Media & Sport, 28 June 2021; *Decision on the Adequate Protection of Personal Data by the United Kingdom – General Data Protection Regulation*, EU Commission, 28 June 2021.
8   Ibid.
9   Ibid.
10 Ibid.
11 Ibid.

commitment to establish a smooth transition for the UK's departure from the bloc.

The government plans to promote the *free flow of personal data globally and across borders*, including through ambitious new trade deals and through new data adequacy agreements with some of the fastest growing economies, while ensuring people's data continues to be protected to a high standard.'[12] (Emphasis added).

The statement also indicates an apparent indication to lean to industry over rights, or a balance between industry and rights, when it states '[a]ll future decisions will be based on what maximises innovation and keeps up with evolving tech. As such, the government's approach will seek to minimise burdens on organisations seeking to use data to tackle some of the most pressing global issues, including climate change and the prevention of disease.'[13]

The DCMS also refers to a number of statements made by interested parties, which are contained in the announcement. The respective statements are as follows.

The Secretary of State for Digital Oliver Dowden said:

'After more than a year of constructive talks it is right the European Union has formally recognised the UK's high data protection standards.

This will be welcome news to businesses, support continued cooperation between the UK and the EU and help law enforcement authorities keep people safe.

We will now focus on unlocking the power of data to drive innovation and boost the economy while making sure we protect people's safety and privacy.'[14]

John Foster, the CBI Director of Policy said:

'This breakthrough in the EU – UK adequacy decision will be welcomed by businesses across the country.

The free flow of data is the bedrock of the modern economy and essential for firms across all sectors– from automotive to logistics – playing an important role in everyday trade of goods and services.

This positive step will help us move forward as we develop a new trading relationship with the EU.'[15]

Julian David, techUK CEO, said:

'Securing an EU-UK adequacy decision has been a top priority for techUK and the wider tech industry since the day after the 2016 referendum. The

---

12 Ibid.
13 Ibid.
14 Ibid.
15 Ibid.

decision that the UK's data protection regime offers an equivalent level of protection to the EU GDPR is a vote of confidence in the UK's high data protection standards and is of vital importance to UK – EU trade as the free flow of data is essential to all business sectors.

The data adequacy decision also provides a basis for the UK and EU to work together on global routes for the free flow of data with trust, building on the G7 Digital and Technology declaration and possibly unlocking €2 trillion of growth.

The UK must also now move to complete the development of its own international data transfer regime in order to allow companies in the UK not just to exchange data with the EU, but also to be able to access opportunities across the world.'[16]

Example

2.05 Let us consider an example with a UK manufacturer of bikes (UK Bikes). It markets and sells bikes over the internet. One of its markets is the EU consumer market where it, amongst other things, seeks to sell directly to EU-based customers on its website. When it is selling to customers in Belgium, for example, it is collecting personal data (including financial data) from the EU, and such data is transferred to the UK. The company may also have a reseller based in Brussels selling its bikes. This reseller is collecting and transferring personal data on these purchasers, eg, payment data, address data, deliver data (eg, the UK company is fulfilling the orders from the UK). The company will need to consider the new EU-UK adequacy decision, and may also look to terms, contracts, etc.

16 Ibid.

CHAPTER 3

UK-International Data Transfer Stream

Data Flow Key	
Stream:	Data Stream 2
Data flow:	UK to international
Origin:	UK
Destination:	International
Data type:	EU data

DATA STREAM 2

3.01   Organisational recipients of EU data cannot solely think of the EU-UK data stream of EU data needed for their business activities. While, depending on the circumstances, the EU-UK data stream may be lawful, there may be an additional data stream to consider when dealing with the same data.

UK ➡ International

transfer of EU data

Stream 2

There may be business circumstances where the UK company seeks to transfer-on the same EU data to some international jurisdictional outside of the UK. Such data may be in the same state as it was originally received from the EU. Alternatively, there may be some add-on processing or other use activities which work with the original data and may incorporate it, enhance it, expand it, or some other value-added activity. There may be some new second database created or involved which incorporates a new or updated version of the original EU data. Business activities may arise where the company would like to transfer-on the original data or the enhanced data (each incorporating EU data) to a related company in another international jurisdiction. This is the *UK-international data stream*, involving data derived and received from the EU.

The question arises, therefore, as to whether these proposed UK-international data stream transfers are lawful and permitted. This is an important issue to be considered.

Companies must identity whether there are any potential UK-international data stream transfers. Where these are identified, it is then necessary to determine if they are lawful and permissible. Specifically, the company must identify under what basis these transfers would be permitted under the data protection rules.

Obviously, part of this activity requires assessment for permissibility and lawfulness of this data stream under UK data protection rules.

However, that may not be the end of the matter. Given that the data in this instance originates from the EU, it may be necessary to consider whether there are any issues that present themselves as they may impact this onward transfer of the data to outside of the UK. It may be permitted to transfer it into the UK, but that does not in and of itself mean that it is automatically permitted to then make onward transfers.

Example

3.02 UK Bikes has a related company in a third-party country. It may also have some of its product lines manufactured in third party countries as opposed to other products which are manufactured in the UK. The company may decide that it wishes to send customer data for these product lines direct to the sister company or whatever entity is doing the manufacturing hoping that the products may be sent directly from the third-party locations. However, where some of these customers are EU customers and thus involve EU data, while it may be permissible for the data to be sent to the UK, it may not be permissible to pass this data from the UK to third countries.

CHAPTER 4

UK-EU Data Transfer Steam

Data Flow Key	
Stream:	Data Stream 3
Data flow:	UK to EU
Origin:	UK
Destination:	EU
Data type:	EU data

DATA STREAM 3

4.01 Business activities are not aways linear. Data flows and business transactions are not merely one directional. Of course, the UK economy and the EU economy are linked on many levels. UK businesses – especially in the financial and technology sectors – engage in significant levels of EU-UK data stream transfers. Some of the issues involved are referred to above, in Chapter 12 and below in Part C.

UK ⟹ EU

transfer of EU data

Stream 3

In the real world of frenetic business transactions, data can flow two ways, back and forth. This can flow and repeat in an almost endless cycle. So while there are EU-UK data transfers of EU personal data, some of this same data may also be returned to the EU in a UK-EU data transfer stream.

While at least intuitively, many may perceive fewer potential issues with EU data being transferred back into the EU, it is still important for entities to identify this as a separate data stream flow. At least then it is possible to assess what further diligence is required under data law rules.

Example

4.02 UK Bikes may seek to fulfil an order in the EU by sending details of intended deliveries to a warehouse in the EU. It ships advance batches of bikes to the warehouse so that they are available closer to the customer and to speed up delivery. As part of this process, it may be sending (ie transferring) received EU customer data back into the EU.

17

CHAPTER 5

UK-EU Data Transfer Stream

Data Flow Key	
Stream:	Data Stream 4
Data flow:	UK to EU
Origin:	UK
Destination:	EU
Data type:	UK data

DATA STREAM 4

5.01   Naturally UK businesses wish to trade with the large EU marketplace. As part of these activities there may be cause to send UK personal data to entities in the EU. These can be referred to as Stream 4 or the data stream of UK personal data being transferred to the EU.

UK ➡ EU

transfer of UK data

Stream 4

UK business will need to assess the legal basis and circumstances under which these Stream 4 data transfers may legally occur.

Separate to the above transfers by UK companies, there may also be examples of EU companies dealing directly with UK consumers obviating any direct engagement with UK-based companies. These EU companies will themselves need to look at the nature of the legal relationships and how these data collections and data transfers may be considered under the UK and EU data protection regimes.

Example

5.02   UK Bikes may have some of its products manufactured in China, and these are delivered in bulk to a warehouse in Belgium after being shipped from China to Rotterdam. It may be that these product lines are sent from the warehouse direct to customers. The company may seek to send UK customer data to the warehouse in the EU to then forward the product to each UK customer. Perhaps the company is more economical and efficient as there may be more sales for particular product lines in the EU than there are in the UK. In this instance, the company needs to consider UK data protection rules as UK personal data is being transferred outside of the UK. As there is similarity between UK and EU data laws (and a shared history in relation to data laws), this may be an easier data transfer as opposed to a non-EU third country. Diligence is still required, however.

CHAPTER 6

UK-International Data Transfer Steam

Data Flow Key	
Stream:	Data Stream 5
Data flow:	UK to international
Origin:	UK
Destination:	International
Data type:	UK data

DATA STREAM 5

6.01 Many UK businesses will be dealing with a data stream which does not involve any EU originating personal data at all. They will be dealing with the personal data of UK citizens. On some occasions this data will remain in the UK and local data law rules will apply.

UK ➡ International

transfer of UK data

Stream 5

In other situations, the UK companies may wish to send such UK personal data abroad to specified international locations (other than the EU). These Stream 5 data transfers will need to be assessed under the UK data protection rules in order to see if they are permissible, and also what conditions may need to be complied with.

Example

6.02 For certain product lines the company may consider that it is more streamlined and economic if it tries to fulfil UK orders directly from a factory in China (at least for those product lines). The question then arises as to whether it is permissible under UK data protection law to send UK customer data to China. This may not be permitted as envisaged. Similar queries will also arise in relation to other third-party countries. A further problem is discovered which will alarm the DPO in the company. The fulfilment department thinks it is easier to allow a third-party factory in China to get log in access to the full purchase and fulfillment system for all products. This raises many alerts. The first is on data transfers. Another is regarding a third-party company. The factory is also getting access to all the customers' files, not just customers of the specific products it manufactures. In addition, it can see payment and bank details, not just product purchased and delivery destination. Many problems arise to be considered.

CHAPTER 7

US-UK Data Transfer Stream

Data Flow Key	
Stream:	Data Stream 6
Data flow:	US to UK
Origin:	US
Destination:	UK
Data type:	US data

DATA STREAM 6

7.01   While it is clear that there are a large number of data flows under data stream 5 (above), given the importance attached to US-UK relations and US-UK trade interactions it is reasonable to consider data flows from the US to the UK as a separate data stream. This is in terms of the data of US citizens. Unlike some of the other data flows, this is a data flow into the UK.

US ➡ UK

transfer of US data

Stream 6

While there are UK data law considerations, there will clearly also be US data law considerations. In addition, these US data law considerations can be twofold, in terms of US federal data laws, and also US state law(s) in terms of the specific US state(s) in which the individuals in question reside.

These assessments may become more complicated if there are a large number of individuals involved in different US states. Each local state data law may need to be considered as well as the US federal data law.

Example

7.02   UK Bikes may have US-based customers. The company will need to assess if there are any requirements or restrictions in the US which may restrict these data transfers, or impose some other obligations. Unfortunately,

23

the company may have to consider both US federal law issues as well as the law of the particular state in which each US customer is based. The company may well have provided on its website that UK law, including UK data protection laws, will apply. This does not obviate the need to consider local US issues.

CHAPTER 8

UK-US Data Transfer Stream

Data Flow Key	
Stream:	Data Stream 7
Data flow:	UK to US
Origin:	UK
Destination:	US
Data type:	UK data

DATA STREAM 7

8.01   The UK has significant business relations and business transactions with the US. While there is consideration of data flows from the UK to international jurisdictions under Stream 5 above, the significance of relations and data flows with the US ensure that it is reasonable to also consider the data flows from the UK to the US individually, as regards UK citizens' personal data.

transfer of UK data

Stream 7

Example

8.02   UK Bikes may sell other products in addition to its bikes. One of these may be bike lights, which are made by a company in the US which the company partners with. So, when a UK customer orders a particular light, the purchase details may be sent to the US and the US company will directly send the light to the customer in the UK. It is important for the UK company to assess on what legal basis it is justified in transferring UK customer personal data to the company in the US. The company will need to assess the new UK model contract options. While the EU has only recently agreed a new EU-US Data Privacy Framework, a formal EU decision must follow, which may carry into 2023. There is as yet no equivalent with the UK-US Data Privacy Framework which the US company has signed up to. Careful analysis will be needed.

CHAPTER 9

International-UK Data Transfer Stream

Data Flow Key	
Stream:	Data Stream 8
Data flow:	International to UK
Origin:	International
Destination:	UK
Data type:	International data

DATA STREAM 8

9.01 The government is making a number of comments post Brexit in relation to how it wishes to foster more international trade relations, and expressly those involving data and data transfers. It is professed that official policy wishes to facilitate as best as possible the use and transfer of data. The UK is even intending to be an international data hub for commerce and for research regarding data. This will involve numerous changes to UK data protection rules.

One of the earliest such new post Brexit deals was with Japan. However, an initial assessment appears to have discovered that not as much new trade resulted between the parties as was initially hoped for. While official sources do not get into this level of detail, if the level of trade is down, it is also possible that the level of data transfers might also be down. That could mean that, at least in this instance or at least in the early stages, there is not as much data stream 8 international data coming to the UK. As a general comment, there have also been some recent polling suggesting that popularity for Brexit is dipping. No doubt, however, this data stream will be an area that will require monitoring as developments and trade continue.

International ➡️ UK

transfer of international data

Stream 8

As such the current and proposed UK data protection rules need to be assessed.

In addition and to the extent that foreign personal data may be coming to the UK, it needs to be considered how such data transfers under this data stream may be impacted on, permitted, and/or prohibited by foreign data law rules. This will apply to each potential data sender/transferer jurisdiction to the UK.

Example

9.02 UK Bikes may sell other products to customers internationally other than to the US and EU. It may be necessary to assess each of these third-party countries individually as to whether data laws exist, and what rules they may apply on the transfer of their citizens' data to the UK. In addition, the company may have to consider where fulfilment deliveries may be sent from in the event that these are from locations other than the UK itself.

CHAPTER 10

International-UK-International Data Transfer Stream

Data Flow Key	
Stream:	Data Stream 9
Data flow:	UK to international
Origin:	UK
Destination:	International
Data type:	International data

DATA STREAM 9

10.01   Under this data stream we are looking at internationally originating data which makes its way to the UK, and is then subsequently sent from the UK to an international destination. This is data stream 9. This is a good example of how an entity in the UK will need to look at not just local law, but also international laws, as each may have an impact on the data and what may and may not be permitted. The worst situation for a UK entity – and not least their data lawyers – will be a situation where one law contradicts the other. Equally, problems may arise where one of these laws may not be as express in permitting a particular activity as the parties would ideally like. Grey areas and uncertainty are unwelcome when one is seeking to approve a particular data transfer model and related business transactions.

UK   ➡   International

transfer of international data

Stream 9

Example

10.02 The UK company needs to consider a range of issues. In terms of international third countries, it needs to assess what specific countries the customers may be located in. The local data protection laws need to be understood. In addition, it needs to monitor international/UK data protection laws as to whether there is a specific agreement in place between the UK and the specific country in question. Even if there is no specific bilateral agreement, the company needs to determine if the UK and or minister and or ICO has in some way recognised particular rules for that country. Even where data originates from a particular international jurisdiction and is sent to the UK, it does not automatically mean that it can then be sent to some other third country. Greater consideration of the data flows, actual data, purposes, and jurisdictions would be required by the company.

PART C

LAWS

CHAPTER 11

Data Transfer Laws

INTRODUCTION

11.01   Organisations are ever increasing the amount of data that they collect and hold. Often, but not always, this includes personal data. Frequently, these data sets are sought to be transferred whether in whole or in part to other locations, even across borders. They can also be collected across borders. This can sometimes also involve consideration of outsourcing to countries outside of the jurisdiction. In addition, the global nature of commercial activities means that organisations as part of normal business processes may seek to transfer particular sets of personal data to group entities whom may be located outside of the jurisdiction. There can be similar situations where an organisation wishes to make cross border data transfers to agents, partners or outsourced processors. Increasingly, any transfers of personal data outside of the jurisdiction are restricted.

DEFAULT DATA TRANSFER BANS

11.02   An increasing number of data laws and data rules will apply to these intended collections, outsourcing or other data transfer activities. The data protection regime of a country will control and regulate the transfers of personal data[1] from that country to other third-party countries. The EU data protection regime, for example, regulates what, if any, data transfers of personal data may occur with EU data intended to be sent to non-EU countries (which now includes the UK). This has been the position for decades now, at least as it relates to the EU environment. Equally, UK data protection law regulates what UK personal data may or may not be sent to other countries. Other jurisdictions around the world operate on a similar basis.

The transfer of personal data outside of the jurisdiction are known as transfers, data transfers, trans border data flows (TBDFs), or cross border transfers.[2] Frequently organisations would have transferred personal data to other sections

---

1   See Nugter, *Transborder Flow of Personal Data within the EC* (Kluwer Law and Taxation Publishers, 1990).

2   Beling, 'Transborder Data Flows: International Privacy Protection and the Free Flow of Information' (1983) 6 *Boston College International and Comparative Law Review* 591–624; 'Declaration on Transborder Data Flows' (1985) 24 *International Legal Materials* 912–913; 'Council Recommendation Concerning Guidelines Governing the Protection of Privacy and Transborder Flows of Personal Data' (1981) 20 *International Legal Materials* 422–450; 'Draft Recommendation of the Council Concerning Guidelines the Protection of Privacy and Transborder Flows of Personal Data' (1980) 19 *International Legal Materials* 318–324.

within their international organisation, such as banks. This could be personal data in relation to customers as well as employees (eg, where the personnel or payroll section may be in a different country). This too is included in the data transfer restrictions, unless specifically exempted. The trend of transfers has increased, however, as more and more activity is carried out online, such as eCommerce and social media. Personal data is frequently transferred or mirrored on computer servers in more than one country as a matter of apparent technical routine.

However, organisations need to be aware that any transfer of personal data of UK and EU citizens needs to be in compliance with the data protection regime. One of the rules is that transfers of personal data may not occur.[3] This default position can be derogated from if one of a limited number of criteria are satisfied. If none of the permission criteria apply, the default position in the data protection regime applies and the transfer cannot take place.

It is important to appreciate that the default position or starting position when considering these matters is that there is often a default data transfer ban. Data transfers to outside of the given jurisdiction are restricted at the very outset. They are banned as a default position. Transfers are prohibited per se. The focus is directed upon the privacy protection elsewhere and the dangers of uncontrolled transfers of personal data. While there may be circumstances which may be satisfied which will later permit a given data transfer, this should not be assumed, and certainly will not be possible in every circumstance. One must also identify and satisfy in advance a given data transfer channel which is exempted and permitted and ensure ongoing compliance.

The Data Protection Act 1998 (DPA 1998) stated previously that 'Personal data shall not be transferred to a country or territory outside the European Economic Area [EEA] unless that country or territory ensures an adequate level of protection for the rights and freedoms of Data Subjects in relation to the processing of personal data.'

This has since been updated by the Data Protection Act 2018 and the UK GDPR. Proposals also exist for further updates in the form of the Data Protection and Digital Information Bill 2022. Section 18 of the Data Protection Act 2018, referring to transfers of personal data to third countries etc, provides that the Secretary of State may by regulations specify, for the purposes of Article 49(1)(d) of the [UK] GDPR, circumstances in which a transfer of personal data to a third country or international organisation is to be taken to be necessary for important reasons of public interest. The Secretary of State may by regulations restrict the transfer of a category of personal data to a third country or international organisation.

---

3   For one article noting the difficulties that the data protection regime creates in terms of trans border data flows, see Kong, 'Data Protection and Trans Border Data Flow in the European and Global Context' (2010) 21 *European Journal of International Law* 441–456.

ADEQUATE PROTECTION

11.03   If the recipient country has already been deemed by the UK or EU to already have an adequate level of protection for personal data, then the transfer may be permitted. However, the specific rules need to be consulted.

A transfer may occur where there has been a positive Community finding in relation to the type of transfer proposed. A decision finding refers to a finding that a country or territory outside the EU/EEA does, or does not, ensure an adequate level of protection.

Therefore, if there has been a positive decision finding in relation to a named country outside of the jurisdiction, this means that that country may be deemed to have a level of protection in its laws comparable to the UK and EU data protection regime. This then makes it possible for organisations to make transfers to that specific country, subject to data type, transfer channel option rules applicable, and the destination country.

The EU Commission provides a list of Commission decisions on the adequacy of the protection of personal data in named third countries.[4] The EU Commission has thus far recognised that the UK, Andorra, Canada (commercial organisations), Faroe Islands, Israel, Japan, Switzerland, Argentina, Guernsey, Isle of Man, Jersey, New Zealand, Uruguay, the EU-US Privacy Shield rules (if signed up and adhered to) [note however, that the Privacy Shield was invalidated in a caselaw challenge and has been replaced in 2022 by the EU-US Privacy Framework, and as a result of which a further adequacy decision finding is expected], and the transfer of air passenger name records to the United States Bureau of Customs and Border Protection (as specified) as providing adequate protection for personal data. This list will expand over time.

SAVERS

11.04   If the recipient country's protection for personal data is not adequate, or not ascertainable, but it is intended that transfers are still commercially desired, the organisation should ascertain if the transfer comes within one of the other potentially permitted categories. Transfers of personal data from the EU, for example, to outside jurisdictions cannot occur unless it falls within one of the transfer permission channels.

The permission channels from the transfer restrictions in the EU regime are (and similarly the UK to the extent that similar rules are applied in UK data law):

- the data subject has given consent;

- the transfer is necessary for performance of contract between data subject and controller;

4   At http://ec.europa.eu/justice/data-protection/international-transfers/adequacy/index_en.htm.

- the transfer is necessary for taking steps at the request of the data subject with a view to entering into a contract with the controller;

- the transfer is necessary for conclusion of a contract between controller and a person other than the data subject that is entered into at the request of the data subject and is in the interests of the data subject;

- the transfer is necessary for the performance of such a contract;

- the transfer is required or authorised under any enactment or instrument imposing international obligation on UK;

- the transfer is necessary for reasons of substantial public interest;

- the transfer is necessary for purposes of, or in connection with, legal proceedings or prospective legal proceedings;

- the transfer is necessary in order to prevent injury or damage to the health of the data subject or serious loss of or damage to the property of the data subject or otherwise to protect vital interests;

- subject to certain conditions the transfer is only part of personal data on a register established by or under an enactment;

- the transfer has been authorised by a supervisory authority where the controller adduces adequate safeguards;

- the transfer is made to a country that has been determined by the EU Commission as having 'adequate levels of [data] protection' ie a Community finding (see above);

- the transfer is made to a US entity that has signed up to the EU-US 'safe harbour' arrangements (as replaced by the new EU-US Privacy Framework);

- EU Commission contract provisions: the model contracts (the EU has set out model contracts which if incorporated into the data exporter – data importer/recipient relationship can act as an exemption thus permitting the transfer to occur.[5]

In determining whether a third country ensures an adequate level of protection, factors taken into account include:

- 'any security measures taken in respect of the data in that country or territory';

---

5   Chapter V of the GDPR refers to data transfers and transfer of personal data to third countries or international organisations. Cross border data transfers are referred to in Recitals 6, 48, 101–103, 107, 108, 110–115, 153. Transfers of personal data which are undergoing processing or are intended for processing after transfer to a third country or to an international organisation shall only take place if, subject to the other provisions of the GDPR, the conditions laid down in this Chapter are complied with by the controller and processor, including for onward transfers of personal data from the third country or an international organisation to another third country or to another international organisation. All provisions in this Chapter shall be applied in order to ensure that the level of protection of natural persons guaranteed by the GDPR is not undermined. See GDPR, Art 44.

- the transfer is necessary for obtaining legal advice or in connection with legal proceedings or prospective proceedings;

- (subject to certain conditions) it is necessary in order to prevent injury or damage to the health or property of the data subject, or in order to protect their vital interests;

- the transfer is required or authorised by law;

- the ICO has authorised the transfer where the controller has given or adduced adequate safeguards; or

- the contract relating to the transfer of the data embodies appropriate contract clauses as specified in a 'Community finding.'

Other potential permitted categories are where:

- the transfers are substantially in the public interest;

- the transfers are made in connection with any (legal) claim;

- the transfers are in the vital interests of the data subject;

- there are public protections;

- the transfer is necessary for the performance of a contract.

CONCLUSION

11.05 Data protection compliance practice for organisations means that they will have to include a compliance assessment as well as an assessment of the risks associated with transfers of personal data outside of the jurisdiction. This applies to transfers from parent to subsidiary or to a branch office in the same way as a transfer to an unrelated company or entity. However, different exemptions can apply in different scenarios.

The ICO also provides guidance in relation to various current (and ever evolving) UK data protection issues.[6]

EU organisations (including subsidiaries of UK entities) should be aware that if they wish to transfer personal data outside of the EU/EEA, that additional considerations arise and that unless there is a specific exemption, then the transfer may not be permitted. Once a transfer possibility arises, the organisation should undertake a compliance exercise to assess if the transfer can be permitted, and if so, how. Additional compliance documentation and contracts may be required.

---

6 Some examples of ICO guidance and commentary include: Assessing Adequacy; Model Contract Clauses; Binding Corporate Rules; Outsourcing; Data Protection Act; International Data Transfers; The Information Commissioner's Recommended Approach to Assessing Adequacy Including Consideration of the Issue of Contractual Solutions, Binding Corporate Rules; Brexit guidance; and even new post Brexit guidance and especially on foot of the new Data Protection Act and proposed further new data laws.

Various review processes will need to be considered. One of the questions to consider is what is a data 'transfer'? Is there a difference between a data transfer versus a data transit through one country to another? Where is the dividing line between 'data' as defined and anonymised data which may not be restricted (or as restricted)? Is there a restriction on transfers of anonymised data to the same extent? For example, perhaps certain anonymised data fall outside the definition of personal data, in which case there may be corporate benefit is seeking to filter and anonymise certain data or data sets. 'Third country' needs to be considered. Currently from the EU perspective, it includes the EU countries and EEA countries of Iceland, Norway, Liechtenstein. The EU countries are expanding over time. In addition, the list of permitted additional third countries is also expanding over time. However, as the new UK data rules develop, a 'third country' may come to mean any country other than the UK.

The increasing locations and methods by which personal data may be collected by organisations, in particular internet, communications and social media, will increasingly be scrutinised in terms of transparency, consent and compliance. Equally, cloud computing is receiving particular data protection attention. Apps are also being considered as is the developing area of the Internet of Things (IoT), metaverse, and related data protection compliance issues.

CHAPTER 12

EU Laws

INTRODUCTION

12.01 The EU data protection rules, including data transfer rules, are important for a number of reasons. These rules are provided for in the GDPR.[1] In the first instance many would consider the GDPR to be the most influential set of data rules internationally. It is legally required in the EU and is also very influential elsewhere. In addition, the EU rules need to be considered from the UK perspective because prior to Brexit these rules were also the UK rules, as the GDPR (as a formal Regulation instrument) was directly effective in the UK. Even post Brexit, the UK needs to maintain relations and trading relationships with the EU. This requires complying with EU law or equivalents when it comes to UK companies seeking to receive the personal data of EU customers.

TRANSFERS BANNED AS DEFAULT

12.02 Transfers of personal data to locations outside of the EU/EEA are prohibited per se. The focus is directed upon the privacy protections elsewhere and the dangers of uncontrolled transfers of personal data.

Chapter V of the GDPR refers to data transfers and transfer of personal data to third countries or international organisations. Data transfers are referred to in Recitals 6, 48, 101–103, 107, 108, 110–115, 153 of the GDPR.

Any transfer of personal data which are undergoing processing or are intended for processing after transfer to a third country or to an international organisation shall only take place if the conditions are complied with by the controller and processor, including for onward transfers of personal data from the third country or an international organisation to another third country or to another international organisation. All provisions must be applied in order to ensure that the level of protection of natural persons guaranteed by the GDPR are not undermined.[2]

---

1 Stoilova, 'Regulation Of International Data Transfers Under EU Data Protection Law' (2021) XIII(1) *CES Working Papers* 1; Bu-Pasha, 'Cross-Border Issues Under EU Data Protection Law With Regards To Personal Data Protection' (2017) 26(3) *Information & Communications Technology Law* 213.

2 See GDPR, Art 44. The UK Data Protection Act 1998 (DPA 1998), also following a default data transfer ban, stated previously that 'Personal data shall not be transferred to a country or territory outside the European Economic Area [EEA] unless that country or territory ensures an adequate level of protection for the rights and freedoms of Data Subjects in relation to the processing of personal data.'

Data protection compliance practice for organisations means that they will have to include a compliance assessment as well as an assessment of the risks associated with transfers of personal data outside of the jurisdiction. This applies to transfers from parent to subsidiary or to a branch office in the same way as a transfer to an unrelated company or entity. However, different transfer permission channels can apply in different scenarios.

CHANNELS TO OVERCOME BAN

12.03 Despite the default data transfer ban, there are channel mechanisms whereby certain data transfers may be permitted. These should be considered channel enabling mechanisms as opposed to outright exceptions.

The fixed list of permission channels from the transfer ban restrictions are:

- the data subject has given consent;

- the transfer is necessary for performance of contract between data subject and controller;

- the transfer is necessary for taking steps at the request of the data subject with a view to entering into a contract with the controller;

- the transfer is necessary for the conclusion of a contract between the controller and a person other than the data subject that is entered into at the request of the data subject and is in the interests of the data subject;

- the transfer is necessary for the performance of such a contract;

- the transfer is required or authorised under any enactment or instrument imposing international obligation on UK;

- the transfer is necessary for reasons of substantial public interest;

- the transfer is necessary for purposes of, or in connection with, legal proceedings or prospective legal proceedings;

- the transfer is necessary in order to prevent injury or damage to the health of the data subject or serious loss of, or damage to, the property of the data subject or otherwise to protect vital interests;

- subject to certain conditions the transfer is only part of personal data on a register established by or under an enactment;

- the transfer has been authorised by a supervisory authority where the controller adduces adequate safeguards;

- the transfer is made to a country that has been determined by the EU Commission as having 'adequate levels of [data] protection' ie a Community finding;

- the transfer is made to a US entity that has signed up to the EU-US 'Safe Harbour' arrangements (although less have signed up than originally envisaged) [Note that the Safe Harbour mechanism was challenged and had to be replaced with a Privacy Shield mechanism. This, however, was also successfully challenged. It was only replaced in late 2022 with a new EU-US Data Privacy Framework mechanism. (For further details see Chapter 17, and Schedules 9 and 10)];

- EU Commission contract provisions: the model contracts (the EU has set out model contracts which if incorporated into the data exporter – data importer/recipient relationship can act as an exemption thus permitting the transfer to occur.

Permission Channel Options
Consent
Contract
International obligation
Substantial public interest
Proceedings
Health/property/vital interests
Register
Supervisory authority authorised
Adequacy finding
EU-US Data Privacy Framework

If the recipient country's protection for personal data is not adequate, or not ascertainable, but it is intended that transfers are still commercially desired, the organisation should ascertain if the transfer comes within one of the other excepted categories. Transfers of personal data from the UK to outside of the EU/EEA jurisdiction cannot occur unless it falls within one of the transfer exemptions.

In determining whether a third country ensures an adequate level of protection factors taken into account include:

- 'any security measures taken in respect of the data in that country or territory';

- the transfer is necessary for obtaining legal advice or in connection with legal proceedings or prospective proceedings;

- (subject to certain conditions) it is necessary in order to prevent injury or damage to the health or property of the data subject, or in order to protect their vital interests;

- the transfer is required or authorised by law;

- the supervisory authority has authorised the transfer where the controller has given or adduced adequate safeguards; or

- the contract relating to the transfer of the data embodies appropriate contract clauses as specified in a 'Community finding.'

Other potential exempted categories are where:

- the transfers are substantially in the public interest;

- the transfers are made in connection with any (legal) claim;

- the transfers are in the vital interests of the data subject;

- there are public protections;

- the transfer is necessary for the performance of a contract. (This will depend on the nature of the goods or services provided under the contract. The transfer must be necessary for the benefit of the individual and not just convenient for the organisation).

CHANNEL EXAMPLES

Adequate country protection channel

12.04   One of the channels available to overcome the default data transfer ban is if there is a formal adequacy decision from the EU in favour of a specified country. If the recipient country has already been formally deemed by the EU to already have an adequate level of protection for personal data, then the transfer may be permitted.

A transfer can occur where there has been a positive Community finding in relation to the type of transfer proposed. A Community finding means a formal finding and decision that a country or territory outside the EU/EEA does, or does not, ensure an adequate level of protection. The benefit accrues to the country specifically identified, and hence to the companies or controllers within that country.

Therefore, if there has been a positive community finding in relation to a named country outside of the jurisdiction, this means that that country is deemed to have a level of protection in its laws comparable to the UK and EU data protection regime. This then makes it possible for organisations to make transfers to that specific country.

The EU Commission provides a list of Commission decisions on the adequacy of the protection of personal data in named third countries.[3] The EU Commission has thus far recognised that Andorra, Canada (commercial organisations), Faroe Islands, Israel, Japan, Switzerland, Argentina, Guernsey, Isle of Man, Jersey, New Zealand, Uruguay, the EU-US Data Privacy Framework rules (if signed up and adhered to), and the transfer of air passenger name records to the United

---

3   At http://ec.europa.eu/justice/data-protection/international-transfers/adequacy/index_en.htm.

States Bureau of Customs and Border Protection (as specified) as providing adequate protection for personal data. The UK has now been added to this list of deemed adequate counties (see Chapter 13). This list will potentially expand further over time.

12.05 A transfer of personal data to a third country or an international organisation may take place where the Commission has decided that the third country, a territory or one or more specified sectors within that third country (eg, Canada), or the international organisation in question ensures an adequate level of protection. Such transfer shall not require any specific authorisation.[4] It therefore includes organisations as well as countries.

When assessing the adequacy of the level of protection, the Commission shall, in particular, take account of the following elements:

- the rule of law, respect for human rights and fundamental freedoms, relevant legislation, both general and sectoral, including concerning public security, defence, national security and criminal law and the access of public authorities to personal data, as well as the implementation of such legislation, data protection rules, professional rules and security measures, including rules for onward transfer of personal data to another third country or international organisation, which are complied with in that country or international organisation, case law, as well as effective and enforceable data subject rights and effective administrative and judicial redress for the data subjects whose personal data are being transferred;

- the existence and effective functioning of one or more independent supervisory authorities in the third country or to which an international organisation is subject, with responsibility for ensuring and enforcing compliance with the data protection rules, including adequate enforcement powers, for assisting and advising the data subjects in exercising their rights and for co-operation with the supervisory authorities of the states; and

- the international commitments the third country or international organisation concerned has entered into, or other obligations arising from legally binding conventions or instruments as well as from its participation in multilateral or regional systems, in particular in relation to the protection of personal data.[5]

The Commission, after assessing the adequacy of the level of protection, may decide, by means of implementing act, that a third country, a territory or one or more specified sectors within a third country, or an international organisation ensures an adequate level of protection within the meaning of Article 45(3). The implementing act shall provide for a mechanism for a periodic review, at least every four years, which shall take into account all relevant developments in the third country or international organisation. The implementing act shall specify its

4   GDPR, Art 45(1).
5   Ibid, Art 45(2).

territorial and sectorial application and, where applicable, identify the supervisory authority or authorities referred to in Article 45(2)(b). The implementing act shall be adopted in accordance with the examination procedure referred to in Article 93(2).[6]

The Commission shall, on an on-going basis, monitor developments in third countries and international organisations that could affect the functioning of decisions adopted pursuant to paragraph 3 and decisions adopted on the basis of Article 25(6) of the EU Data Protection Directive 1995 (DPD).[7] This applies to the UK as well as other countries.

The Commission shall, where available information reveals, in particular following the review referred to in Article 45(3), that a third country, a territory or one or more specified sectors within a third country, or an international organisation *no longer* ensures an adequate level of protection within the meaning of Article 45(2), to the extent necessary, repeal, amend or suspend the decision referred to in Article 45(3) without retro-active effect. Those implementing acts shall be adopted in accordance with the examination procedure referred to in Article 87(2), or, in cases of extreme urgency, in accordance with the procedure referred to in Article 93(2).[8] On duly justified imperative grounds of urgency, the Commission shall adopt immediately applicable implementing acts in accordance with the procedure referred to in Article 93(3).[9] This is of particular relevance to the UK given recent and anticipated changes to the UK data protection regime (and changes to a wider set of laws). One concern is that there could be so much divergence or change away from EU equivalence that the basis of the adequacy decision might be challenged or otherwise called into question.

However, the Commission shall enter into consultations with the third country or international organisation with a view to remedying the situation giving rise to the decision made pursuant to Article 45(5).[10]

A decision pursuant to Article 45(5) is without prejudice to transfers of personal data to the third country, territory or one or more specified sectors within that third country, or the international organisation in question pursuant to Articles 46 to 49.[11]

The Commission shall publish in the Official Journal of the EU and on its website a list of those third countries, territories and specified sectors within a third country and international organisations for which it has decided that an adequate level of protection is or is no longer ensured.[12]

---

6   Ibid, Art 45(3).
7   Ibid, Art 45(4).
8   Ibid, Art 45(5).
9   Ibid, Art 45(5).
10   Ibid, Art 45(6).
11   Ibid, 45(7).
12   Ibid, 45(8).

Decisions adopted by the Commission on the basis of Article 25(6) of the DPD 1995 shall remain in force until amended, replaced or repealed by a Commission Decision adopted in accordance with Article 45(3) or (5).[13] This obviated the need for new individual measures to be introduced, and associated review processes.

UK adequacy decision

12.06 See Chapter 13 with regard to the UK and Brexit adequacy decision issues.

Consent channel

12.07 One of the possible transfer solutions is 'creating adequacy' through consent.

Obtaining consent of pre-existing customers may pose a problem so in some cases may not be possible or practical. For example, it may not be possible to retrospectively change existing contracts, consent clauses, and terms.

However, going forward it may be possible to include 'transfer' issues in any data protection compliance and related models.

The EU has recently updated its model contract precedents (see Chapters 21–23) which may be relevant to review even in the context of considering the drafting of consent processes and clauses.

Contract channel

12.08 One of the other channels relates to transfers permitted as a result of adopting the EU model contracts into the legal relationship between the data exporter and the data importer/recipient.

A permission channel relates to transfers permitted as a result of adopting the EU model contracts into the legal relationship between the data exporter and the data importer/recipient.

Transfers of data to a third country may be made even though there is no adequate protection in place in the third country, if the controller secures the necessary level of protection through contractual obligations.

These contractual protections are the model contract clauses emanating from the Commission. The Commission has issued what it considers to be adequate

13   Ibid, 45(9).

clauses which are incorporated into the contract relationship of the data exporter and data importer as then provide an adequate level of consent.

Appropriate safeguards channel

12.09   In the absence of a decision pursuant to Article 45(3), a controller or processor may transfer personal data to a third country or an international organisation only if the controller or processor has provided appropriate safeguards, and on condition that enforceable data subject rights and effective legal remedies for data subjects are available.[14]

The appropriate safeguards referred to in Article 46(1) may be provided for, without requiring any specific authorisation from a supervisory authority, by:

- a legally binding and enforceable instrument between public authorities or bodies;

- binding corporate rules in accordance with Article 47;

- standard data protection clauses adopted by the Commission in accordance with the examination procedure referred to in Article 93(2); or

- standard data protection clauses adopted by a supervisory authority and approved by the Commission pursuant to the examination procedure referred to in Article 93(2); or

- an approved code of conduct pursuant to Article 40 together with binding and enforceable commitments of the controller or processor in the third country to apply the appropriate safeguards, including as regards data subjects' rights; or

- an approved certification mechanism pursuant to Article 42 together with binding and enforceable commitments of the controller or processor in the third country to apply the appropriate safeguards, including as regards data subjects' rights.[15]

Subject to the authorisation from the competent supervisory authority, the appropriate safeguards referred to in Article 46(1) may also be provided for, in particular, by:

- contractual clauses between the controller or processor and the controller, processor or the recipient of the personal data in the third country or international organisation; or

- provisions to be inserted into administrative arrangements between public authorities or bodies which include enforceable and effective data subject rights.[16]

14   Ibid, 46(1).
15   Ibid, 46(2).
16   Ibid, 46(3).

The supervisory authority shall apply the consistency mechanism referred to in Article 63 in the cases referred to in Article 46(3) (Article 46(4)).

Authorisations by a state or supervisory authority on the basis of Article 26(2) of DPD 1995 shall remain valid until amended, replaced or repealed, if necessary, by that supervisory authority. Decisions adopted by the Commission on the basis of Article 26(4) of DPD 1995 shall remain in force until amended, replaced or repealed, if necessary, by a Commission Decision adopted in accordance with Article 46(2) (Article 42(5)).

Binding corporate rules channel

12.10 The Commission and the WP29[17] (now replaced by the EDPB) have also developed a policy of recognising adequate protection of the policies of multinational organisations transferring personal data that satisfy the determined binding corporate rules (BCR).[18] This relates to transfers internally between companies within a related group of large multinational companies. It therefore, differs from the model contract clauses above which generally relate to non-related companies, rather than group companies.

Organisations which have contracts, policies and procedure which satisfy the BCR and are so accepted as doing so *after* a review process with the Commission or one of the national data protection supervisory authorities can transfer personal data outside of the EU within the group organisation. This review process can take a considerable time (even over years), be extensive in its detail, and involve a lot of resources.

The WP29 has issued the following documents in relation to the BCRs, namely:

- Working Document on Transfers of personal data to third countries: Applying Article 26(2) of the EU Data Protection Directive to Binding Corporate Rules for International Data Transfers (WP74);

- Model Checklist, Application for approval of Binding Corporate Rules (WP102);

- Working Document setting forth a Co-Operation Procedure for Issuing Common Opinions on Adequate Safeguards Resulting from Binding Corporate Rules (WP107);

---

17 WP29, Recommendation 1/2007 on the Standard Application for Approval of Binding Corporate Rules for the Transfer of Personal Data; Working Document setting up a table with the elements and principles to be found in Binding Corporate Rules, WP 153 (2008); Working Document Setting up a framework for the structure of Binding Corporate Rules, WP154 (2008); Working Document on Frequently Asked Questions (FAQs) related to Binding Corporate Rules, WP155 (2008).
18 See http://ec.europa.eu/justice/data-protection/international-transfers/binding-corporate-rules/index_en.htm; Moerel, *Binding Corporate Rules, Corporate Self-Regulation of Global Data Transfers* (OUP, 2012).

- Working Document Establishing a Model Checklist Application for Approval of Binding Corporate Rules (WP108);

- Recommendation on the Standard Application for Approval of Binding Corporate Rules for the Transfer of Personal Data;

- Working Document setting up a table with the elements and principles to be found in Binding Corporate Rules (WP153);

- Working Document Setting up a framework for the structure of Binding Corporate Rules (WP154);

- Working Document on Frequently Asked Questions (FAQs) related to Binding Corporate Rules.

The BCRs[19] appear to be increasingly popular to large multinational organisation in relation to their data processing and data transfer compliance obligations. Readers will also need to consult the advice and recommendations from the EDPB which replaces the WP29. The ICO also refers to the BCR rules.

It is envisaged that the popularity of the BCR option for exemption from the data protection regime transfer restrictions will increase. However, the review process with the Commission or one of the national data protection supervisory authorities (or the ICO) can take some time given the complexity involved.

The GDPR provides that a competent supervisory authority shall approve binding corporate rules (BCR) in accordance with the consistency mechanism set out in Article 63, provided that they:

- are legally binding and apply to and are enforced by every member concerned of the group of undertakings or groups of enterprises engaged in a joint economic activity, including their employees;

- expressly confer enforceable rights on data subjects with regard to the processing of their personal data;

- fulfil the requirements laid down in Article 47(2).[20]

The BCRs must specify at least:

- the structure and contact details of the concerned group of undertakings or group of enterprises engaged in a joint economic activity and of each of its members;

- the data transfers or set of transfers, including the categories of personal data, the type of processing and its purposes, the type of data subjects affected and the identification of the third country or countries in question;

- their legally binding nature, both internally and externally;

---

19   See also Moerel, ibid.
20   GDPR, Art 47(1).

- the application of the general data protection principles, in particular purpose limitation, data minimisation, limited storage periods, data quality, data protection by design and by default (DPbD), legal basis for the processing of special categories of personal data, measures to ensure data security, and the requirements in respect of onward transfers to bodies not bound by the binding corporate rules [d];

- the rights of data subjects in regard to processing and the means to exercise these rights, including the right not to be subject to decisions based solely on automated processing, including profiling in accordance with Article 22, the right to lodge a complaint before the competent supervisory authority and before the competent courts of the states in accordance with Article 79, and to obtain redress and, where appropriate, compensation for a breach of the binding corporate rules [e];

- the acceptance by the controller or processor established on the territory of a state of liability for any breaches of the binding corporate rules by any member concerned not established in the EU; the controller or the processor shall be exempted from this liability, in whole or in part, only if it proves that that member is not responsible for the event giving rise to the damage [f];

- how the information on the binding corporate rules, in particular on the provisions referred to in this Article 47(2)(d), (e) and (f) is provided to the data subjects in addition to Articles 13 and 14;

- the tasks of any DPO designated in accordance with Article 37 or any other person or entity in charge of the monitoring compliance with the binding corporate rules within the group of undertakings, or group of enterprises engaged in a joint economic activity, as well as monitoring the training and complaint handling;

- the complaint procedures;

- the mechanisms within the group of undertakings, or group of enterprises engaged in a joint economic activity, for ensuring the verification of compliance with the binding corporate rules. Such mechanisms shall include data protection audits and methods for ensuring corrective actions to protect the rights of the data subject. Results of such verification should be communicated to the person or entity referred under point (h) and to the board of the controlling undertaking or of the group of enterprises engaged in a joint economic activity, and should be available upon request to the competent supervisory authority [i];

- the mechanisms for reporting and recording changes to the rules and reporting these changes to the supervisory authority;

- the co-operation mechanism with the supervisory authority to ensure compliance by any member of the group of undertakings, or group of enterprises engaged in a joint economic activity, in particular by making available to the supervisory authority the results of verifications of the measures referred to in this Article 47(2)(j);

- the mechanisms for reporting to the competent supervisory authority any legal requirements to which a member of the group of undertakings, or group of enterprises engaged in a joint economic activity is subject in a third country which are likely to have a substantial adverse effect on the guarantees provided by the binding corporate rules; and

- the appropriate data protection training to personnel having permanent or regular access to personal data.[21]

There may be future changes and requirements too. The Commission may specify the format and procedures for the exchange of information between controllers, processors and supervisory authorities for binding corporate rules. Those implementing acts shall be adopted in accordance with the examination procedure set out in Article 93(2).[22]

Transfers not authorised by EU law

12.11   Any judgment of a court or tribunal and any decision of an administrative authority of a third country requiring a controller or processor to transfer or disclose personal data may only be recognised or enforceable in any manner if based on an international agreement, such as a mutual legal assistance treaty, in force between the requesting third country and the EU or a state, without prejudice to other grounds for transfer pursuant to this chapter.[23]

Country and international organisation derogations

12.12   In the absence of an adequacy decision pursuant to Article 45(3), or of appropriate safeguards pursuant to Article 46, including binding corporate rules, a transfer or a set of transfers of personal data to a third country or an international organisation shall take place only on one of the following conditions:

- the data subject has explicitly consented to the proposed transfer, after having been informed of the possible risks of such transfers for the data subject due to the absence of an adequacy decision and appropriate safeguards; [a]

- the transfer is necessary for the performance of a contract between the data subject and the controller or the implementation of pre-contractual measures taken at the data subject's request; [b]

- the transfer is necessary for the conclusion or performance of a contract concluded in the interest of the data subject between the controller and another natural or legal person; [c]

- the transfer is necessary for important reasons of public interest;

---

21   Ibid, 47(2).
22   Ibid, 48(3).
23   Ibid, 48.

- the transfer is necessary for the establishment, exercise or defence of legal claims;

- the transfer is necessary in order to protect the vital interests of the data subject or of other persons, where the data subject is physically or legally incapable of giving consent;

- the transfer is made from a register which according to EU or state law is intended to provide information to the public and which is open to consultation either by the public in general or by any person who can demonstrate a legitimate interest, but only to the extent that the conditions laid down in EU or state law for consultation are fulfilled in the particular case. [g]

Where a transfer could not be based on a provision in Articles 45 or 46, including the provision of binding corporate rules, and none of the derogations for a specific situation pursuant to para (1) is applicable, a transfer to a third country or an international organisation may take place only if the transfer is not repetitive, concerns only a limited number of data subjects, is necessary for the purposes of compelling legitimate interests pursued by the controller which are not overridden by the interests or rights and freedoms of the data subject, and the controller has assessed all the circumstances surrounding the data transfer and has on the basis of that assessment provided suitable safeguards with respect to the protection of personal data. The controller shall inform the supervisory authority of the transfer. The controller shall in addition to the information referred to in Articles 13 and 14, inform the data subject about the transfer and on the compelling legitimate interests pursued by the controller.[24] [h]

A transfer pursuant to paragraph Article 49(1)(g) shall not involve the entirety of the personal data or entire categories of the personal data contained in the register. Where the register is intended for consultation by persons having a legitimate interest, the transfer shall be made only at the request of those persons or if they are to be the recipients.[25]

Article 49(1)(a), (b) and(c) and Article 49(2) shall not apply to activities carried out by public authorities in the exercise of their public powers.[26]

The public interest referred to in Article 49(1)(g) shall be recognised in EU law or in the law of the state to which the controller is subject.[27]

In the absence of an adequacy decision, EU law or state law may, for important reasons of public interest, expressly set limits to the transfer of specific categories of personal data to a third country or an international organisation. States shall notify such provisions to the Commission.[28]

---

24   Ibid, 49(1).
25   Ibid, 49(2).
26   Ibid, 49(3).
27   Ibid, 49(5).
28   Ibid, 49(5).

The controller or processor shall document the assessment as well as the suitable safeguards referred to in Article 49(1) (second subparagraph) in the records referred to in Article 30.[29]

International cooperation

12.13   In relation to third countries and international organisations, the Commission and supervisory authorities are obliged to take appropriate steps to:

- develop international co-operation mechanisms to facilitate the effective enforcement of legislation for the protection of personal data;

- provide international mutual assistance in the enforcement of legislation for the protection of personal data, including through notification, complaint referral, investigative assistance and information exchange, subject to appropriate safeguards for the protection of personal data and other fundamental rights and freedoms;

- engage relevant stakeholders in discussion and activities aimed at furthering international co-operation in the enforcement of legislation for the protection of personal data;

- promote the exchange and documentation of personal data protection legislation and practice, including on jurisdictional conflicts with third countries.[30]

National rules

12.14   Chapter III, Section 5 of the new GDPR refers to restrictions. EU or state law to which the controller or processor is subject may restrict by way of a legislative measure the scope of the obligations and rights provided for in Articles 12 to 22 and Article 34, as well as Article 5 in so far as its provisions correspond to the rights and obligations provided for in Articles 12 to 20, when such a restriction respects the essence of the fundamental rights and freedoms and is a necessary and proportionate measure in a democratic society to safeguard:

- national security [a];

- defence [b];

- public security [c];

- the prevention, investigation, detection or prosecution of criminal offences or the execution of criminal penalties, including the safeguarding against and the prevention of threats to public security [d];

---

29   Ibid, 44(6).
30   Ibid, 50.

- other important objectives of general public interests of EU or of a state, in particular an important economic or financial interest of EU or of a state, including monetary, budgetary and taxation matters, public health and social security [e];

- the protection of judicial independence and judicial proceedings;

- the prevention, investigation, detection and prosecution of breaches of ethics for regulated professions [g];

- . a monitoring, inspection or regulatory function connected, even occasionally, to the exercise of official authority in cases referred to in (a) to (e) and (g);

- the protection of the data subject or the rights and freedoms of others;

- the enforcement of civil law claims.[31]

In particular, any legislative measure referred to in Article 23(1) shall contain specific provisions at least, where relevant, as to:

- the purposes of the processing or categories of processing;

- the categories of personal data;

- the scope of the restrictions introduced;

- the safeguards to prevent abuse or unlawful access or transfer;

- the specification of the controller or categories of controllers;

- the storage periods and the applicable safeguards taking into account the nature, scope and purposes of the processing or categories of processing;

- the risks for the rights and freedoms of data subjects; and

- the right of data subjects to be informed about the restriction, unless this may be prejudicial to the purpose of the restriction.[32]

NEW EU STANDARD CONTRACT CLAUSES

12.15   One of the transfer channel exemptions from the default transfer ban under the GDPR which is relevant in relation to stream one data transfers from the EU to the UK is what are known as the Commission-endorsed standard contractual clauses to govern such transfers.

The Commission recently endorsed a second generation of such clauses. The Commission states:

> 'According to the General Data Protection Regulation (GDPR), contractual clauses ensuring appropriate data protection safeguards can be used as a ground for data transfers from the EU to third countries. This includes model

---

31   Ibid, 23(1).
32   Ibid, 23(2).

contract clauses – so-called standard contractual clauses (SCCs) – that have been "pre-approved" by the European Commission.

On 4 June 2021, the Commission issued modernised standard contractual clauses under the GDPR for data transfers from controllers or processors in the EU/EEA (or otherwise subject to the GDPR) to controllers or processors established outside the EU/EEA (and not subject to the GDPR):

These modernised SCCs replace the three sets of SCCs that were adopted under the previous Data Protection Directive 95/46. Since 27 September 2021, it is no longer possible to conclude contracts incorporating these earlier sets of SCCs.

Until 27 December 2022, controllers and processors can continue to rely on those earlier SCCs for contracts that were concluded before 27 September 2021, provided that the processing operations that are the subject matter of the contract remain unchanged.'[33]

The following innovations are referred to in the new generation of the standard contractual clauses:

- update in line with the GDPR;

- one single entry-point covering a broad range of transfer scenarios, instead of separate sets of clauses;

- more flexibility for complex processing chains, through a 'modular approach' and by offering the possibility for more than two parties to join and use the clauses;

- practical toolbox to comply with the *Schrems II* judgment; ie, an overview of the different steps companies have to take to comply with the *Schrems II* judgment as well as examples of possible 'supplementary measures', such as encryption, that companies may take if necessary.[34]

The European Commission adopted

'two sets of standard contractual clauses, one for use between controllers and processors and one for the transfer of personal data to third countries. They reflect new requirements under the GDPR and take into account the *Schrems II* judgement of the Court of Justice (see Chapter 17), ensuring a high level of data protection for citizens. These new tools will offer more legal predictability to European businesses and help, in particular, SMEs to ensure compliance with requirements for safe data transfers, while allowing data to move freely across borders, without legal barriers.'[35]

---

33   'Standard Contractual Clauses For International Transfers, Modernised Standard Contractual Clauses For The Transfer Of Personal Data To Third Countries' EU Commission, JUSTICE AND CONSUMERS, 4 June 2021.
34   'European Commission Adopts New Tools For Safe Exchanges Of Personal Data' EU Commission, Press Release, 4 June 2021.
35   Ibid.

There are therefore two types of standard contract for a business to be aware of. The activities of the business and its relationship with the counterparty in the EU will influence which is the appropriate contract that the business will need to consider implementing.

CONTROLLER TO PROCESSOR CONTRACTS

12.16   The new EU model contracts decision states that:

'The standard contractual clauses as set out in the Annex fulfil the requirements for contracts between controllers and processors in Article 28(3) and (4) of Regulation (EU) 2016/679 and of Article 29(3) and (4) of Regulation (EU) 2018/1725.' (Article 1)

'The standard contractual clauses as set out in the Annex may be used in contracts between a controller and a processor who processes personal data on behalf of the controller.' (Article 2)

The Annex to the decision states in relation to purpose and scope that:

'The purpose of these Standard Contractual Clauses (the Clauses) is to ensure compliance with [choose relevant option: OPTION 1: Article 28(3) and (4) of Regulation (EU) 2016/679 of the European Parliament and of the Council of 27 April 2016 on the protection of natural persons with regard to the processing of personal data and on the free movement of such data, and repealing Directive 95/46/EC (General Data Protection Regulation)] / [OPTION 2: Article 29(3) and (4) of Regulation (EU) 2018/1725 of the European Parliament and of the Council of 23 October 2018 on the protection of natural persons with regard to the processing of personal data by the Union institutions, bodies, offices and agencies and on the free movement of such data, and repealing Regulation (EC) No 45/2001 and Decision No 1247/2002/ EC].'

CONTRACTS AND TRANSFERS TO THIRD COUNTRIES

12.17   The new rules for international data transfers requires review of both the Commission decision document pursuant to the GDPR, and the related contract clauses document. The decision is Commission Implementing Decision on standard contractual clauses for the transfer of personal data to third countries pursuant to Regulation (EU) 2016/679.[36] It states that:

'The standard contractual clauses set out in the Annex are now considered to 'provide appropriate safeguards' within the meaning of Article 46(1) and (2) (c) of Regulation (EU) 2016/679 for the transfer by a controller or processor of personal data processed subject to that Regulation (data exporter) to a

---

36   Commission Implementing Decision (EU) 2021/914 of 4 June 2021 on standard contractual clauses for the transfer of personal data to third countries pursuant to Regulation (EU) 2016/679 of the European Parliament and of the Council (Text with EEA relevance), C/2021/3972, [2021] OJ L199, 31–61.

controller or (sub-)processor whose processing of the data is not subject to that Regulation (data importer).'[37]

'The standard contractual clauses also set out the rights and obligations of controllers and processors with respect to the matters referred to in Article 28(3) and (4) of Regulation (EU) 2016/679, as regards the transfer of personal data from a controller to a processor, or from a processor to a sub-processor.'[38]

EU – US DATA TRANSFERS

12.18   The US and EU have agreed a new data transfer mechanism for the transfer of data from the EU to the US. After all, there are significant numbers of commercial transactions occurring on a daily basis. A large number of US companies also have branches located in the EU. The new EU-US Data Privacy Framework agreed in 2022 replaces the prior Privacy Shield which was struck down after being legally challenged (see Chapter 17 for further details). (Indeed, the Privacy Shield was itself a replacement mechanism after the even earlier Safe Harbour arrangement was also struck down in separate proceedings).

CONCLUSION

12.19   Data protection compliance practice for organisations means that they will have to include a compliance assessment, as well as an assessment of associated risks, in relation to potential transfers of personal data outside of the jurisdiction. This applies to transfers from parent to subsidiary or to a branch office as well as transfers to any unrelated company or entity.

Organisations should be aware that if they wish to transfer personal data outside of the EU/EEA, that additional considerations arise and that unless there is a specific exemption, then the transfer may not be permitted. Once a transfer possibility arises, the organisation should undertake a compliance exercise to assess if the transfer can be permitted, and if so, how. Additional compliance documentation and contracts may be required.

The increasing locations and methods by which personal data may be collected by organisations, in particular internet, communications and social media, will increasingly be scrutinised in terms of transparency, consent and compliance. Equally, cloud computing is receiving particular data protection attention. Apps are also being considered as is the developing area of the Internet of Things (IoT) and related data protection compliance issues.

---

37   Article 1(1).
38   Article 1(2).

CHAPTER 13

UK Laws

INTRODUCTION

13.01 Data protection rules can be complex generally, and data transfer rules no less so. The general principle of restricting data transfers unless otherwise provided for, and complied with, also applies in the UK. The prior Data Protection Act (Data Protection Act 1998 (DPA 1998)), for example, stated previously that: 'Personal data shall not be transferred to a country or territory outside the European Economic Area [EEA] unless that country or territory ensures an adequate level of protection for the rights and freedoms of data subjects in relation to the processing of personal data.'

GDPR AS UK LAW

13.02 The GDPR was effectively the law in the UK governing data protection and data transfer issues. This was from the period of the go-live of the GDPR to the date that Brexit became effective. Of course, in addition to the GDPR which was directly effective in the UK, there was also the UK Data Protection Act 2018, and the PECR rules in relation to electronic communications and electronic marketing issues.

BREXIT BREAK

13.03 The UK left the EU on 31 January 2020. The issue of Brexit generally, and in particular what will happen in terms of data protection and data transfers has been an obvious concern for commercial entities and their advisors.

EU data rules are increasingly followed, if not applied, internationally. The GDPR has been replicated as a model for data laws in other countries. The UK GDPR is also broadly similar to the EU GDPR, and indeed starts from the same text and then makes amendments. The UK Data Protection Act 2018 is also similar to EU law.

BREXIT AND DATA PROTECTION

13.04 The EU and UK reached an agreement in December 2020 which enabled continuing data transfers for six months to 30 June 2021. The EU has now deemed UK legislation 'adequate' in June 2021.

The ICO issued lots of guidance in the period up to the end of the post-Brexit transition period. However, in the end the UK and EU reached an agreement that data exports and imports may continue as before, so much of the guidance is no longer relevant. However, as the UK data protection legal landscape is still undergoing significant change, careful attention to these ongoing changes are recommended.

EUWA

13.05   The EU Withdrawal Act (EUWA) is part of the mechanism for achieving Brexit. As such it can be considered relevant in terms of data events.

Since the post-Brexit interim period ended on 31 December 2020, the DPA 2018 and UK GDPR (both as amended) are the (primary) governing UK legislation in this area.

Post-Brexit data protection law

13.06   UK data protection law currently comprises the UK GDPR, the Data Protection Act 2018, and the Privacy and Electronic Communications Regulations (PECR) and various secondary legislation or statutory instruments.

There is also new proposed legislation referred to as the Data Protection and Digital Information Bill 2022; and also new rules in relation to artificial intelligence (AI) regulation and usage.

The GDPR brought the most significant changes to the rules surrounding the use of personal data in over 20 years. Recall also that the EU GDPR was initially directly effective in the UK (pre-Brexit finalisation). If that was not enough tumult to practitioners, the divorce rules consequent upon the implementation of Brexit has meant that companies and advisors have had to assess what the detailed specifics of the UK GDPR mean in practice – and in conjunction with the Data Protection Act 2018. Some have suggested that the 2018 Act is not the most user-friendly of legislative documents. Adding to the confusion is that the UK GDPR is not a statute.

One of the legitimate concerns of industry was whether the EU would deem UK legislation 'adequate'. This did occur in June 2021 (see EU Decision on the adequate protection of personal data by the United Kingdom: General Data Protection Regulation, 28 June 2021; also see EU Decision on the adequate protection of personal data by the United Kingdom: Law Enforcement Directive, 28 June 2021). This general concern will not be alleviated to everyone's satisfaction as data protection legal changes are still continuing. (See Chapter 16).

A wide range of changes from EU rules were set forth by the government in a list of DPA 2018 Keeling Schedule amendments. At the same time, a separate wide range of changes form the GDPR were outlined in a GDPR Keeling Schedule amendment. (See further details in Chapter 16).

DPA 2018 TRANSFER RULES

13.07 The UK DPA 2018 refers to data transfers. Section 18 specifically refers to transfers of personal data to third countries etc. It is also noted that Section 18 comes within Chapter 2 of the Act which refers to 'The GDPR', and which itself falls under Part 2 of the Act referring to 'General processing.'

Section 18 provides that:

'(1) The Secretary of State may by regulations specify, for the purposes of Article 49(1)(d) of the GDPR—

(a) circumstances in which a transfer of personal data to a third country or international organisation is to be taken to be necessary for important reasons of public interest, and

(b) circumstances in which a transfer of personal data to a third country or international organisation which is not required by an enactment is not to be taken to be necessary for important reasons of public interest.

(2) The Secretary of State may by regulations restrict the transfer of a category of personal data to a third country or international organisation where—

(a) the transfer is not authorised by an adequacy decision under Article 45(3) of the GDPR, and

(b) the Secretary of State considers the restriction to be necessary for important reasons of public interest.

(3) Regulations under this section—

(a) are subject to the made affirmative resolution procedure where the Secretary of State has made an urgency statement in respect of them;

(b) are otherwise subject to the affirmative resolution procedure.

(4) For the purposes of this section, an urgency statement is a reasoned statement that the Secretary of State considers it desirable for the regulations to come into force without delay.'

UK GDPR

13.08 The UK has made changes from the GDPR as is directly applied in the UK for a period, which vary between changes to the DPA 2018 and to the UK GDPR. Some of these are necessary and inconsequential in terms of being necessary merely to reflect that Brexit has occurred. Others may transpire to be more consequential differences. The direction of more consequential changes would also appear to reflect some of the political policy rhetoric which seems to wish to portray quite a different data protection regime from that which applies in the EU or even which might be considered broadly equivalent to the GDPR. As changes are potentially still ongoing, this is an area which readers will be required to pay continued attention to.

In the UK GDPR, Article 44 refers to general principle for transfers.[1] It provides that

> '[a]ny transfer of personal data which are undergoing processing or are intended for processing after transfer to a third country or to an international organisation shall take place only if, subject to the other provisions of this Regulation, the conditions laid down in this Chapter are complied with by the controller and processor, including for onward transfers of personal data from the third country or an international organisation to another third country or to another international organisation. All provisions in this Chapter shall be applied in order to ensure that the level of protection of natural persons guaranteed by this Regulation is not undermined.'

Article 45 of the UK GDPR refers to transfers on the basis of an adequacy decision.[2] Additions are provided in bold, while deletions are marked in strike through. Article 45 as amended in the UK is as follows:

> '1. A transfer of personal data to a third country or an international organisation may take place where the Commission has decided that the third country, a territory or one or more specified sectors within that third country, or the international organisation in question ensures an adequate level of protection **where it is based on adequacy regulations (see section 17A of the 2018 Act)**.[3] Such a transfer shall not require any specific authorisation.
>
> 2. When assessing the adequacy of the level of protection, the Commission **"for the purposes of sections 17A and 17B of the 2018 Act, the Secretary of State"**[4] shall, in particular, take account of the following elements:
>
>> (a) the rule of law, respect for human rights and fundamental freedoms, relevant legislation, both general and sectoral, including concerning public security, defence, national security and criminal law and the access of public authorities to personal data, as well as the implementation of such legislation, data protection rules, professional rules and security measures, including rules for the onward transfer of personal data to another third country or international organisation which are complied with in that country or international organisation, case-law, as well as effective and enforceable data subject rights and effective administrative and

1   The potentially most relevant Recitals to this Article are Recitals 101, and 102.
2   The potentially most relevant Recitals to this Article are Recitals 103, 104, 105, 106, and 107.
3   Data Protection, Privacy and Electronic Communications (Amendments etc) (EU Exit) Regulations 2019 (2019 No. 419), Regulation 38(2) in Article 45(1), deletes '"where the Commission' to the end of the first sentence" and inserts '"where it is based on adequacy regulations (see section 17A of the 2018 Act)'.
4   Data Protection, Privacy and Electronic Communications (Amendments etc) (EU Exit) Regulations 2019 (2019 No. 419), Regulation 38(3)(a) in Article 45(2), deletes ',the Commission' and inserts 'for the purposes of sections 17A and 17B(12) of the 2018 Act, the Secretary of State'.

judicial redress for the data subjects whose personal data are being transferred;

(b) the existence and effective functioning of one or more independent supervisory authorities in the third country or to which an international organisation is subject, with responsibility for ensuring and enforcing compliance with the data protection rules, including adequate enforcement powers, for assisting and advising the data subjects in exercising their rights and for cooperation with the supervisory authorities of the Member States **the Commissioner**[5]; and

(c) the international commitments the third country or international organisation concerned has entered into, or other obligations arising from legally binding conventions or instruments as well as from its participation in multilateral or regional systems, in particular in relation to the protection of personal data.

3. [Deleted].[6]

4. [Deleted].[7]

5. [Deleted].[8]

6. [Deleted].[9]

7. A decision pursuant to paragraph 5 of this Article **The amendment or revocation of regulations under section 17A of the 2018 Act**[10] is without prejudice to transfers of personal data to the third country, a territory or one or more specified sectors within that third country, or the international organisation in question pursuant to Articles 46 to 49.

8. [Deleted].[11]

9. [Deleted].[12]

---

5 Data Protection, Privacy and Electronic Communications (Amendments etc) (EU Exit) Regulations 2019 (2019 No. 419), Regulation 38(3)(b) in Article 45(2), deletes 'the supervisory authorities of the Member States' and inserts 'the Commissioner'.

6 Data Protection, Privacy and Electronic Communications (Amendments etc) (EU Exit) Regulations 2019 (2019 No. 419), Regulation 38(4) in Article 45(3)-(6), deletes 'paragraphs 3, 4, 5 and 6'.

7 Data Protection, Privacy and Electronic Communications (Amendments etc) (EU Exit) Regulations 2019 (2019 No. 419), Regulation 38(4) in Article 45(3)-(6), deletes 'paragraphs 3, 4, 5 and 6'.

8 Data Protection, Privacy and Electronic Communications (Amendments etc) (EU Exit) Regulations 2019 (2019 No. 419), Regulation 38(4) in Article 45(3)-(6), deletes 'paragraphs 3, 4, 5 and 6'.

9 Data Protection, Privacy and Electronic Communications (Amendments etc) (EU Exit) Regulations 2019 (2019 No. 419), Regulation 38(4) in Article 45(3)-(6), deletes 'paragraphs 3, 4, 5 and 6'.

10 Data Protection, Privacy and Electronic Communications (Amendments etc) (EU Exit) Regulations 2019 (2019 No. 419), Regulation 38(5) in Article 45(7), deletes 'A decision pursuant to paragraph 5 of this Article' and inserts 'The amendment or revocation of regulations under section 17A of the 2018 Act'.

11 Data Protection, Privacy and Electronic Communications (Amendments etc) (EU Exit) Regulations 2019 (2019 No. 419), Regulation 38(6) in Article 45(7), deletes 'paragraphs 8 and 9'.

12 Data Protection, Privacy and Electronic Communications (Amendments etc) (EU Exit) Regulations 2019 (2019 No. 419), Regulation 38(6) in Article 45(7), deletes 'paragraphs 8 and 9'.

Article 46 of the UK GDPR refers to transfers subject to appropriate safeguards.[13] It provides that:

1. In the absence of a decision pursuant to Article 45(3) **adequacy regulations under section 17A of the 2018 Act**[14], a controller or processor may transfer personal data to a third country or an international organisation only if the controller or processor has provided appropriate safeguards, and on condition that enforceable data subject rights and effective legal remedies for data subjects are available.

2. The appropriate safeguards referred to in paragraph 1 may be provided for, without requiring any specific authorisation from a supervisory authority **the Commissioner**[15], by:

   (a) a legally binding and enforceable instrument between public authorities or bodies;

   (b) binding corporate rules in accordance with Article 47;

   (c) standard data protection clauses adopted by the Commission in accordance with the examination procedure referred to in Article 93(2); **(c) standard data protection clauses specified in regulations made by the Secretary of State under section 17C(13) of the 2018 Act and for the time being in force;**[16]

   (d) standard data protection clauses adopted by a supervisory authority and approved by the Commission pursuant to the examination procedure referred to in Article 93(2); **(d) standard data protection clauses specified in a document issued (and not withdrawn) by the Commissioner under section 119A(14) of the 2018 Act and for the time being in force;**[17]

   (e) an approved code of conduct pursuant to Article 40 together with binding and enforceable commitments of the controller or processor in the third country to apply the appropriate safeguards, including as regards data subjects' rights; or

   (f) an approved certification mechanism pursuant to Article 42 together with binding and enforceable commitments of the controller or processor in the third country to apply the appropriate safeguards, including as regards data subjects' rights.

13 The potentially most relevant Recitals to this Article are Recitals 108, and 109.
14 Data Protection, Privacy and Electronic Communications (Amendments etc) (EU Exit) Regulations 2019 (2019 No. 419), Regulation 39(2) in Article 46(1), deletes 'a decision pursuant to Article 45(3)' and inserts 'adequacy regulations under section 17A of the 2018 Act'.
15 Data Protection, Privacy and Electronic Communications (Amendments etc) (EU Exit) Regulations 2019 (2019 No. 419), Regulation 39(3)(a) in Article 46(2), deletes 'a supervisory authority' and inserts 'the Commissioner'.
16 Data Protection, Privacy and Electronic Communications (Amendments etc) (EU Exit) Regulations 2019 (2019 No. 419), Regulation 39(3)(b) in Article 46(2), deletes 'paragraph (c)' and inserts '(c) standard data protection clauses specified in regulations made by the Secretary of State under section 17C(13) of the 2018 Act and for the time being in force;'.
17 Data Protection, Privacy and Electronic Communications (Amendments etc) (EU Exit) Regulations 2019 (2019 No. 419), Regulation 39(3)(c) in Article 46(2), deletes 'paragraph (d)' and inserts '(d) standard data protection clauses specified in a document issued (and not withdrawn) by the Commissioner under section 119A of the 2018 Act and for the time being in force;'.

3. Subject to the authorisation from the competent supervisory authority **With authorisation from the Commissioner,**[18] the appropriate safeguards referred to in paragraph 1 may also be provided for, in particular, by:

   (a) contractual clauses between the controller or processor and the controller, processor or the recipient of the personal data in the third country or international organisation; or

   (b) provisions to be inserted into administrative arrangements between public authorities or bodies which include enforceable and effective data subject rights.

4. The supervisory authority shall apply the consistency mechanism referred to in Article 63 in the cases referred to in paragraph 3 of this Article.[19]

5. Authorisations by a Member State or supervisory authority on the basis of Article 26(2) of Directive 95/46/EC shall remain valid until amended, replaced or repealed, if necessary, by that supervisory authority. Decisions adopted by the Commission on the basis of Article 26(4) of Directive 95/46/EC shall remain in force until amended, replaced or repealed, if necessary, by a Commission Decision adopted in accordance with paragraph 2 of this Article.[20]

Article 47 of the UK GDPR refers to binding corporate rules (BCR).[21] It refers as follows:

1. The competent supervisory authority **The Commission**[22] shall approve binding corporate rules in accordance with the consistency mechanism set out in Article 63,[23] provided that they:

   (a) are legally binding and apply to and are enforced by every member concerned. of the group of undertakings, or group of enterprises engaged in a joint economic activity, including their employees;

   (b) expressly confer enforceable rights on data subjects with regard to the processing of their personal data; and

   (c) fulfil the requirements laid down in paragraph 2.

18 Data Protection, Privacy and Electronic Communications (Amendments etc) (EU Exit) Regulations 2019 (2019 No. 419), Regulation 39(4) in Article 46(3), deletes 'Subject to the authorisation from the competent supervisory authority" and inserts "With authorisation from the Commissioner'.

19 Data Protection, Privacy and Electronic Communications (Amendments etc) (EU Exit) Regulations 2019 (2019 No. 419), Regulation 39(5) in Article 46(4)-(5), deletes 'paragraphs 4 and 5'.

20 Data Protection, Privacy and Electronic Communications (Amendments etc) (EU Exit) Regulations 2019 (2019 No. 419), Regulation 39(5) in Article 46(4)-(5), deletes 'paragraphs 4 and 5'.

21 The potentially most relevant Recitals to this Article are Recital 110.

22 Data Protection, Privacy and Electronic Communications (Amendments etc) (EU Exit) Regulations 2019 (2019 No. 419), Regulation 40(2) in Article 47(1)(a), deletes 'The competent supervisory authority' and inserts 'The Commissioner'.

23 Data Protection, Privacy and Electronic Communications (Amendments etc) (EU Exit) Regulations 2019 (2019 No. 419), Regulation 40(2) in Article 47(1)(b), deletes 'in accordance with the consistency mechanism set out in Article 63'.

2. The binding corporate rules referred to in paragraph 1 shall specify at least:

(a) the structure and contact details of the group of undertakings, or group of enterprises engaged in a joint economic activity and of each of its members;

(b) the data transfers or set of transfers, including the categories of personal data, the type of processing and its purposes, the type of data subjects affected and the identification of the third country or countries in question;

(c) their legally binding nature, both internally and externally;

(d) the application of the general data protection principles, in particular purpose limitation, data minimisation, limited storage periods, data quality, data protection by design and by default, legal basis for processing, processing of special categories of personal data, measures to ensure data security, and the requirements in respect of onward transfers to bodies not bound by the binding corporate rules;

(e) the rights of data subjects in regard to processing and the means to exercise those rights, including the right not to be subject to decisions based solely on automated processing, including profiling in accordance with Article 22, the right to lodge a complaint with the competent supervisory authority and before the competent courts of the Member States in accordance with Article 79 **the Commissioner and before a court in accordance with Article 79 (see section 180 of the 2018 Act)**,[24] and to obtain redress and, where appropriate, compensation for a breach of the binding corporate rules;

(f) the acceptance by the controller or processor established on the territory of a Member State **established in the United Kingdom**[25] of liability for any breaches of the binding corporate rules by any member concerned not established in the Union **not established in the United Kingdom**[26]; the controller or the processor shall be exempt from that liability, in whole or in part, only if it proves that that member is not responsible for the event giving rise to the damage;

(g) how the information on the binding corporate rules, in particular on the provisions referred to in points (d), (e) and (f) of this paragraph is provided to the data subjects in addition to Articles 13 and 14;

---

24 Data Protection, Privacy and Electronic Communications (Amendments etc) (EU Exit) Regulations 2019 (2019 No. 419), Regulation 40(3) in Article 47(2)(e), deletes 'the competent supervisory authority and before the competent courts of the Member States in accordance with Article 79' and inserts 'the Commissioner and before a court in accordance with Article 79 (see section 180 of the 2018 Act)'.

25 Data Protection, Privacy and Electronic Communications (Amendments etc) (EU Exit) Regulations 2019 (2019 No. 419), Regulation 40(4)(a) in Article 47(2)(f), deletes 'established on the territory of a Member State' and inserts 'established in the United Kingdom'.

26 Data Protection, Privacy and Electronic Communications (Amendments etc) (EU Exit) Regulations 2019 (2019 No. 419), Regulation 40(4)(b) in Article 47(2)(f), deletes 'not established in the Union' and inserts 'not established in the United Kingdom'.

(h) the tasks of any data protection officer designated in accordance with Article 37 or any other person or entity in charge of the monitoring compliance with the binding corporate rules within the group of undertakings, or group of enterprises engaged in a joint economic activity, as well as monitoring training and complaint-handling;

(i) the complaint procedures;

(j) the mechanisms within the group of undertakings, or group of enterprises engaged in a joint economic activity for ensuring the verification of compliance with the binding corporate rules. Such mechanisms shall include data protection audits and methods for ensuring corrective actions to protect the rights of the data subject. Results of such verification should be communicated to the person or entity referred to in point (h) and to the board of the controlling undertaking of a group of undertakings, or of the group of enterprises engaged in a joint economic activity, and should be available upon request to the competent supervisory authority **the Commissioner**;[27]

(k) the mechanisms for reporting and recording changes to the rules and reporting those changes to the supervisory authority **the Commissioner**;[28]

(l) the cooperation mechanism with the supervisory authority **the Commissioner**[29] to ensure compliance by any member of the group of undertakings, or group of enterprises engaged in a joint economic activity, in particular by making available to the supervisory authority **the Commissioner**[30] the results of verifications of the measures referred to in point (j);

(m) the mechanisms for reporting to the competent supervisory authority **the Commissioner**[31] any legal requirements to which a member of the group of undertakings, or group of enterprises engaged in a joint economic activity is subject in a third country which are likely to have a substantial adverse effect on the guarantees provided by the binding corporate rules; and

(n) the appropriate data protection training to personnel having permanent or regular access to personal data.

---

27 Data Protection, Privacy and Electronic Communications (Amendments etc) (EU Exit) Regulations 2019 (2019 No. 419), Regulation 40(5) in Article 47(2)(j), deletes 'the competent supervisory authority' and inserts 'the Commissioner'.

28 Data Protection, Privacy and Electronic Communications (Amendments etc) (EU Exit) Regulations 2019 (2019 No. 419), Regulation 40(6) in Article 47(2)(k), deletes 'the supervisory authority' and inserts 'the Commissioner'.

29 Data Protection, Privacy and Electronic Communications (Amendments etc) (EU Exit) Regulations 2019 (2019 No. 419), Regulation 40(7) in Article 47(2)(l), deletes 'the supervisory authority' (in both places) and inserts 'the Commissioner'.

30 Data Protection, Privacy and Electronic Communications (Amendments etc) (EU Exit) Regulations 2019 (2019 No. 419), Regulation 40(7) in Article 47(2)(l), deletes 'the supervisory authority' (in both places) and inserts 'the Commissioner'.

31 Data Protection, Privacy and Electronic Communications (Amendments etc) (EU Exit) Regulations 2019 (2019 No. 419), Regulation 40(8) in Article 47(2)(m), deletes 'the competent supervisory authority' and inserts 'the Commissioner'.

3. [Deleted].[32]

Article 48[33] of the UK GDPR had referred to transfers or disclosures not authorised by Union law. However, it is now deleted from the UK GDPR.

Article 49 of the UK GDPR refers to derogations for specific situations.[34] It provides that:

1. In the absence of an adequacy decision pursuant to Article 45(3) **adequacy regulations under section 17A of the 2018 Act,**[35] or of appropriate safeguards pursuant to Article 46, including binding corporate rules, a transfer or a set of transfers of personal data to a third country or an international organisation shall take place only on one of the following conditions:

    (a) the data subject has explicitly consented to the proposed transfer, after having been informed of the possible risks of such transfers for the data subject due to the absence of an adequacy decision and appropriate safeguards;

    (b) the transfer is necessary for the performance of a contract between the data subject and the controller or the implementation of pre-contractual measures taken at the data subject's request;

    (c) the transfer is necessary for the conclusion or performance of a contract concluded in the interest of the data subject between the controller and another natural or legal person;

    (d) the transfer is necessary for important reasons of public interest;

    (e) the transfer is necessary for the establishment, exercise or defence of legal claims;

    (f) the transfer is necessary in order to protect the vital interests of the data subject or of other persons, where the data subject is physically or legally incapable of giving consent;

    (g) the transfer is made from a register which according to Union or Member State law **domestic law**[36] is intended to provide information to the public and which is open to consultation either by the public in general or by any person who can demonstrate a legitimate interest, but only to the extent that the conditions laid down by Union or Member State law **domestic law**[37] for consultation are fulfilled in the particular case.

---

32 Data Protection, Privacy and Electronic Communications (Amendments etc) (EU Exit) Regulations 2019 (2019 No. 419), Regulation 40(9) in Article 47(3), deletes 'paragraph 3'.

33 Data Protection, Privacy and Electronic Communications (Amendments etc) (EU Exit) Regulations 2019 (2019 No. 419), Regulation 41 at Article 48, deletes 'Article 48'. Article 48 is therefore deleted and does not apply in the UK.

34 The potentially most relevant Recitals to this Article are Recitals 111, 112, 113, 114, and 115.

35 Data Protection, Privacy and Electronic Communications (Amendments etc) (EU Exit) Regulations 2019 (2019 No. 419), Regulation 42(2)(a) in Article 49, in the opening words deletes 'an adequacy decision pursuant to Article 45(3)' and inserts 'adequacy regulations under section 17A of the 2018 Act'.

36 Data Protection, Privacy and Electronic Communications (Amendments etc) (EU Exit) Regulations 2019 (2019 No. 419), Regulation 42(2)(b) in Article 49(1)(g), deletes 'Union or Member State law' (in both places) and inserts 'domestic law'.

37 Data Protection, Privacy and Electronic Communications (Amendments etc) (EU Exit) Regulations 2019 (2019 No. 419), Regulation 42(2)(b) in Article 49(1)(g), deletes 'Union or Member State law' (in both places) and inserts 'domestic law'.

Where a transfer could not be based on a provision in Article 45 or 46, including the provisions on binding corporate rules, and none of the derogations for a specific situation referred to in the first subparagraph of this paragraph is applicable, a transfer to a third country or an international organisation may take place only if the transfer is not repetitive, concerns only a limited number of data subjects, is necessary for the purposes of compelling legitimate interests pursued by the controller which are not overridden by the interests or rights and freedoms of the data subject, and the controller has assessed all the circumstances surrounding the data transfer and has on the basis of that assessment provided suitable safeguards with regard to the protection of personal data. The controller shall inform the supervisory authority **the Commissioner**[38] of the transfer. The controller shall, in addition to providing the information referred to in Articles 13 and 14, inform the data subject of the transfer and on the compelling legitimate interests pursued.

2. A transfer pursuant to point (g) of the first subparagraph of paragraph 1 shall not involve the entirety of the personal data or entire categories of the personal data contained in the register. Where the register is intended for consultation by persons having a legitimate interest, the transfer shall be made only at the request of those persons or if they are to be the recipients.

3. Points (a), (b) and (c) of the first subparagraph of paragraph 1 and the second subparagraph thereof shall not apply to activities carried out by public authorities in the exercise of their public powers.

4. The public interest referred to in point (d) of the first subparagraph of paragraph 1 shall be recognised in Union law or in the law of the Member State to which the controller is subject **must be public interest that is recognised in domestic law (whether in regulations under section 18(1) of the 2018 Act or otherwise)**.[39]

5. [Deleted].[40]

5A. This Article and Article 46 are subject to restrictions in regulations under section 18(2) of the 2018 Act.[41]

6. The controller or processor shall document the assessment as well as the suitable safeguards referred to in the second subparagraph of paragraph 1 of this Article in the records referred to in Article 30.'

---

38 Data Protection, Privacy and Electronic Communications (Amendments etc) (EU Exit) Regulations 2019 (2019 No. 419), Regulation 42(2)(c) in Article 49(1)(g) second subparagraph, deletes 'the supervisory authority' and inserts 'the Commissioner'.

39 Data Protection, Privacy and Electronic Communications (Amendments etc) (EU Exit) Regulations 2019 (2019 No. 419), Regulation 42(3) in Article 49(4), deletes 'shall be recognised in Union law or in the law of the Member State to which the controller is subject' and inserts 'must be public interest that is recognised in domestic law (whether in regulations under section 18(1) of the 2018 Act or otherwise)'.

40 Data Protection, Privacy and Electronic Communications (Amendments etc) (EU Exit) Regulations 2019 (2019 No. 419), Regulation 42(4) in Article 49(5), deletes 'paragraph 5'.

41 Data Protection, Privacy and Electronic Communications (Amendments etc) (EU Exit) Regulations 2019 (2019 No. 419), Regulation 42(5) in Article 49, after Article 49(5), inserts '5A. This Article and Article 46 are subject to restrictions in regulations under section 18(2) of the 2018 Act.'.

Article 50 of the UK GDPR refers to international cooperation for the protection of personal data.[42] It states that:

> 'In relation to third countries and international organisations, the Commission and supervisory authorities **the Commissioner**[43] shall take appropriate steps to:
>
> (a) develop international cooperation mechanisms to facilitate the effective enforcement of legislation for the protection of personal data;
>
> (b) provide international mutual assistance in the enforcement of legislation for the protection of personal data, including through notification, complaint referral, investigative assistance and information exchange, subject to appropriate safeguards for the protection of personal data and other fundamental rights and freedoms;
>
> (c) engage relevant stakeholders in discussion and activities aimed at furthering international cooperation in the enforcement of legislation for the protection of personal data;
>
> (d) promote the exchange and documentation of personal data protection legislation and practice, including on jurisdictional conflicts with third countries.'

ADEQUACY CHANNEL FOR EU-UK DATA STREAM

13.09   The EU agreed to an adequacy decision such as to permit data transfers to continue from the EU to the UK. This occurred on 28 June 2021. This is very important as is applies countrywide and not just to individual companies. It is important for business to assess how to ensure adherence. It will also be necessary for entities to consider how the government may put this adequacy in jeopardy.

The Department for Digital, Culture, Media & Sport (DCMS) issued commentary on and announced the new Adequacy Decision.[44] It states that the 'European Union (EU) has formally recognised the UK's high data protection standards after more than a year of constructive talks' and that '[t]his will allow the continued seamless flow of personal data from the EU to the UK.'[45]

The Department states that '[p]ersonal data can continue to flow freely between Europe and the UK following agreement by the European Union to adopt "data adequacy" decisions.'[46]

---

42   The potentially most relevant Recitals to this Article are Recital 116.

43   Data Protection, Privacy and Electronic Communications (Amendments etc) (EU Exit) Regulations 2019 (2019 No. 419), Regulation 43 in Article 50, deletes 'the Commission and supervisory authorities' and inserts 'the Commissioner'.

44   'EU Adopts "Adequacy" Decisions Allowing Data to Continue Flowing Freely to the UK"' *Press Release*, Department for Digital, Culture, Media & Sport, 28 June 2021; *Decision on the Adequate Protection of Personal Data by the United Kingdom – General Data Protection Regulation*, EU Commission, 28 June 2021.

45   Ibid.

46   Ibid.

Officially, the

> 'government welcomes the move, which rightly recognises the country's high data protection standards. Formal adoption of the decisions under the EU General Data Protection Regulation (GDPR) and Law Enforcement Directive (LED) allows personal data to flow freely from the EU and wider European Economic Area (EEA) to the UK. The decisions mean that UK businesses and organisations can continue to receive personal data from the EU and EEA without having to put additional arrangements in place with European counterparts.'[47]

It is indicated that '[t]his free flow of personal data supports trade, innovation and investment, assists with law enforcement agencies tackling crime, and supports the delivery of critical public services sharing personal data as well as facilitating health and scientific research.'[48]

If examined more critically, the statements following may portent some contention and potential trouble for the just announced adequacy decision. The following statements are made, namely:

> 'The UK, which now operates a *fully independent* data policy, has already recognised the EU and EEA member states as "adequate", as part of its commitment to establish a smooth transition for the UK's departure from the bloc.
>
> The government plans to promote the *free flow of personal data globally and across borders*, including through ambitious new trade deals and through new data adequacy agreements with some of the fastest growing economies, while ensuring people's data continues to be protected to a high standard.'[49] (Emphasis added).

The statement also indicates an apparent indication to lean to industry over rights, or a balance between industry and rights, when it states '[a]ll future decisions will be based on what maximises innovation and keeps up with evolving tech. As such, the government's approach will seek to minimise burdens on organisations seeking to use data to tackle some of the most pressing global issues, including climate change and the prevention of disease.'[50]

The DCMA also refers to a number of statements made by interested parties, which are contained in the announcement. The respective statements are as follows.

The Secretary of State for Digital Oliver Dowden said that:

> 'After more than a year of constructive talks it is right the European Union has formally recognised the UK's high data protection standards.

47 Ibid.
48 Ibid.
49 Ibid.
50 Ibid.

This will be welcome news to businesses, support continued cooperation between the UK and the EU and help law enforcement authorities keep people safe.

We will now focus on unlocking the power of data to drive innovation and boost the economy while making sure we protect people's safety and privacy.'[51]

John Foster, the CBI Director of Policy said that:

'This breakthrough in the EU-UK adequacy decision will be welcomed by businesses across the country.

The free flow of data is the bedrock of the modern economy and essential for firms across all sectors– from automotive to logistics – playing an important role in everyday trade of goods and services.

This positive step will help us move forward as we develop a new trading relationship with the EU.'[52]

Julian David, techUK CEO, said that:

'Securing an EU-UK adequacy decision has been a top priority for techUK and the wider tech industry since the day after the 2016 referendum. The decision that the UK's data protection regime offers an equivalent level of protection to the EU GDPR is a vote of confidence in the UK's high data protection standards and is of vital importance to UK-EU trade as the free flow of data is essential to all business sectors.

The data adequacy decision also provides a basis for the UK and EU to work together on global routes for the free flow of data with trust, building on the G7 Digital and Technology declaration and possibly unlocking €2 trillion of growth.

The UK must also now move to complete the development of its own international data transfer regime in order to allow companies in the UK not just to exchange data with the EU, but also to be able to access opportunities across the world.'[53]

The official EU Adequacy Decision[54] for the UK states that the following decision has been made by the Commission, namely:

'For the purposes of Article 45 of Regulation (EU) 2016/679, the United Kingdom ensures an adequate level of protection for personal data transferred within the scope of Regulation (EU) 2016/679 from the European Union to the United Kingdom.'[55]

---

51   Ibid.
52   Ibid.
53   Ibid.
54   Commission Implementing Decision of 28.6.2021 pursuant to Regulation (EU) 2016/679 of the European Parliament and of the Council on the adequate protection of personal data by the United Kingdom, Brussels, 28.6.2021, C(2021) 4800 final.
55   Ibid, Art 1(1).

There is also a provision referring to ongoing monitoring to ensure that the UK maintains compliance. It states that:

> 'The Commission shall continuously monitor the application of the legal framework upon which this Decision is based, including the conditions under which onward transfers are carried out, individual rights are exercised and United Kingdom public authorities have access to data transferred on the basis of this Decision, with a view to assessing whether the United Kingdom continues to ensure an adequate level of protection within the meaning of Article 1.'[56]

If there is non compliance, the Commission may 'may suspend, repeal or amend this Decision'.[57] In addition, 'The Commission may suspend, repeal or amend this Decision if the lack of cooperation of the United Kingdom government prevents the Commission from determining whether the finding in Article 1(1) is affected.'[58]

The UK adequacy decision also has an expiry date. So, further UK changes can be reviewed in terms of there being continued compliance and equivalency between UK laws and UK laws. It is provided that:

> 'This Decision shall expire on 27 June 2025, unless extended in accordance with the procedure referred to in Article 93(2) of Regulation (EU) 2016/679.'[59]

FURTHER CHANGE

13.10 Further changes are now in prospect to UK data protection law. More change is promised in the form of the Data Protection and Digital Information Bill 2022, new AI rules, new codes, new statutory instruments, new Ministerial orders, and new rules from the ICO itself on foot of the new governmental changes.

In September 2021, the Department for Digital, Culture, Media & Sport announced some further major intended changes to UK data protection laws.[60] This consultation period ended on 19 November 2021. The government issued its response to this consultation process on 23 June 2022, referred to as Data: a new direction – government response to consultation. Annex A to the response document contains a list of the proposed changes.

The proposals cover areas such as cookies, online marketing and ecommerce activities. Currently, some companies are required to have a Data Protection Officer and it is possible that this requirement may be abolished. Significant

---

56 Ibid, 2(1).
57 Ibid, 3(4).
58 Ibid, 3(5).
59 Ibid, 4.
60 See Department for Digital, Culture, Media & Sport, Open consultation, 'Data: a new direction', 10 September 2021.

change to the role, office and powers of the Information Commissioner's Office (ICO) are proposed. This may move UK law away from the EU legislation position.

UK data protection law comprises of, at a headline level, the UK GDPR, the Data Protection Act 2018, and the Privacy and Electronic Communications Regulations (PECR) – and the new proposed Data Protection and Digital Information Bill once enacted.

The government revealed the new Data Protection and Digital Information Bill 2022 on 18 July 2022. Some might note the apparent short temporal distance between the government response to the consultation and the new Bill.

The overall announced intention is to assist the UK in being more competitive in terms of trade, and also claiming to maintain high standards of protection for data. No doubt, the proposals may be controversial to some, when issues regarding reduced risk audits, and changes to the data regulator are more fully considered.

Some of the proposed changes include:

- clarifying that further processing for an incompatible purpose may be lawful when based on a law that safeguards an important public interest or when the data subject has re-consented (consultation response 1.2.9, 1.3.1, 1.3.2, Annex A);

- clarifying when further processing may occur when the original lawful ground was consent (consultation response 1.3.4, Annex A);

- extending the 'disproportionate effort' exemption on information provision requirements for further processing for research purposes of personal data collected directly from the data subject (consultation response 1.2.10, 1.2.11, Annex A);

- creating a limited list of legitimate interests for businesses to process personal data without applying the balancing test (consultation response 1.4.1, 1.4.2, 1.4.4, Annex A);

- enable organisations to use sensitive personal data for the purpose of managing the risk of bias in their AI systems by clarifying that Schedule 1 Paragraph 8 can be used for the processing necessary for the purpose of ensuring bias monitoring, detection and correction (consultation response 1.5.11, 1.5.12, 1.5.13, Annex A);

- clarifying the limits and scope of Article 22 UK GDPR (consultation response 1.5.14, 1.5.15, 1.5.16, 1.5.17, Annex A);

- adopting the Council of Europe's test for anonymisation into legislation (consultation response 1.6.1, 1.6.2, Annex A);

- confirming that the test for anonymisation is a relative one (consultation response 1.6.3, Annex A);

- require organisations to operate a privacy management programme (consultation response 2.2.2, 2.2.3, 2.2.14, 2.2.15, Annex A);

- replace the requirement to appoint a DPO with a requirement to designate a suitable individual to oversee the organisation's DP compliance (consultation response 2.2.5, 2.2.6, Annex A);

- remove the requirement for Data Protection Impact Assessments (consultation response 2.2.8, Annex A);

- remove the requirement for Prior Consultation with the ICO on high-risk processing (consultation response 2.2.9, Annex A);

- to amend the threshold for refusing to respond to/charge a reasonable fee for a subject access request from 'manifestly unfounded or excessive' to 'vexatious or excessive' (consultation response 2.3.1, 2.3.2, 2.3.3, Annex A);

- requiring data controllers to have complaints-handling mechanisms (consultation response 5.6.2, 5.6.3, Annex A);

- align key terms that are used across the different data processing frameworks to drive consistency (consultation response 4.5.1, Annex A);

- new statutory framework setting out the ICO's strategic objectives and duties (consultation response 5.2.1, Annex A);

- a new overarching duty for the ICO to uphold data rights and to encourage trustworthy and responsible data use (consultation response 5.2.2, Annex A);

- new duty for the ICO to have regard to economic growth and innovation (consultation response 5.2.4, Annex A);

- new duty for the ICO to have regard to competition issues (consultation response 5.2.5, Annex A);

- new duty for the ICO to consult with relevant regulators and any other relevant bodies when exercising its duties to have regard to growth, innovation and competition (consultation response 5.2.6, 5.2.7, Annex A);

- new duty for the ICO to have regard to public safety (consultation response 5.2.10, Annex A);

- new power for the DCMS SoS to prepare a statement of strategic priorities which the ICO must respond to (consultation response 5.2.11, Annex A);

- establish an independent Board and Chief Executive for the ICO (consultation response 5.3.1, Annex A);

- appointing the Chair by the same process as that for appointing the ICO under DPA 2018 (consultation response 5.3.2, Annex A);

- appointing the non-executive board members by the DCMS SoS (consultation response 5.3.3, Annex A);

- removing parliamentary approval to amend ICO's salary (consultation response 5.4.1, Annex A);

- requirement for the ICO to develop and publish KPIs (consultation response 5.4.2, Annex A);

- requirement for the ICO to publish key strategies and processes guiding its work (consultation response 5.4.3, Annex A);

- requirement for ICO to publish other information to aid transparency (consultation response 5.4.3, Annex A);

- a process for the DCMS Secretary of State to approve statutory codes of practice and statutory guidance ahead of laying them in Parliament (consultation response 5.5.3, Annex A);

- a power for the DCMS Secretary of State to require the ICO to set up a panel of experts when developing all codes of practice and statutory guidance, unless exempt (consultation response 5.5.1, Annex A);

- to require the ICO to undertake and publish impact assessments when developing all codes of practice and statutory guidance unless exempt (consultation response 5.5.2, Annex A);

- set out in legislation the criteria the ICO can use to determine whether to pursue a complaint in order to provide clarity and enable the ICO to take a more risk-based and proportionate approach to complaints (consultation response 5.6.2, 5.6.3, 5.6.4, Annex A);

- new power to commission a technical report to aid breach investigations (consultation response 5.7.2, 5.7.3, 5.7.4, Annex A);

- introducing a provision to permit the ICO additional time beyond the six-month statutory deadline to issue a penalty, under certain circumstances (consultation response 5.7.8, Annex A);

- introducing a requirement for the ICO to set out to the relevant data controller/s at the beginning of an investigation the anticipated timelines for phases of its investigation (consultation response 5.7.9, Annex A);

- new power for the ICO to compel witnesses to interview during investigations and answer questions (consultation response 5.7.6, Annex A).

There are specific proposals in relation to data transfers. The government refers to proposals:

- to reform the DCMS Secretary of State's adequacy making power (consultation response 3.3.7, Annex A);

- to remove the requirement for the DCMS Secretary of State to conduct a review adequacy decisions every four years (consultation response 3.2.3, Annex A);

- clarifying that either judicial or administrative redress is acceptable for international transfers (consultation response 3.3.7, Annex A);

- creating a new power for the DCMS Secretary of State to formally recognise new ATMs [adaptable transfer mechanisms] (consultation response 3.3.1, 3.3.8, Annex A);

- reinforcing the importance of proportionality when using ATMs (consultation response 3.2.3, Annex A).

In terms of electronic marketing and PECR related rules, the proposed Data Protection and Digital Information Bill makes a number of changes, including:

- empowering the ICO to take action against organisations for the number of unsolicited direct marketing calls 'sent' as well as calls 'received' and connected (consultation response 2.4.10, Annex A);

- empowering the ICO to impose assessment notices on companies suspected of PECR breaches (consultation response 2.4.17, 2.4.18, Annex A);

- introducing a 'duty to report' on communication service providers to report suspicious traffic transiting their networks (consultation response 2.4.11, Annex A);

- requiring websites to respect preferences set by individuals through their browser (consultation response 2.4.6, 2.4.7, Annex A);

- increasing fines under PECR to GDPR levels (consultation response 2.4.16, Annex A);

- other measures to help ensure the enforcement regime is effective, proportionate and dissuasive (consultation response 2.4.16, Annex A);

- to remove the consent requirement for analytics cookies and similar technologies (governed by Regulation 6 of PECR); treat them in a similar way as 'strictly necessary' cookies (consultation response 2.4.1, Annex A);

- to remove the consent requirements in Regulation 6 of PECR for a wider range of circumstances where the controller can demonstrate legitimate interest for processing the data (consultation response 2.4.3, Annex A);

- to remove the consent requirements in Regulation 6 of PECR when controllers are using cookies or similar technology in compliance with an ICO-approved sector code or regulatory guidance (consultation response 2.4.2, Annex A);

- extending the soft opt-in for direct marketing to communications from political parties (consultation response 2.4.9, Annex A);

- extending the soft opt-in for direct marketing to other political entities such as candidates and registered (with the Electoral Commission) third-party campaign groups (consultation response 2.5.3, Annex A);

- extending the soft opt-in for direct marketing to communications from other non-commercial organisations (consultation response 2.4.9, Annex A);

- to remove the requirement for prior consent for all types of cookies (governed by Regulation 6 of PECR) (consultation response 2.4.4, Annex

A). However, it adds that the government plans to proceed with this proposal in the future for websites, once automated technology is widely available to help users manage online preferences.

There are also particular changes being proposed in relation to scientific and academic research. Those affected should examine these particular proposals further (see consultation response at questions 1.2.1, 1.2.2, 1.2.8, Annex A).

Separate change proposals also relate to public bodies (see consultation response at questions 4.3.1, 4.3.2, 4.2.1, 4.4.7, Annex A) and the police (see consultation response at questions 4.4.8, 5.8.1, 5.8.2, Annex A), so those affected should examine these proposals in detail.

The Data Protection and Digital Information Bill comprises six parts plus 13 schedules. The six parts span 113 sections.

- Part 1 refers to: definitions; data protection principles; data subjects' rights; automated decision making; obligations of controllers and processors; international transfers of personal data; safeguards for processing for research etc purposes; national security; intelligence services; Information Commissioner's role; enforcement; protection of prohibitions and restrictions;

- Part 2 refers to: digital verification services; trust marks;

- Part 3 refers to: customer data and business data;

- Part 4 refers to: other provisions about digital information; privacy and electronic communications; trust services; sharing of data; registers of births and deaths; information standards for health and social care;

- Part 5 refers to: regulation and oversight; the ICO; biometric;

- Part 6 refer to: final provisions.

In addition to the Data Protection and Digital Information Bill the government announced proposals for a separate set of rules regarding the governance of AI.

This is intended to involve a range of regulators including the ICO, Ofcom, Financial Conduct Authority, Medicine and Healthcare Products Regulatory Authority, and the Competition and Markets Authority. Included in the wider proposal is an AI Paper[61] and press release.[62] This is overall referred to as the

---

61 Policy paper, 'Establishing a pro-innovation approach to regulating AI', available at https://www.gov.uk/government/publications/establishing-a-pro-innovation-approach-to-regulating-ai/establishing-a-pro-innovation-approach-to-regulating-ai-policy-statement.
62 'UK sets out proposals for new AI rulebook to unleash innovation and boost public trust in the technology', available at https://www.gov.uk/government/news/uk-sets-out-proposals-for-new-ai-rulebook-to-unleash-innovation-and-boost-public-trust-in-the-technology, dated 18 July 2022.

National AI Strategy. These proposals will no doubt be relevant to vendors but also a range of companies which directly (and perhaps even indirectly) use AI software and capabilities.

Interestingly, while the proposed act reduces or eliminates the need for a DPO, the AI proposals appear to require the designation of a responsible person. Other aspects of the AI proposal refer to the use of safe AI, security, transparency, and fairness.

There are currently announced policy proposals in terms of making large scale amendments and deletions of so-called retained EU laws in the UK. It remains uncertain, at least at this stage, what sort of impact these changes would have in terms of UK data protection rules, and in particular how the EU – and privacy groups – may view such impacts on the EU-UK data stream.

FUTURE INTERNATIONAL COOPERATION

13.11 Prior to Brexit there was close institutional cooperation with EU bodies and institutions. This included the Commission and the data protection bodies referred to as the Article 29 Working Party and the later European Data Protection Board. The ICO would also be a participating member of these bodies. Cooperation also existed with the European Data Protection Supervisor. Other international bodies and organisations would also have shared interests and cooperation with the ICO. It remains to be seen how the UK may cooperate with EU bodies, EU data regulators, and other interested bodies internationally in the future.

CONCLUSION

13.12 The above highlights the complexities of UK data protection law, Brexit, adequacy decisions, etc. A UK adequacy decision is critical for the UK. Given the economic importance of continued access to EU trade and data from the EU, it is not difficult to imagine that data protection and adequacy issues are one of the most important pressing Brexit problems for those dealing with the negotiations, not to mention those sectors of the economy potentially most affected.

Data protection compliance practice for organisations means that they will have to include a compliance assessment, as well as an assessment of associated risks, in relation to potential transfers of personal data outside of the jurisdiction. This applies to transfers from parent to subsidiary or to a branch office as well as transfers to any unrelated company or entity.

The ICO also provides useful guidance in relation to a number of Brexit and post Brexit data protection issues, and which will have to continue as further UK data law changes occur, such as: Assessing Adequacy; Model Contract Clauses; Binding Corporate Rules; Outsourcing; Data Protection Act; International

Data Transfers; The Information Commissioner's Recommended Approach to Assessing Adequacy Including Consideration of the Issue of Contractual Solutions, etc.

The increasing locations and methods by which personal data may be collected by organisations, in particular internet, communications and social media, will increasingly be scrutinised in terms of transparency, consent and compliance. Equally, cloud computing is receiving particular data protection attention. Apps are also being considered as is the developing area of the Internet of Things (IoT) and related data protection compliance issues.

Organisations should be aware that if they wish to transfer personal data outside of the EU/EEA, that additional considerations arise and that unless there is a specific exemption, then the transfer may not be permitted. This is important to consider as UK businesses will naturally wish to be able to deal with EU entities and EU customers and which may need EU personal data to be sent to the UK for transactions to occur. Once a transfer possibility arises, the organisation should assess if the transfer can be permitted, and if so, how. Additional compliance documentation and contracts may be required. Potentially a party in the EU may request warranties as to compliance and permissibility from a UK company.

Certain issues may arise in relation to:

• What is a 'transfer'? Is there a difference between transfer versus transit?

• 'Data' and anonymised data, is there a restriction on transfers of anonymised data? For example, can certain anonymised data fall outside the definition of personal data?

• 'Third country' currently includes the EU countries and EEA countries of Iceland, Norway and Liechtenstein. The EU countries are expanding over time. In addition, the list of permitted additional third countries is also expanding over time, for example, safe harbour, privacy framework, etc.

• How EU-US transfers will evolve after the ECJ/CJEU has struck down the original EU-US Safe Harbour data transfer agreement and the EU-US Privacy Shield replacement – and the new EU-US Data Privacy Framework.[63] Many organisations use these agreements as the legitimising basis for the lawful transfer of personal data from the EU to the US. Big questions arise as to how these operate and may be challenged further, and also how the UK may seek to mimic these arrangements.

The important issue of a UK adequacy decision and the complicating issues involved are necessary considerations. Many issues remain unclear at this stage and there will be potential for continued uncertainty as we continue in a period of

---

63 *Digital Rights Ireland and Seitlinger and Others*, joined Cases C-293/12 and C-594/12, Court of Justice, 8 April 2014.

amendment as regards UK data protection law and policy change. Two researchers commenting on Brexit and data protection issues once said that the only certainty is uncertainty.[64] I am not entirely sure as yet that we have yet reached terra firma. (See Chapter 16 for further details in relation to certainty issues.) While it is difficult to speculate upon, the potential for data transfer type litigation from Max Schrems and/or others in relation to the UK cannot be ruled out.

Readers should also note that separate to formal laws and rule the data regulator (ICO) also issues guidance which it hopes can assist in summarising and clarifying the best ways to achieve data transfer compliance. This includes the recent International Data Transfer Agreement and Guidance, and the earlier International Data Transfers; International Transfers; International Data Transfer Agreement and Addendum and Transitional Provisions Laid Before Parliament; International Data Transfer Agreement and Guidance; Contracts and Data Sharing, Overview – Data Protection and the EU; For Organisations, Encryption and Data Transfer; International Transfers; Your Right to Data Portability; EU-US Privacy Shield; and more. This serves to demonstrate, if it was not already clear, that data transfer rules are complex and evolving. It is essential, however, to be familiar with official guidance in addition to specific data transfer rules. One of the themes evident from the official guidance is to ensure an (advance) assessment of what data and transfer channels are involved prior to transfers commencing, and even prior to formal contacts and documentation. Accountability is also key (eg who is responsible; who has the risk), as is proportionality (do we need to transfer; are we transferring too much data), and restrictions (how is data restricted and protected in the destination). No doubt, more guidance will also arise.

---

64 Diker Vanberg and Maunick, 'Data Protection In The UK Post-Brexit: The Only Certainty Is Uncertainty' (2018) 32(1) *International Review of Law, Computers & Technology* 190.

CHAPTER 14

International Laws

INTRODUCTION

14.01   Data protection is important, and despite some misunderstandings it reflects policy concerns to protect personal data but also facilitate responsible commercial activities. In one sense, therefore, there is a balance struck between overly protective measures in one extreme, and overly intrusive business practices in the other. In reality, data laws seek to strike a reasonable balance.[1]

DEFAULT BANS

14.02   In many jurisdictions there is an established model of seeking to protect the personal data of citizens by establishing a default data transfer ban. These bans aim to ensure that if and when personal data is to leave a given jurisdiction, that the citizens can still expect that their data will be protected and secured. This is the model in the GDPR, but in addition was already established in the prior data protection laws in the EU. Other countries and data laws also seek to follow this model. This is arguably expected as one might assume that every country will have some concerns as to how to deal with the risks that may occur if the personal data of citizens were to be transferred to a third-party country. These types of risks are increasingly appreciated.

GDPR REFERENCE POINT

14.03   The GDPR is increasingly recognised as the norm or at least the starting point to understanding how to legislate for data protection rules in the modern world. Regardless of ones' positions and location in the world, one should be consulting what the GDPR says on specific issues when these come to be considered elsewhere. That is merely to say that the GDPR is a relevant and appropriate document to consider and reference.

---

1   Some might suggest that technology has so far advanced that the balance of data laws is arguably a little skewed in favour of industry data collection and insufficient rules to protect online safety and needs some recalibration.

GDPR FOLLOWED

14.04 Many jurisdictions which may not have had data rules are now following the GDPR model and implementing their own national laws – including rules restricting data transfers and regulating when and how transfers may occur. An increasing number of countries when implementing their data laws for the first time, and also when updating their laws, seek to follow the general model of the GDPR.

EU AND EEA

14.05 The EEA refers to the European Economic Area. The countries of Iceland, Liechtenstein and Norway are EEA Member States but they are not members of the EU. However, their data protection laws and rules bear close relationships with the GDPR legal landscape. The UK is no longer an EU/ EEA Member State since 31 January 2020.

EU AND CLOSE NEIGHBOURS

14.06 There are also other countries which while not EU members also follow closely the rules of the EU, including the GDPR. This includes Switzerland which is not a member of the EU nor the EEA. As an example, once the ECJ/ CJEU invalidated the EU-US Privacy Shield arrangement, the EU and later also Switzerland formally cancelled their respective recognition of the mechanics of these transfer arrangements. Switzerland had a similar arrangement in place comparable to that in the EU as regards data transfers to the US.

INTERNATIONAL RELATIONS AND COOPERATION

14.07 Both before and after the GDPR, many countries internationally have data protection laws and privacy laws. While data flows occur around the globe, these national data laws will need to be considered on an individual level when national data and national data law is triggered. A wide array of commentary and guidance exists on a country by country basis – from academics, practitioners, officials, and others.[2] Guidance will also exist in relation to specific issues (eg,

---

2   Jimenez-Gomez, 'Cross-Border Data Transfers Between The EU And The U.S.: A Transatlantic Dispute' (2021) 19(2) *Santa Clara Journal of International Law* 1; Keser Berber, and Atabey, 'Evaluation Of The Recent Developments In Laws and Policies Relating To Cross-Border Data Transfers In Turkey' (2022) 8(2) *European Data Protection Law Review* (EDPL) 302; Zalnieriute, 'Developing A European Standard For International Data Transfers After Snowden: Opinion 1/15 On The EU–Canada PNR Agreement' (2018) 81(6) *Modern Law Review* 1046; Suda, 'Japan's Personal Information Protection Policy Under Pressure: The Japan-EU Data Transfer Dialogue and Beyond' (2020) 60(3) *Asian Survey* 510; 'Brazil Bill Implements New Provisions for International Data Transfers' (2015) Q1 *Venulex Legal Summaries* 1. In relation to the UK, see, eg, Lambert, *A Users Guide to Data Protection* (Bloomsbury, 2020).

contracts, BCRs, etc), or from specific industry perspectives (eg, health sector,[3] banking sector, marketing and advertising sector, etc), or in relation to specific bilateral relations (eg, the US and EU,[4] the EU and Japan,[5] the UK and EU,[6] Asia and EU,[7] etc).

Many countries and blocs, not least the UK and EU, seek to establish friendly rules and norms with other desired trading countries. These discussions and relations in the modern connected world naturally also include seeking to establish rules for the transfer of personal data – especially in relation to commerce but also in relation to law enforcement. (Just to note, this book refers to the former but not the later issues).

In relation to third countries and international organisations, the Commission and supervisory authorities take appropriate steps to:

- develop international co-operation mechanisms to facilitate the effective enforcement of legislation for the protection of personal data;

- provide international mutual assistance in the enforcement of legislation for the protection of personal data, including through notification, complaint referral, investigative assistance and information exchange, subject to

---

3   Bradford, Aboy, and Liddell, 'Standard Contractual Clauses For Cross-Border Transfers Of Health Data After Schrems II' (2021) 8(1) *Journal of Law and the Biosciences* 36; Konicki, Wasmuht-Perroud, Aaron and Caplan, 'Virtual Surgical Planning And Data Ownership: Navigating The Provider-Patient-Vendor Relationship' (2022) 36(5) *Bioethics* 494; Corrales Compagnucci, Minssen, Seitz and Aboy, 'Lost On The High Seas Without A Safe Harbor Or A Shield? Navigating Cross-Border Transfers In The Pharmaceutical Sector After Schrems II Invalidation Of The EU-US Privacy Shield' (2020) 4(3) *European Pharmaceutical Law Review* 153; Minssen, Seitz, Aboy and Corrales Compagnucci, 'The EU-US Privacy Shield Regime For Cross-Border Transfers Of Personal Data Under The GDPR: What Are The Legal Challenges And How Might These Affect Cloud-Based Technologies, Big Data, And AI In The Medical Sector?'(2020) 4(1) *European Pharmaceutical Law Review* 34.
4   Burke, 'EU-US Reach An Agreement On Data Transfers: Will It Lead To Schrems III?' (2022) 135(69) *Los Angeles Daily Journal* 1; Jimenez-Gomez, 'Cross-Border Data Transfers Between the EU and the U.S.: A Transatlantic Dispute' (2021) 19(2) *Santa Clara Journal of International Law* 1; 'European Union and United States Conclude Agreement to Regulate Transatlantic Personal Data Transfers' (2016) 110(2) *American Journal of International Law* 360; Archick and Fefer, 'U.S.-EU Privacy Shield and Transatlantic Data Flows' Report, Congressional Research Service: Report (9/22/2021) 1; Minssen, Seitz, Aboy and Corrales Compagnucci, M, 'The EU-US Privacy Shield Regime For Cross-Border Transfers Of Personal Data Under The GDPR: What Are The Legal Challenges And How Might These Affect Cloud-Based Technologies, Big Data, And AI In The Medical Sector?' (2020) 4(1) *European Pharmaceutical Law Review* 34; Manny, 'Data Transfers From The EU To The U.S. After Schrems' (2016) 49(1) *Business Law Review*.
5   Suda, 'Japan's Personal Information Protection Policy Under Pressure: The Japan-EU Data Transfer Dialogue and Beyond' (2020) 60(3) *Asian Survey* 510.
6   For example, Lambert, *A Users Guide to Data Protection* (Bloomsbury, 2020); Diker Vanberg and Maunick, 'Data Protection In The UK Post-Brexit: The Only Certainty Is Uncertainty' (2018) 32(1) *International Review of Law, Computers & Technology* 190.
7   Sullivan, 'EU GDPR Or APEC CBPR? A Comparative Analysis Of The Approach Of The EU And APEC To Cross Border Data Transfers And Protection Of Personal Data In The IoT Era' (2019) 35(4) *Computer Law & Security Review* 380.

appropriate safeguards for the protection of personal data and other fundamental rights and freedoms;

- engage relevant stakeholders in discussion and activities aimed at furthering international co-operation in the enforcement of legislation for the protection of personal data;

- promote the exchange and documentation of personal data protection legislation and practice, including on jurisdictional conflicts with third countries.[8]

This is required by the GDPR itself. In the absence of the Commission and the GDPR, the UK is required to consider such efforts and arrangements on its own. Indeed, various government statements and the official consultation process of 2021–2022 have referenced such desires.

UNITED NATIONS

14.08   The United Nations (UN) is also concerned with personal data issues and recently referred to research in relation to data transfer rules.[9] The UN launched what it calls a 'privacy lab' in relation to international data sharing. It indicates that:

- experts from national statistical offices, private sector and academia launch service to enable the use of privacy enhancing technologies (PETs);

- secure data sharing could unlock nearly US$3 trillion of annual GDP over the next 20 years, according to research;

- crucial national policy decisions could benefit from data provided by partner countries, but international data sharing is almost non-existent due to privacy concerns;

- pilot project with UK, US, Netherlands and Italy will demonstrate shared sensitive data can be analysed in a privacy-compliant and ethical way.[10]

This is a developing space. It is also noted that the UN and other international bodies (such as the Council of Europe) have also been long concerned to recognise the need for protection for personal data in the electronic age.

---

8   GDPR, Art 50.
9   See: 'UN Launches Privacy Lab Pilot to Unlock Cross-Border Data Sharing Benefits', *Information-age.com*, 25 January 2022.
10   'UN Launches First Of Its Kind "Privacy Lab" To Unlock Benefits Of International Data Sharing' UN, 25 January 2022, available at https://unstats.un.org/bigdata/events/2022/unsc-un-pet-lab/UN%20PET%20Lab%20-%20Press%20Release% 20-%2025%20Jan%202022.pdf.

CONCLUSION

14.09 The importance of international commerce will ensure that efforts to research and create legal policy to assist data transfer mechanisms will continue.[11] The recent Covid-19 pandemic also pushed towards greater international data transfers, albeit for a wholly different imperative. At least for the continued near future, the EU and international organisations will be at the forefront of developing the infrastructures and safeguards that will be used. Existing forms of documentation will be expanded upon and will become more complex. New methods may also be tested and if successful also added to the transfer permission channels.[12] There will no doubt be additional obstacles and unexpected developments,[13] but risks must be identified and when catered for appropriately and not to the total detriment of individuals nor business,[14] reasonable and fair data transfers will likely continue.

---

11 Archick and Fefer, 'U.S.-EU Privacy Shield and Transatlantic Data Flows' Report, Congressional Research Service: Report (9/22/2021) 1; Wang, 'The Best Data Plan Is To Have A Game Plan: Obstacles and Solutions To Reaching International Data Privacy Agreements' (2022) 28(2) *Michigan Telecommunications & Technology Law Review* 385; Velli, 'The Issue of Data Protection in EU Trade Commitments: Cross-Border Data Transfers in GATS and Bilateral Free Trade Agreements' (2019) 4(3) *European Papers – A Journal on Law and Integration* 881; Marengo, 'Regulating Data Transfers through the International Trade Regime' (2020) 17(2) *Manchester Journal of International Economic Law* 266; 'Brazil Bill Implements New Provisions for International Data Transfers' (2015) Q1 *Venulex Legal Summaries* 1; Hahn, 'Saving The Global Internet: Towards A Rights-Based Approach To Regulating Cross-Border Data Transfers' (2021) 53(2) *George Washington International Law Review* 357.

12 Consider Hutt and Boardman, 'New UK Standard Contractual Clauses for Personal Data Transfers' (2022) 39(7) *Computer & Internet Lawyer* 12; De Boel, Dhont and Fol, 'New Model Clauses For Personal Data Transfers Outside the UK' (2022) 39(6) *Computer & Internet Lawyer* 12. Also consider the recent UK consultation, and also the Data Protection and Digital Information Bill 2022.

13 Voss, 'Cross-Border Data Flows, The GDPR, And Data Governance' (2020) 29(3) *Washington International Law Journal* 485.

14 Neuman, Kavanagh, Balbirnie and White, 'Schrems II: European Data Protection Board Data Transfers Guidance' (2021) 33(3) *Intellectual Property & Technology Law Journal* 18; Jurcys, Compagnucci and Fenwick, 'The Future Of International Data Transfers: Managing Legal Risk With A "user-held" data model"' [2022] *Computer Law* 46; Breitbarth, 'A Risk-Based Approach to International Data Transfers' (2021) 7(4) *European Data Protection Law Review* (EDPL) 539.

PART D

PRACTICE ISSUES

PART D

PRACTICAL ISSUES

CHAPTER 15

Practice and transfers

INTRODUCTION

15.01   Those in the UK who collect, process, or otherwise use personal data as defined under the data protection legal regime need to comply with various legal rules. These rules set out compliance obligations as well as refer to various data rights which must be respected.

There are various levels of rules. Some are general in nature while others refer to additional precautions needed for special or sensitive personal data.

Data laws increasingly set out additional levels of rules, such as for risk assessment tools, or when it is proposed to transfer personal data abroad (data exporting). That does not mean that an entity does not need to concern itself if it is the recipient of personal data from a foreign location (data recipients). Data recipients will also have data law, contracting, and due diligence responsibilities. In fact, the obligations on recipients are growing and becoming more express as data laws expand.

DATA STREAMS

15.02   Brexit was and is a significant event and has many ongoing consequences, some practical while others are political and legal.

Entities in the UK, especially those dealing with international issues or customers in more than one country, will have been aware of the significance of Brexit Day and the implication (subject to time limited extension periods) that the UK would become a de facto third country outside of the EU. The implication under EU data laws (currently the GDPR), is that the UK would be subject to the default ban on transfers of personal data to third countries (now including the UK) from the EU. This would mean that the transfer of such data to the UK would have to be stopped.

There are obvious business consequences. These are even more enhanced for certain sectors, such as banking and financial.

Such data can be transferred to the UK *only if* one of a limited number of circumstances or exceptions to the default transfer ban can be satisfied.

Some of the exemption criteria refer to acts that an individual entity can try to satisfy, some refer to acts that a group of companies can try to satisfy, and some relate to a large-scale exemption to all relevant entities in a particular country. The benefit of the latter is that if the country itself can satisfy the EU that its laws and processes are equivalent to those in the EU relating to personal data, the EU may designate that country as a whole as adequate in order to send personal data to and from the EU. This is known as an adequacy decision.

Hence, there has been significant discussion on the ability of the UK to apply to the EU as quickly as possible after Brexit to be considered for a successful data transfer adequacy decision.

Perhaps to the surprise of some, the EU granted not only an Adequacy Decision for transfers of data from the EU to the UK,[1] but also that this occurred relatively quickly as compared to some past such application processes.

The first stream that many businesses would be concerned with would be the EU-UK data stream.

Another data stream relates to data going from the UK to third countries. This relates to UK data originally received from the EU and data from elsewhere. As the UK data protection laws hold the potential to split (further) away from the EU and the GDPR, this data stream may come to be considered quite different from the rules relating to the EU data received in the UK.

As official policy is being directed to UK trade and other relationships with third countries outside of the EU, there is potential for large amounts of personal data to be received in the UK from such counties. Increasingly, therefore, business will need to assess what data laws and obligations arise for this (increasing) data stream. This is a third data stream.

An important aspect of ensuring compliance will require careful attention to an arguably increasing set of data laws dealing with separate data streams, and the contracts and related legal documentation directed to each of these separate data streams.

It goes without saying that there will be an increasing need for internal diligence as well as external legal advice.

The respective businesses will also need to consider their particular role in the respective data processing activities, and whether they are a prime data controller or an outsourced processor entity acting for and at the direction of the prime controller of the personal data in question.

---

1 'EU Adopts "Adequacy" Decisions Allowing Data to Continue Flowing Freely to the UK," Press Release, Department for Digital, Culture, Media & Sport, 28 June 2021; *Decision on the Adequate Protection of Personal Data by the United Kingdom – General Data Protection Regulation*, EU Commission, 28 June 2021.

These data transfer issues are important because so many businesses will be involved either as a data exporter or data recipient. The data transfer compliance issues will be further complicated when a given business entity is involved not just in one data stream, but rather involved in numerous data streams all at once.

PRACTICAL STEPS

15.03 Assessing if the export ban applies, includes asking the following questions:

- Does the organisation wish to transfer personal data?

- Is there a transfer to a 'third country'?

- Does that third country have an adequate level of protection?

- Does it involve transfers to the EU-US Privacy Shield or other transfer mechanism?

- Does it involve whitelist countries?

- What constitutes adequacy?

- What is the nature of the data?

- How is it to be used?

- What laws and practices are in place in the third country?

- Is it a transfer by controller to processor?

- Are they transfers within an international or multinational company or group of companies where an internal privacy code or agreement is in place?

- Are they transfers within a consortium established to process international transactions, for example, banking?

- Are they transfers between professionals such as lawyers or accountants where a clients' business has on international dimension?

- The Commission has identified core principles which must be present in the foreign laws or codes of practice or regulations in order to achieve the requisite standard of 'adequacy' in third party countries – are these principles present?

- Has the personal data been processed for a specific purpose?

- Is the personal data accurate and up to date?

- Has the data subject been provided with adequate information in relation to the transfer?

- Have technical and organisational security measures been taken by the controller?

- Is there a right of access to the data by the data subject?

- Is there a prohibition on onward transfer of data?

- Is there an effective procedure or mode of enforcement?

Contracts, consent and binding corporate rules take on a new significance as the concepts of permissibility and adequacy receive renewed scrutiny. Given the controversy and striking out of the EU-US Privacy Shield arrangement, all controllers engaged in processing, and those considering transfers, should very carefully consider all of the implications, current changes and the potential for change and additional measures in the short to medium term. For example, while official policymakers have agreed proposals for the EU-US Privacy Shield, the WP29 (now EDPB) suggests further clarity, if not amendment. The Commission, and the new EDPB, are likely to consider transfer legitimising mechanisms in future. Despite not being directly effective, UK entities will still have to consider the new updated standard contracts issued by the EU Commission.

Organisations should consider the following queries when considering data transfer issues:

- Does the organisation transfer customer, etc, personal data outside of the jurisdiction?

- Is there a transfer to the US? If so, is the recipient of the data a EU-US Privacy Framework recipient or any equivalent as may be agreed in relation to UK-US data transfers? If yes, then the organisation can transfer the data. If not, the organisation needs to: (i) assess the adequacy of the protection measures in place; (ii) see if that transfer is exempted; (iii) create adequacy through consent or appropriate contract.

- Is the recipient country a Commission permitted whitelist country? If so, transfer is permitted.

- Are there data protection rules in place or codes of practice and if so did they incorporate the adequate and equivalent protections?

- If there is inadequate protection is it practical to obtain the consent of the data subject?

- If not, then is it practical to enter into an appropriate contract with the recipient?

- Are the Commission model data contract clauses available?

The ICO also asks:

1. does the organisation need to transfer personal data abroad?

2. is the organisation transferring the personal data to a country outside of the jurisdiction or will it just be in transit through a non-EEA country?

3. has the organisation complied with all the other principles of data protection?

4. is the transfer to a country on the EU Commission's white list of countries or territories (per a Community finding) accepted as providing adequate levels

of protection for the rights and freedoms of Data Subjects in connection with the processing of their personal data?

5. if the transfer is to the US, has the US recipient of the personal data signed up to the EU – US Department of Commerce Privacy Shield scheme [or any alternative mechanism]?

6. is the personal data passenger name record information (PNR)? If so, particular rules may apply.

8. can the organisation assess that the level of protection for data subjects' rights as 'adequate in all the circumstances of the case'?

9. if not, can the organisation put in place adequate safeguards to protect the rights of the data subjects whose data is to be transferred?

10. can the organisation rely on another exception from the restriction on international transfers of personal data?

[Note: No 7 missing in the original]

Readers should note that the ICO issues guidance, and commentary, on an ongoing basis. Some examples include guidance documentation in relation to a number of data transfer consideration. The ICO also provides useful guidance in relation to:

- Assessing Adequacy;

- Model Contract Clauses;

- Binding Corporate Rules; and

- Outsourcing;

- Data Protection Act;

- International Data Transfers;

- The Information Commissioner's Recommended Approach to Assessing Adequacy Including Consideration of the Issue of Contractual Solutions, Binding Corporate Rules;

- Etc.

CONCLUSION

15.04 Data protection compliance practice for organisations means that they will have to include a compliance assessment, as well as an assessment of associated risks, in relation to potential transfers of personal data outside of the jurisdiction. This applies to transfers from parent to subsidiary or to a branch office as well as transfers to any unrelated company or entity.

EU organisations (including subsidiaries of UK entities) should be aware that if they wish to transfer personal data outside of the EU/EEA, that additional considerations arise and that unless there is a specific exemption, then the transfer may not be permitted. Once a transfer possibility arises, the organisation should undertake a compliance exercise to assess if the transfer can be permitted, and if so, how. Additional compliance documentation, notices, consent clauses, and contracts may be required.

The increasing locations and methods by which personal data may be collected by organisations, in particular internet, communications and social media, will increasingly be scrutinised in terms of transparency, consent and compliance. Equally, cloud computing is receiving particular data protection attention. Apps are also being considered as is the developing area of the Internet of Things (IoT) and related data protection compliance issues.

CHAPTER 16

Legal and business certainty

INTRODUCTION

16.01   Naturally there is a lot of discussion focused on how Brexit might work and what the implications will be. It is a momentous event. It is extremely complex both politically and legally. Vanberg and Maunick describe how the only certainty is uncertainty.[1] Many may feel a general frustration with developments and the potential implications.[2] One of the significant issues, which is receiving greater attention, is how Brexit impacts issues of data protection, its impact on particular industries,[3] wider institutional issues[4] – and especially cross border data transfer issues.[5]

After Brexit, the GDPR is no longer directly effective in the UK, so a critical review of the UK DPA 2018, the so-called UK GDPR and the new adequacy decision needs to be undertaken to reveal the impact and how they relate to each other. Despite political intentions, it may never be possible to ignore EU development of data laws and cases relating to data laws. Overall, it appears that understanding how to comply with data transfer laws has become more complex in the UK. Indeed, with the new Consultation, it may become even more complex.

Businesses were already under pressure to ascertain how Brexit data changes would impact their activities, especially where they sought to interact with business partners and customers abroad.

DATA TRANSFER PROBLEMS

16.02   The data transfer issues after Brexit are significant and underestimated. Only after the possibility of a no deal Brexit increased did the attention of many begin to fix on the data transfer problem, arguably the biggest problem or data problem at the heart of Brexit. The UK could apply for an adequacy decision to

1   Vanberg and Maunick, 'Data Protection in the UK Post-Brexit: The Only Certainty Is Uncertainty' (2018) 32(1) *International Review of Law, Computers & Technology* 190.
2   Day, 'Isn't Brexit Frustrating?' (2019) 78(2) *Cambridge Law Journal* 270.
3   Lewis, 'A Dramatic Brexit: Why the United Kingdom's EU Referendum Vote Could Send the UK Film Industry Reeling' (2017) 45(1) *Syracuse Journal of International Law and Commerce* 83; Butler, 'Obligations Imposed on Private Parties by the GDPR and UK Data Protection Law: Blurring the Public-Private Divide' (2018) 24(3) *European Public Law* 555.
4   Chang, 'Brexit and the EU Economic & Monetary Union: From EMU Outsider to Instigator' [2017] *The Law and Politics of Brexit* 163.
5   Lambert, 'Data Protection and Brexit Threats – Will Adequacy Work?' (2018) 23(4) *Communications Law* 1.

(re)commence EU-UK data transfer post Brexit.[6] After all, one of the intentions of the new UK DPA 2018 was to comply with EU level rules set out in the GDPR.

The UK GDPR must also be considered. Unfortunately, this is not established in a stand-alone statute/Act per se, which would give it added certainty and clarity.

As Article 45(1) makes clear, the EU Commission makes the decision on whether the destination jurisdiction of the transfer is deemed acceptable and adequate to exempt such transfers from the default transfer ban. It also seems clear that before such a decision may be arrived at, the intended destination country must apply for an adequacy assessment culminating in an adequacy decision.

While there is reference to an adequacy decision, it would seem that an application can result in a negative as well as a positive outcome. It is less clear if there is a positive and negative adequacy decision or rather if an adequacy decision only arises from a positive assessment. While this may be a semantic differentiation, practically speaking it may be that most applications are well considered in advance of application as to the merits and chances of a successful outcome. There is also the possibility of advance discussions between the parties.

An adequacy decision has now been granted for a period of four years. The implications of the Consultation related data protection law changes will need to be carefully scrutinised as to whether they may change the basis upon which the adequacy decision was granted, and call its continuance into question. Adequacy decisions can be suspended, cancelled, or not renewed.

The general (EU) rule or principle is that transfers of personal data outside the EU are prohibited per se. This is a longstanding bedrock position in data protection rules. It is a default transfer ban. Therefore, on Brexit day, the use and transfer of personal data required for countless transactions from and between the EU must cease. This would have undoubted consequences for commerce and City financial entities.

Article 44 of the GDPR sets out the general principle for transfers within the EU under the data protection regime. The rule provides that:

> 'Any transfer of personal data which are undergoing processing or are intended for processing after transfer to a third country or to an international organisation shall take place only if, subject to the other provisions of this Regulation, the conditions laid down in this Chapter are complied with by the controller and processor, including for onward transfers of personal data from the third country or an international organisation to another third country or to another international organisation. All provisions in this Chapter shall be applied in order to ensure that the level of protection of natural persons guaranteed by this Regulation is not undermined.'

---

6   The following countries and territories have also successful adequacy decisions (whether in whole or in part): Andorra, Argentina, Canada (partial), Faroe Islands, Guernsey, Israel, the Isle of Man, Jersey, New Zealand, Switzerland, Uruguay and the US (EU-US Privacy Shield only).

Therefore, 'any' transfer to a third country outside of the EU or EEA[7] may 'take place only *if*[8] certain conditions are met. So, the default position is that external transfers should not occur. *Only if* specified conditions are satisfied by way of exemption from the default rule might the transfer become permissible.

Once Brexit occurred, the UK was no longer a member country of either the EU or the EEA. The default rule kicks in and post-Brexit transfers by default are no longer permitted between the EU and the UK. One can only imagine the consequences and the imperative, therefore, to consider whether the UK can fit within one of the exceptions for (continued) data transfers. The decision was therefore very important for the UK and respective entities within the UK.

PRESSURE FOR OFFICIAL ADVICE AND CLARITY

16.03   Business needed clarity and certainty from official sources as to what would happen to the UK data transfer regime. There was significant worry as Brexit negotiations continued (and even stalled on occasion) There was and is increased focus on seeking to provide official guidance on these issues.

The following will highlight some of the many official comments and official guidance which were issued at various stages leading up to and following Brexit. From one perspective some of these (particularly those pre-Brexit and pre any deal on Brexit between the UK and EU), may now be more historic and less immediately relevant. That may be correct. However, they are extremely apt in assisting to convey the sheer uncertainty and headaches which have faced businesses.

Importantly, however, reference to this large amount of official guidance and commentary is still relevant in emphasising the point that there remains an ongoing need for such guidance. Businesses still need as much legal and business certainty as possible. Yet, businesses are still even faced with varying levels of legal and business certainty not least from new rules having to be introduced in the UK as a direct result of Brexit, the correlations between the UK and EU, divergences between the UK and EU, draft new data laws being introduced, results of the consultation of 2021/2022 announcing additional areas of data law and policy being actively reviewed for potential future change, and separate more recent announcements that close to 2,500 laws will be amended with EU related relevance. At the very least, one can say that the UK data protection regime (and to include the UK data transfer regime) is far from settled. As long as this remains the case, the UK and international businesses will face at least some uncertainty, and even some significant uncertainty depending on individual changes. There is also a potential for litigation. Litigation could include litigation against individual

---

7   The EEA is the European Economic Area, which currently comprises the EU countries plus
     Iceland, Liechtenstein, and Norway.
8   Emphasis added.

companies, against data regulators, against the EU and or EU Commission, and/ or against the UK and/or UK government.

A number of external data protection supervisory authorities also issued guidance for dealing with entities inside the UK. Organisations inside the UK receive queries that external partners have to plan and respond to accordingly.

These issues in terms of data protection generally and data transfers is an obvious concern for commercial entities and their advisors.

An example of the various, and ongoing, guidance comes from the ICO such as:

• ICO announcements, descriptions and statements on no deal Brexit;

• ICO Six Steps to Take guide on no deal Brexit;

• ICO 'Broader' guidance document on leaving EU if no withdrawal agreement;

• ICO Overview FAQs guidance on no deal Brexit;

• advice on the European Union (Withdrawal) Act 2018; and

• departmental data protection updates.

The ICO acknowledged that:

> '[w]hile the basis on which the UK will leave the EU has still to be decided, the ICO has today published new guidance and practical tools to help organisations understand the implications in the event of a no deal'.

The set of ICO documentation includes:

• announcements and descriptions (press statement, blog post, etc);

• Six Steps to Take guide;

• 'broader' guidance document on leaving EU if no withdrawal agreement; and

• overview FAQs guidance.

The ICO blog post is more detailed than the press release. It notes that the 'Government has made clear that the [GDPR] will be absorbed into UK law at the point of exit, so there will be no substantive change'. However, readers will note that the DPA 2018 does not absorb or implement the GDPR.

The blog also suggests that the 'two-way free flow of personal information will no longer be the case if the UK leaves the EU without a withdrawal agreement that specifically provides [and hopefully expressly so provide] for the continued flow of personal data'. However, it may also be that an official EU adequacy decision may be needed also, and indeed which later occurred..

The ICO blog advises organisations to take 'precautionary preparations' to 'ensure these data flows continue'. Previously, there was uncertainty as to whether there would be a deal. The official advice is to 'carefully consider alternative transfer mechanisms to maintain data flows'. If the EU-UK adequacy decision is challenged by a third party this will create a new level of uncertainty. Bear in mind also that an EU adequacy decision is subject to review. Such review is mandated. The EU Commission must at the time of such review consider whether the criteria and conditions in the third-party recipient state (in this case the UK) continue to satisfy the data transfer rules.

Notwithstanding that there was ultimately a deal and Brexit has occurred, there will, even in the normal course, remain a need for added diligence by entities seeking to engage in data transfers. Regard will have to be had to the categories of data, where the data is, what UK rules apply, what EU rules may apply (and what additional rules may apply depending on the data stream). Post Brexit data laws in the UK are and will be very important. If that was not complicated enough, there is at least a proposal to get rid of a whole variety of retained EU law in the UK, with some suggestion referring to close to 2,500 laws. This is obviously a complicated, if not controversial, issue.

One of the additional rules may relate to the standard contractual clauses route. It is indicated that there will be further official guidance and assistance in relation to these contracts. Another route, but one generally reserved for multinational organisations is approved binding corporate rules. These take time. However, it is suggested in the guidance that they may need to be reviewed.

The ICO also issued a six-step assistance guide. It states that '[i]f you operate in the EEA, you may need to comply with both the UK data protection regime and the EU regime after the UK exits the EU. You may also need to appoint a representative in the EEA'. The six steps for 'Leaving the EU' are:

1.   continue to comply;

2.   transfers to the UK;

3.   transfers from the UK;

4.   European operations;

5.   documentation; and

6.   organisational awareness.

Point 1 (Continue to comply) states, inter alia, that:

> 'The [DPA 2018] will remain in place. The government intends to bring the GDPR directly into UK law on exit, to sit alongside it. There will be some technical adjustments to the UK version of the GDPR so that it works in a UK-only context – for example, amending provisions referring to EU law and enforcement cooperation.'

Point 1 (transfers to the UK) states, inter alia, that organisations must:

'Review your data flows and identify where you receive data from the EEA, including from suppliers and processors. Think about what GDPR safeguards you can put in place to ensure that data can continue to flow once we are outside the EU.'

It continues that this 'means the sender needs to make sure there are adequate safeguards in place, or one of the exceptions listed in the GDPR'.

It also refers to the importance of the adequacy decision issue. It states that:

'If the EU makes a formal adequacy decision that the UK regime offers an adequate level of protection, there will be no need for specific safeguards. However, on exit date there may not be such a decision in place. So you should plan to implement adequate safeguards.'

The ICO guidance advises that '[y]ou may want to consider putting standard contractual clauses (SCCs) in place if you are receiving data from the EEA'.

Point 3 (transfers from the UK) refers to transfers from the UK to the EU; and to transfers from the UK to countries outside the EEA. In terms of the latter, the guidance states, inter alia, '[w]e expect the UK government to confirm that the UK will reflect existing EU adequacy decisions, approved EU SCCs and BCRs'. It then cross-refers to the more detailed guidance. Readers will note that this is descriptive of some future governmental and legal decisions and rules. It is unclear specifically what this refers to, or when.

Point 4 (European operations) states, inter alia, that '[i]f you operate across Europe, you should review your structure, processing operations and data flows to assess how the UK's exit from the EU will affect the data protection regimes that apply to you'.

It also refers to data protection regimes and reiterates that organisations may need to comply with EU and the UK data protection regimes, highlighting the need for dual compliance exercises. Issues of branches and establishments within the post-Brexit EU must be considered. A further consideration is having to deal with the UK and one or more respective data protection authorities.

It refers also to lead authority and One-Stop-Shop, and states, inter alia, that '[i]f the UK is currently your lead [data protection] supervisory authority, you should review the structure of your European operations to assess whether you will continue to be able to have a lead authority and benefit from One-Stop-Shop'.

The need to appoint a representative located in the EU is also highlighted.

Point 5 (documentation) highlights the need to review the organisation's locations, documentation flows, processes and relationships. This applies to both inward and outward facing. Once changes occur there will be additional changes, such as identifying and differentiating EU and UK legal references in documentation, policies, notices, etc.

Point 6 (organisational awareness) reiterates the need for training and internal awareness raising processes. This is needed generally, but also needs to be utilised as Brexit related data changes arise, as well as engagement and consultation to identify these issues in advance and make appropriate preparations. Reference is also made to the need for organisations to have, and to update, their risk register.

The ICO also issued a broader Brexit transfer guidance. This highlights that the (various) guidance is particularly relevant to organisations which:

- operate in the EEA, which includes the EU;

- send personal data outside the UK; or

- receive personal data from the EU/EEA.

It is also indicated to be relevant where the following apply to the organisation:

- the Privacy and Electronic Communications (EC Directive) Regulations (PECR);[9]

- the Network and Information Systems Regulations (NIS);[10] or

- EU Regulation 910/2014 on electronic identification and trust services for electronic transactions in the internal market (eIDAS).

The guidance refers to the DPA 2018. It points out that it came into force at the same time as the GDPR, and covers four data protection regimes, namely:

1. Part 2, Chapter 2: General processing – the GDPR – 'this chapter supplements the GDPR so that it operates in a UK context'.

2. Part 2, Chapter 3: Other general processing – 'this chapter applies a UK version of the GDPR (the "applied GDPR") to those areas outside the scope of EU law, such as defence'.

3. Part 3: Law enforcement processing – 'this chapter brings into UK law the EU Data Protection Directive 2016/680 (the Law Enforcement Directive)'.

4. Part 4: Intelligence services processing.

The ICO frequently asked questions (FAQs) guidance refers to the following:

- will the GDPR still apply if we leave EU without a deal?

- what will the UK data protection law be if we leave without a deal?

- is the old ICO guidance still relevant?

- can we still transfer data to and from Europe if we leave without a deal?

- do PECR rules still apply?

---

9   Privacy and Electronic Communications (EC Directive) Regulations 2003 (SI 2003/2426) (PECR).
10 Network and Information Systems Regulations 2018 (SI 2018/506) (NIS).

- do network and information system (NIS) rules still apply?

- do the electronic identification and trust services for electronic transactions in the internal market (eIDAS) rules still apply?

- do FOIA still apply?

- do the environmental information regulations (EIR) still apply?

- will ICO be producing more guidance?

The first question advises that:

> 'The GDPR is an EU Regulation and, in principle, it will no longer apply to the UK if we leave the EU on 29 March 2019 without a deal. However, if you operate inside the UK, you will need to comply with UK data protection law. The government *intends* to incorporate the GDPR into UK data protection law when we exit the EU – so in practice there will be little change to the core data protection principles, rights and obligations found in the GDPR' (emphasis added and as of 29 March 2019 has now been superseded by extensions).

In terms of organisations wishing to continue dealing with the EU, its adds that the 'GDPR may also still apply directly to you if you operate in Europe, offer goods or services to individuals in Europe, or monitor the behaviour of individuals in Europe'. The GDPR will also 'still apply to any organisations in Europe who send you data, so you may need to help them decide how to transfer personal data to the UK in line with the GDPR'. The guidance cross-refers to the six points above.

Question 2 above indicates that the DPA 2018 'which currently supplements and tailors the GDPR within the UK, will continue to apply'. Again, referring to the future intent, it states that the 'government also intends to incorporate the provisions of the GDPR directly into UK law if we leave the EU without a deal, to sit alongside the DPA 2018'. In addition, the ICO 'expect the government to use new legislation to make technical amendments to the GDPR so that it works in a UK-only context'.

Question 4 above asks if an organisation can still transfer data to and from Europe if the UK leaves without a deal. The ICO guidance is as follows:

> 'The government has said that transfers of data from the UK to the European Economic Area (EEA) will not be restricted. However, if we leave the EU without a deal, GDPR transfer rules will apply to any data coming from the EEA into the UK. You need to consider what GDPR safeguards you can put in place to ensure that data can continue to flow into the UK.'

In terms of Question 5, referring to the PECR rules, the ICO states:

> 'Yes. The current PECR rules cover marketing, cookies and electronic communications. They derive from EU law but are set out in UK law. They will continue to apply after we exit the EU.'

Forthcoming EU changes are also noted:

> 'The EU is replacing the current e-privacy law with a new e-privacy Regulation (ePR). The new ePR is not yet agreed. It is unlikely to be finalised before the UK exists the EU. This means the ePR will not form part of UK law if we leave without a deal.'

Question 6 refers to NIS rules. The guidance advises, inter alia, that organisations may need to appoint local representatives in the EU and to review and comply with local NIS rules.

This guidance concludes by saying that '[i]n the meantime, given that we expect UK data protection law to remain aligned with the GDPR, our Guide to GDPR remains a good source of advice and guidance on how to comply with UK and EU data protection rules both now and after we leave the EU'. The guidance will be variously updated as changes and new developments occur.

However, the European Union (Withdrawal) Act 2018 is not referred to.

Given obvious concerns, the ICO decided to issue further guidance referring expressly to the issues arising from a no deal Brexit scenario. This is commercially focused guidance (with the ICO noting that separate guidance may be issued in future for the benefit of individuals). In particular, this no deal Brexit guidance[11] is aimed at businesses and organisations:

- operating in the EU or EEA;

- sending personal data outside the UK; or

- receiving personal data from the EU or EEA.

Obviously a deal was ultimately reached. Hence, the so-called UK GDPR.

The ICO advised that the guidance should be reviewed if the GDPR applies to the organisation (which really does not exclude many). The ICO comments that '[w]hen the UK exits the EU [which it now has], the EU GDPR will no longer be law in the UK. The UK government intends to write the GDPR into UK law, with necessary changes to tailor its provisions for the UK (the "UK GDPR"). The government has published a Keeling Schedule for the GDPR, which shows planned amendments'.[12]

The ICO also advised that the following should be considered:

- 'Data Protection If There's No Brexit Deal';

- 'International data transfers';

---

11 Entitled 'Data Protection If There's No Brexit Deal'.
12 In fact, there are two separate Keeling schedules. See 'Data Protection Regulation Keeling Schedule. Available at: https://assets.publishing.service.gov.uk/government/uploads/system/uploads/attachment_data/file/685632/2018-03-05_Keeling_Schedule.pdf and 'Data Protection Act 2018 Keeling Schedule'. Available at: https://assets.publishing.service.gov.uk/government/uploads/system/uploads/attachment_data/file/779334/Keeling_Schedule_for_Data_Protection_Act_2018.pdf/.

- 'EU representatives';

- 'One-stop Shop regulatory oversight by a lead data protection authority'.

It was the government's intention that:

> 'the UK GDPR will also apply to controllers and processors based outside the UK, where their processing activities relate to:
>
> - offering goods or services to individuals in the UK; or
>
> - monitoring the behaviour of individuals taking place in the UK.'

The ICO gives examples where transfers by a UK business to its consumers outside the UK are permitted; while transfers to third-party organisations or service providers (including cloud service) can trigger the GDPR or UK GDPR.

Those who currently make data transfers outside the EEA should 'already' have compliance strategies in place.

On exit day, organisations needed to consider if they were intending to make restricted transfers outside the UK (permissible IF covered by an adequacy decision; an appropriate safeguard; or an exception); and if it is receiving personal data from outside of the UK.

The ICO also refers to the European Data Protection Board (EDPB) advice in relation to transfers in the event of a no deal Brexit, the ICO data transfers guide as well as any future guidance.

Various detailed references and examples are made to adequacy decisions and appropriate safeguards (eg, standard contractual clauses; binding corporate rules) for restricted transfers. These should be considered in detail as appropriate. Some of this is contingent on future UK legislation.

As regards those in the UK who propose to continue to receive personal data from the EU, it is reiterated that the GDPR applies to such transfers and to the transferor. It is noted that the UK will, on exit day, become a so-called third country (outside the EU), in which case additional restrictions apply to transfers. The ICO has further transfer guidance, as does the EDPB. Organisations should 'take a broad interpretation of [what is] a restricted transfer' (ICO). The EU transferor will 'only' be able to make the transfer to the UK transferee organisation if one of the following apply:

- there is an EU adequacy decision (eg, appropriate safeguards; standard contractual clauses). Additional provisions may apply to public bodies. (Unfortunately, from the UK perspective, '[a]t exit date there may not be an adequacy decision by the European Commission regarding the UK' (ICO) [that would seem to be an understatement at present]);

- an exception outside of the above applies – but which are interpreted very narrowly and restrictively (such as medical emergencies; explicit consent; occasional contract transfers; occasional public interest transfers; occasional legal defence transfers; transfers from public registers; exceptional compelling legitimate interest transfers). The transferor will decide if applicable, not the UK recipient.

There is guidance in relation to transfers from jurisdictions covered by an EU adequacy decision (as opposed to the EU itself). Organisations, therefore, must consider where potential post Brexit transfers to the UK may come from.

The ICO advises that preparation is necessary. The advice states that organisations should:

- assess their data flows and transfers in order to identify problem restricted transfers in advance;

- consider if and how transfers may continue, especially in the absence of a possible future EU adequacy decision which may not have been issued yet;

- consider standard contractual clauses with the counter party (note the ICO tool available and their draft template contracts);

- update binding corporate rules, if previously utilised;

- update documentation and privacy notices; and

- carry out compliance vetting by the transferor entity.

Particular considerations also arise for UK entities that do not have an office, branch or establishment in the EU or EEA after exit day. Other entities may have appointed a representative in the EU for GDPR purposes. The ICO provides commentary on these situations. Indeed, many organisations will already have established branches outside the UK or even moved outside of the UK as a result of preparing for the possibility of Brexit. GDPR compliance must be considered. Details and commentary on these scenarios are referred to in the ICO guidance.

Organisations may need to review their:

- agreements, contracts and appointments;

- terms, contracts, policies and websites;

- rights of data subjects;

- transfer documentation;

- data protection impact assessments (DPIAs);[13]

---

13 See also GDPR Art 35. Also see Warren, Bayley, Bennett, Charlesworth, Clarke and Oppenheim, 'Privacy Impact Assessments: International Experience as a Basis for UK Guidance' (2008) 24(3) *Computer Law and Security Review: The International Journal of Technology and Practice*; Friedewald, Hansen, Bieker, and Obersteller, 'A Process for Data Protection Impact Assessment Under the European General Data Protection Regulation' conference, 4th Annual Privacy Forum, APF 2016 (2016). Also note recent consultation issued in 2021 and which has the potential to amend the risk assessment rules in the UK.

- Data Protection Officer or Officers;[14] and

- further ICO and other official guidance.

Other data protection supervisory authorities were also variously issuing advice and guidance in relation to Brexit, particularly as the possibility of no deal increased.

Additional Brexit advice, guidance, and commentary has also been issued from the ICO.

The European Data Protection Supervisor (EDPS) has also issued guidance in relation to the possibility of a No Deal Brexit.[15]

The EDPS notes that, as of 1 November 2019, the UK will be a third country as referred to under the data protection rules and transfer restrictions automatically kick in. (This was unless the Withdrawal Agreement takes effects prior to that date, which then did not seem likely, in which case transfers should be able to continue until 31 December 2020 (an effective transition period) pending final arrangements and negotiations. Note, the 2020 deadline could be extended by two years. This seems moot presently.)

The EDPS notes that a no deal Brexit 'would have [immediate] repercussions for the protection of personal data ... because ... EU ... law, including data protection law, will cease to apply in the UK'. The GDPR requirements and restrictions on data transfers to less safe or non-equivalent third countries will apply.[16] There is a default transfer ban, unless one of the limited number of transfer mechanisms can be established for particular data transfers or transactions involving personal data.

The level of protection for the data being transferred must not be undermined.[17]

Businesses and their advisers must therefore have considered whether there is a business need for data transfers which will be adversely affected by a no deal Brexit. If so, the organisation needed to assess how best to establish safeguards and the application of one of the limited number of transfer mechanisms in this scenario 'to enable the transfer to a third country' – the UK in this instance.

The EDPS refers to:

- adequacy decisions (see GDPR Article 47 regarding adequate levels of protection);

- appropriate safeguards (GDPR Article 48), eg,

---

14 See also GDPR, Art 39.
15 'Information Note on International Data Transfers After Brexit' 16 July 2019.
16 See GDPR, Ch V.
17 GDPR, Art 46.

- standard contractual clauses expressly adopted by the Commission for such purposes (transfers to controllers 2001/497, 2004/915)(transfers to processors 2010/87);

- binding corporate rules (BCRs)(applicable to a group of companies – and importantly approved by one of the respective data protection supervisory authorities. Note, prior BCRs can continue to apply but may need certain amendments post the GDPR. Currently, BCRs may be applied for in the UK, but this takes time and it remains unclear how the ICO could approve BCRs in a no deal Brexit);[18]

- codes of conduct and certification mechanisms. (However, the exact nature of how this would work is not fully established and more guidance is awaited);

- ad hoc contractual clauses. However, prior authorisation from a data protection supervisory authority would be necessary;[19] and

- derogations.[20]

The EDPS notes that a common feature in the above is that data subject rights must be enforceable and effective. In terms of derogations, the EDPS notes that these are exhaustively mentioned in Article 50:

- explicit consent of the individual to the transfer – 'having been provided with all necessary information about the risks associated with the transfer';

- where the transfer is necessary for contract performance to which the data subject is a part;

- where the transfer is necessary to conclude or perform a contract concluded in the interest of the data subject;

- where the transfer is necessary for important public interest reasons;

- where the transfer is necessary for legal claims;

- where the transfer is necessary to protect the vital interests of the data subject (or someone else) and the data subject is physically or legally incapable of giving consent; and

- where the transfer is made from a public register.

In what may be an important clarification, the EDPS notes that a position paper[21] by the Commission says that personal data transferred (to the UK) before the Withdrawal Date may continue to be processed.

---

18 See GDPR, Arts 46–48.
19 GDPR, Art 48(3)(a).
20 GDPR, Art 50(1).
21 Commission, 'Position paper on the Use of Data and Protection of Information Obtained or Processed Before the Withdrawal Date,' 20 September 2017.

However, a note of caution is advised in that data processing activities must be judged both at the time of collection and the processing and storage. That the initial collection may be lawful and permissible, does not absent an organisation from the assessment of ascertaining a current lawful basis for current processing – especially the further in time the current processing is from the time of the initial date of collection. Moreso, in the event of secondary uses or purposes of processing. Later storage also requires a separate assessment of the basis for ongoing storage.

The EDPS, referring to the Commission Position Paper, stated:

> 'The European Commission in the Position Paper on the Use of Data and Protection of Information Obtained or Processed Before the Withdrawal Date concludes that UK-based controllers and processors may continue to process personal data transferred before the withdrawal date only if these data enjoy the protection of EU data protection law. Such protection will be guaranteed, in the case that a Withdrawal Agreement is put in place.'

The above caution should be noted, however, as anything to do with Brexit and data transfers is far from simple or assured in the current climate and data processing activities can be varied and more nuanced than a headline description may suggest.

The EDPS acknowledges and cautions that '[t]he developments on this sensitive issue should be closely followed and the EDPS [and others] may provide further guidance' as necessary. After all, this is a very fluid situation.

The EDPS set out five steps to prepare for Brexit, which businesses and organisations should consider, namely:

1. map the data processing activities;

2. check available data transfer mechanisms that best suit;

3. implement the correct data transfer mechanism before 1 November 2019;

4. update internal documentation; and

5. update data protection notices.

(These steps are also included in guidance from the EDPB from 12 February 2019.)

In addition to the above Position Paper referred to by the EDPS, the Commission has also issued a 'Notice to Stakeholders Withdrawal of the United Kingdom from the Union and EU Rules in the Field of Data Protection' on 9 January 2018. This notes that given the Article 50 notice submitted by the UK (on 29 March 2017) that EU law ceases to apply in the UK – unless there is a validated Withdrawal Agreement. (Note, the latest extension was granted in October, extending the period to 21 January 2020.) The Commission 'Notice to Stakeholders' notes the 'considerable uncertainties' and that 'all stakeholders processing personal data are reminded of legal repercussions, which need to be considered when the

[UK] becomes a third country'. The Commission highlights the possible needs to consider:

- standard data protection clauses (as approved by Commission);

- binding corporate rules (but which generally only apply to certain large group entities, and in any event require prior approval from a data protection supervisory authority);

- approved codes of conduct; and

- approved certification mechanisms.

The Commission notes that the rules relating to some of these mechanisms have been simplified in the GDPR as compared with the prior DPD95/46.[22]

The EDPB issued guidance entitled 'Information Note on Data Transfers Under the GDPR in the Event of a No Deal Brexit'.[23] In this scenario it reiterates the need to consider:

- standard or ad hoc data protection clauses;

- binding corporate rules;

- codes of conduct and certification mechanisms; and

- derogations.

It also includes reference to the five steps referred to above. It notes that at the time of issue, '[a]ccording to the UK Government, the current practice, which permits personal data to flow freely from the UK to the EEA, will continue in the event of a no-deal Brexit'. However, matters have shifted politically since then and the immediate next steps remain somewhat less certain, which is unfortunate for business entities which require the ability to plan forward. The 'UK Government's and the ICO's website should be regularly consulted'. While there is uncertainty, organisations wishing to continue dealing and receiving personal data from their unconnected business partners located inside the EU must most likely implement standard contractual clauses, given that binding corporate rules will only apply to the largest of organisations and in a pre-approved manner. In addition, there will be increased pressure on parties in the EU wishing to continue to deal with UK entities, to implement appropriate mechanisms and safeguards from their end, in which case they will be raising queries directly with their UK counterparties.

In December 2020, the ICO updated its webpage in light of the EU/UK agreement.[24] This includes the following guidance:

22 Directive 95/46/EC of the European Parliament and of the Council of 24 October 1995 on the protection of individuals with regard to the processing of personal data and on the free movement of such data. [1995] OJ L281, 31–50.
23 European Data Protection Board (EDPB), 'Information Note on Data Transfers Under the GDPR in the Event of a No Deal Brexit' 12 February 2019.
24 See Keep Data Flowing, at https://ico.org.uk/for-organisations/dp-at-the-end-of-the-transition-period/.

'What effect does the trade deal have on data protection?

As part of the new trade deal, the EU has agreed to delay transfer restrictions for at least another four months, which can be extended to six months (known as the bridge). This enables personal data to flow freely from the European Economic Area (EEA) to the UK until either adequacy decisions are adopted, or the bridge ends.

If you receive personal data from the EEA, we recommend you put alternative safeguards in place before the end of April 2021, if you have not done so already.

For more information, read Data Protection at the end of the transition period and our guidance on International Transfers.

We have also produced an interactive tool on using standard contractual clauses for transfers into the UK to help you. [In late 2020, the EU published new draft standard contractual clauses.]

We will keep our guidance under review and update it as necessary to reflect any developments.

Do we need a European representative?

You may need to appoint an EU representative if you are offering goods or services to individuals in the EEA or monitoring the behaviour of individuals in the EEA. For more information, Data protection at the end of the transition period – European representatives.'

Official guidance by way of correspondence (from the Department for Digital, Culture, Media & Sport) indicates that:

'The EU (Withdrawal) Act 2018 (EUWA) retains the GDPR in UK law. The fundamental principles, obligations and rights that organisations and data subjects have become familiar with will stay the same. To ensure the UK data protection framework continues to operate effectively when the UK is no longer as EU Member State, the government will make appropriate changes to the GDPR and Data Protection Act 2018 using regulation-making powers under the EUWA.' [It has now done so by changes to DPA 2018 by the Data Protection, Privacy and Electronic Communications (Amendments etc) (EU Exit) Regulations 2019 (SI 2019/419) which also amend the GDPR. The consolidated amended GDPR (Keeling Schedule) is online at: https://assets. publishing.service.gov.uk/government/uploads/system/ uploads/attachment_ data/file/946117/20201102_-_GDPR_-__MASTER__Keeling_ Schedule__ with_changes_highlighted__V3.pdf, and the consolidated Keeling schedule DPA 2018 is at: https://assets.publishing.service.gov.uk/government/ uploads/system/uploads/ attachment_data/file/946100/20201102_-_DPA_-__MASTER__Keeling_Schedule__with_ changes_highlighted__V3.pdf. Those two files should be read rather than the original GDPR and DPA 2018 in order to see the latest legislation and in particular the 'UK GDPR' which will apply following the end of the post-Brexit interim period.'

The guidance then directs readers to the ICO website.

The ICO also provided guidance in relation to:

- Assessing Adequacy;

- Model Contract Clauses;

- Binding Corporate Rules; and

- Outsourcing.

There is also the following ICO guidance which can be a useful reference for organisations, namely, the:

- Data Protection Act;

- International Data Transfers;

- Information Commissioner's Recommended Approach to Assessing Adequacy Including Consideration of the Issue of Contractual Solutions, Binding Corporate Rules.

ONE SOLUTION TO ONE DATA PROBLEM

16.04 There are a limited number of exceptions to the EU transfer ban and processes through which it may be permitted by way of exemption to undertake transfers of personal data from the EU to an outside jurisdiction. One of these is that the EU has made a determination called an 'adequacy decision' permitting such data transfers to a named country from the EU on the basis that the recipient jurisdiction has an adequate level of protection and rights in relation to personal data that are at least equivalent to those in the EU.

One of the exceptions provided is known as the 'adequacy exception' or condition. This is particularly important for the UK post Brexit. It is difficult to overestimate the importance of this issue – both legally and commercially. The UK sought to avail of the application procedure to have itself deemed adequate for the purposes of data transfers and that the UK laws at the time are sufficient to be deemed compatible and equivalent to those in the EU. Initially, they may not, because the DPA 2018 does not implement the GDPR. There were/are also other potential obstacles to a smooth adequacy decision occurring (eg, human rights, interception of communications).

The UK GDPR also needs to be carefully considered, such as its basis, why it is not a second Data Protection Act in addition to the DPA 2018, whether and how it differs from the GDPR, etc.

Article 45 of the GDPR provides as follows:

'1. A transfer of personal data to a third country or an international organisation may take place where the Commission has decided that the third country, a territory or one or more specified sectors within that third country, or the international organisation in question ensures an adequate level of protection. Such a transfer shall not require any specific authorisation.

2. When assessing the adequacy of the level of protection, the Commission shall, in particular, take account of the following elements:

    (a) the rule of law, respect for human rights and fundamental freedoms, relevant legislation, both general and sectoral, including concerning public security, defence, national security and criminal law and the access of public authorities to personal data, as well as the implementation of such legislation, data protection rules, professional rules and security measures, including rules for the onward transfer of personal data to another third country or international organisation which are complied with in that country or international organisation, case-law, as well as effective and enforceable data subject rights and effective administrative and judicial redress for the data subjects whose personal data are being transferred;

    (b) the existence and effective functioning of one or more independent supervisory authorities in the third country or to which an international organisation is subject, with responsibility for ensuring and enforcing compliance with the data protection rules, including adequate enforcement powers, for assisting and advising the data subjects in exercising their rights and for cooperation with the supervisory authorities of the Member States; and

    (c) the international commitments the third country or international organisation concerned has entered into, or other obligations arising from legally binding conventions or instruments as well as from its participation in multilateral or regional systems, in particular in relation to the protection of personal data.

3. The Commission, after assessing the adequacy of the level of protection, may decide, by means of an implementing act, that a third country, a territory or one or more specified sectors within a third country or an international organisation ensures an adequate level of protection within the meaning of paragraph 2 of this Article. The implementing act shall provide for a mechanism for a periodic review, at least every four years, which shall take into account all relevant developments in the third country or international organisation. The implementing act shall specify its territorial and sectoral application and, where applicable, identify the supervisory authority or authorities referred to in point (b) of paragraph 2 of this Article. The implementing act shall be adopted in accordance with the examination procedure referred to in Article 93(2).

4. The Commission shall, on an ongoing basis, monitor developments in third countries and international organisations that could affect the functioning of decisions adopted pursuant to paragraph 3 of this Article and decisions adopted on the basis of Article 25(6) of Directive 95/46/EC.[25]

5. The Commission shall, where available information reveals, in particular following the review referred to in paragraph 3 of this Article, that a

---

25 Directive 95/46/EC of the European Parliament and of the Council of 24 October 1995 on the protection of individuals with regard to the processing of personal data and on the free movement of such data. [1995] OJ L281, 31–50.

third country, a territory or one or more specified sectors within a third country, or an international organisation no longer ensures an adequate level of protection within the meaning of paragraph 2 of this Article, to the extent necessary, repeal, amend or suspend the decision referred to in paragraph 3 of this Article by means of implementing acts without retro-active effect. Those implementing acts shall be adopted in accordance with the examination procedure referred to in Article 93(2).

On duly justified imperative grounds of urgency, the Commission shall adopt immediately applicable implementing acts in accordance with the procedure referred to in Article 93(3).

6. The Commission shall enter into consultations with the third country or international organisation with a view to remedying the situation giving rise to the decision made pursuant to paragraph 5.

7. A decision pursuant to paragraph 5 of this Article is without prejudice to transfers of personal data to the third country, a territory or one or more specified sectors within that third country, or the international organisation in question pursuant to Articles 46 to 49.

8. The Commission shall publish in the *Official Journal of the European Union* and on its website a list of the third countries, territories and specified sectors within a third country and international organisations for which it has decided that an adequate level of protection is or is no longer ensured.

9. Decisions adopted by the Commission on the basis of Article 25(6) of Directive 95/46/EC shall remain in force until amended, replaced or repealed by a Commission Decision adopted in accordance with paragraph 3 or 5 of this Article.'

This should not be thought of as an exception but rather a mechanism by which to seek an exception from the default transfer ban set out in Article 44 of the GDPR.

It should also be noted that while there are other exceptions or mechanisms, the adequacy mechanism refers not to what each individual company might seek to do but how it operates on a national or nation-state basis. If the adequacy mechanism was to apply, it would apply to the UK per se not company by company. (Individual organisations would benefit to the extent that they are located in the UK.) There is great benefit, therefore, in the UK pursuing and successfully obtaining such an adequacy decision from the EU in relation to the transfer of data to the UK.

The government called for an early adequacy decision from the EU – thus, at least recognising the threat. However, there was no guarantee of this happening or happening as early as the government might have liked.

However, there was a critical problem. In general, an adequacy decision application and review process can take years. That was problematic, to say the least, for Brexit. Optimally, the UK would like a positive adequacy decision to be agreed on day one of Brexit. That seemed unrealistic, if not impossible as the normal process timeframe takes years.

The most recent example of an application for an adequacy decision was filed by Japan. The Commission announced in January 2017 that it had launched a dialogue with the aim of reaching an adequacy decision with Japan.[26] On 17 July 2018, the Commission and Japan concluded the negotiations on a reciprocal finding of an adequate level of protection by the EU and Japan:[27]

> '[t]he Commission will now launch the process leading to the adoption of the adequacy decision under the General Data Protection Regulation. This includes obtaining an opinion from the European Data Protection Board [EDPB], which brings together all the national data protection authorities, and the green light from a committee composed of representatives of the EU Member States. Once this procedure will have been completed, the Commission will adopt the adequacy decision'.[28]

The Commission described the next stages of the process in more detail:

> 'The Commission is planning on adopting the adequacy decision in autumn this year, following the usual procedure:
>
> * approval of the draft adequacy decision by the Commission;
>
> * Opinion from the European Data Protection Board (EDPB), followed by a comitology procedure;
>
> * update of the European Parliament Committee on Civil Liberties, Justice and Home Affairs;
>
> * adoption of the adequacy decision by the Commission.'[29]

Therefore, the process involves even further work.

Ultimately, the Commission announced that the adequacy decision was finalised and adopted on 23 January 2019. It could not be predicted, however, that a UK adequacy decision would be finalised within the same timeframe.

The MPs on the Exiting the EU committee were concerned to issue a report stating that '[t]he UK government should immediately open talks to secure a Data Adequacy Decision from the European Commission, MPs said in a ... report'.[30] The Committee warns that:

> 'An adequacy decision is not automatic and, because this is the first time

---

26 'International Data Flows: Commission Launches the Adoption of Its Adequacy Decision on Japan' European Commission Press Release, 5 September 2018. Available at: http://europa.eu/rapid/press-release_IP-18-5433_en.htm.

27 'Questions & Answers on the Japan Adequacy Decision,' European Commission – Fact Sheet, Tokyo, 17 July 2018. Available at: http://europa.eu/rapid/press-release_MEMO-18-4503_en.htm.

28 Ibid.

29 'The European Union and Japan Agreed to Create the World's Largest Area of Safe Data Flows' European Commission Press Release, 17 July 2018. Available at: http://europa.eu/rapid/press-release_IP-18-4501_en.htm.

30 Fox, 'Seek New Data Deal with EU Immediately, MPs Tell May' *EurActive.com*, 2 July 2018. The Exiting the UK Committee, and it reports are available at: www.parliament.uk/business/committees/committees-a-z/commons-select/exiting-the-european-union-committee/.

a Member State has chosen to leave the UK and then seek an adequacy decision, the timetable is difficult to predict. There is a risk that it could take longer than the transitional period.'[31]

That was not the only problem. The adequacy review process examines compatibility with EU rules, norms and rights in relation to personal data. While a new Data Protection Act has been implemented, there is potential that it: (a) may not have fully implemented the GDPR; (b) a new Data Protection Act is also needed; and (c) some aspect of the existing Act may have omitted to implement some of the GDPR or introduced some element counter to the GDPR. In addition, the UK is proposing many other changes, jettisoning previous European and EU rules (eg, human rights, some of which are considered essential to data protection rules). The potential to undermine a positive adequacy decision should not be underestimated.

CHANGES FROM EU POSITIONS

16.05 Unfortunately, as one solution arrives (in terms of UK adequacy), other problems present themselves. The above pointed to the need for a new Data Protection Act from day one of Brexit which would implement the equivalent of the GDPR into UK law.[32] It remains to be seen if the so-called UK GDPR achieved this. It also remains to be seen if it remains compatible or strictly equivalent after the new Consultation process and any resultant law changes. Even supposing discussions may have commenced in the background, or a request for the review process to commence was made at this stage, a review of the current status of data protections as they exist in the UK would be required and a comparison made to those operating in the EU. In any such current review, issues such as the following would be looked at: how the DPA 2018 does not implement the GDPR; how the Act varies aspects of the GDPR and whether these are permissible or overbroad; how additional changes in the Act may or may not be compatible with the GDPR; how additional legal changes other than in the Act may or may not be compatible with the GDPR (think of human rights, individual rights and freedoms, etc); how announced or proposed changes to UK law would vary and differ from EU law and how this may impact on personal data issues. The government has published a 'Keeling Schedule of possible changes to the GDPR'.[33] It remains to be seen how all of these changes will interact with each other if ever challenged.

---

31 Ibid.
32 On the basis that there is currently no Data Protection Act 2019, any agreed draft or even a recognition or firm proposal for one, one wonders if there is any current basis upon which to make an adequacy application in relation to UK data protection as it will exist post-Brexit.
33 In fact, there are two separate Keeling schedules. See 'Data Protection Regulation Keeling Schedule, at https://assets.publishing.service.gov.uk/government/uploads/system/uploads/attachment_data/file/685632/2018-03-05_Keeling_Schedule.pdf; and 'Data Protection Act 2018 Keeling Schedule' at https://assets.publishing.service.gov.uk/ government/uploads/system/uploads/attachment_data/file/779334/Keeling_Schedule_for_Data_Protection_Act_2018.pdf/.

While there is a new DPA 2018, further additional new changes or (secondary) regulations pursuant to the European Union (Withdrawal) Act 2018, and further amendments were contained in two schedules of amendments, namely:

- the DPA 2018 Keeling Schedule of amendments;[34] and

- the General Data Protection Regulation Keeling Schedule of UK amendments.[35]

The current Consultation, and any consequent law changes, hold potential impacts as to whether UK data protection laws will diverge significantly from the EU.

The DPA 2018 Keeling Schedule of proposed 'illustrative' UK amendments may be made by what was referred to as the Data Protection, Privacy and Electronic Communications (amendments, etc)(EU Exit) Regulations 2019 (DPPEC). It was also indicated in the draft that these were 'subject to Parliamentary approval'. The DPA 2018 Keeling Schedule of amendments include,

- the UK provisions referring to the GDPR are to be changed to refer to the UK GDPR, for example in the heading of Chapter 2;

- deletion of section 9 referring to child's consent in relation to information society services;

- change of 'restriction' to 'exemptions' in sections 15 and 16;

- change of 'accreditation' to 'certification' in section 17;

- insertion of new section 17A regarding transfers based on adequacy regulations;

- insertion of new section 17B regarding transfers based on adequacy regulations: review];

- insertion of new section 17C regarding standard data protection clauses;

- change to headings on Chapter 3;

- changes to section 21 (definitions);

- deletion of sections 21 and 23 regarding application of GDPR;

- national security changes (section 28);

- changes to sections 74, 74A, 74B (re transfers);

- change from GDPR to UK GDPR section 115;

- change to section 118 regarding cooperation, and the Data Protection Convention;

---

34 Ibid.
35 Available at: https://assets.publishing.service.gov.uk/government/uploads/system/uploads/attachment_data/file/685632/ 2018-03-05_Keeling_Schedule.pdf.

- insertion of new section 119A regarding standard clauses for transfers to third countries, etc;

- various new insertions throughout the Act; and

- various changes to the schedules to the Act.[36]

The General Data Protection Regulation Keeling Schedule of proposed 'illustrative' UK amendments may also be made by what was referred to as 'Schedule 6 to the Bill'. These proposed amendments include:

- definitions (Article 4);

- lawful processing (Article 6(2) and (3));

- conditions for consent (Article 7(2));

- conditions applicable to child's consent in relation to information society services (Article 8);

- processing of special categories of personal data (Article 9);

- processing of personal data relating to criminal convictions and offences (Article 10);

- rights of data subjects (Articles 12, 13, 14, 15, 17, 22);

- restrictions (Article 23);

- joint controller (Article 26);

- representatives (Article 27);

- processors (Article 28);

- records (Article 30);

- cooperation (Article 31);

- data protection impact assessments (Article 35);

- prior consultations (Article 36);

- data protection officers (Articles 37, 39);

- codes (Articles 40, 41);

- certification (Articles 42, 43);

- transfers (Articles 44, 45, 46, 47, 48);

- derogations (Article 49);

- data protection supervisory authority (Articles 51, 52, 53, 54, 55, 56, 57, 58, 59, 60, 61, 62, 63, 64, 65, 66);

- EDPB (67, 68, 69, 70, 71, 72, 73, 74, 75, 76);

---

36 See Lambert, *The UK GDPR Annotated* (Kortext.com, 2021).

- complaints (Article 77);

- court remedies (Article 78);

- remedies (Article 79);

- representation (Article 80);

- suspension (Article 81);

- compensation (Article 82);

- fines and penalties (Articles 83, 83);

- specific situations (Articles 85, 86, 87, 88, 89, 90, 91);

- delegated acts (Article 92); and

- further amendments.

There are therefore two references to the GDPPR as it may come to be implemented in the UK, namely, the 'applied GDPR' and 'UK GDPR'.

CONCLUSION

16.06   The above highlights the complexities of Brexit, adequacy decisions and how a UK adequacy decision would be critical for the UK. Given the economic importance of continued access to EU trade and data from the EU, it is not difficult to imagine that data protection and adequacy issues were one of the most important pressing Brexit problems for those dealing with the negotiations, not to mention those sectors of the economy potentially most affected. It is already noted how just recently it has been announced that there is an intention to amend and or delete close to 2,500 UK laws with relevance to the EU. Regardless of any individual direct impact each of these changes may have, it also needs to be considered that as part of the process of considering a data transfer adequacy decision, the EU commission looks at the entire legal regime in the target country. The original review may have noted, for example, that these 2,500 laws existed. If the announced policy results in the intended statute action, the EU Commission may be forced to look at these deletions collectively and individually as to how they may impact an adequacy decision. Even apart from these 2,500 changes, there is already a draft of a new Data Protection Bill 2022/2023. One of the worries raised by various experts is the extent to which this threatens and undermines the role and independence of the UK data regulator, the ICO. This is not an insignificant concern, and there is already some caselaw on the very issue of the independence of data regulators and supervisory authorities.[37]

---

37   See Lambert, *Data Protection, Privacy Regulators and Supervisory Authorities* (Bloomsbury, 2020).

CHAPTER 17

Caselaw on transfers and transfer rules

INTRODUCTION

17.01   Data transfers are important to be sure, but abstractly may not be at the top of things that come to mind when one thinks of personal data, data laws, data rights, and general day to day compliance. Yet, perhaps surprisingly, data transfers have come to be one of the most criticised and litigated areas of the data protection regime. Strictly speaking, some of this ire is directed to particular data transfers as opposed to data transfer permission channels per se. In particular, the focus of these legal challenges have been the arrangements put in place to facilitate transfers of data to the US from the EU.

SAFE HARBOURS

17.02   The data protection regime provides that the designated policymakers can agree and set in place data transfer mechanisms between the EU and third-party states in order to enable the transfer of EU data to the target third country. It is inevitable that the US and EU would be at the forefront of discussions with the EU in terms of seeking to make arrangements in order to facilitate trade, and thus personal data, between the two blocs.

The parties came to such an agreement which came to be known as the EU-US Safe Harbour arrangement. US companies which signed up to and agreed to abide by the terms and policies set out in the US on foot of the Safe Harbour arrangement would be permitted by the EU to satisfy data protection and privacy protections equivalent to the EU data protection regime. As such, they would be permitted to be recipients of personal data coming from the EU to the US. The Safe Harbour Privacy Principles were issued by the US Department of Commerce on 21 July 2000, and are related to the EU Commission Decision 2000/520.

Ultimately, this Safe Harbour arrangement was challenged before the courts in Ireland on foot of complaints to the Irish Data Protection Commissioner (as it then was) by an Austrian privacy activist. The case was called *Schrems v Data Protection Commission.*[1] It has become known as '*Schrems 1.*' The Irish

---

1   *Maximillian Schrems v Data Protection Commissioner, joined party: Digital Rights Ireland Ltd*, Case C-362/14, ECJ, 6 October 2015.

court referred certain questions on the case, which sought to challenge the Safe Harbour arrangement, to the ECJ/CJEU under the preliminary ruling procedure.

The Irish High Court referred the following two questions to the European Court, namely:

- Whether in the course of determining a complaint which has been made to an independent office holder who has been vested by statute with the functions of administering and enforcing data protection legislation that personal data is being transferred to another third country (in this case, the United States of America) the laws and practices of which, it is claimed, do not contain adequate protections for the data subject, that office holder is absolutely bound by the Community finding to the contrary contained in [Decision 2000/520] having regard to Article 7, Article 8 and Article 47 of [the Charter], the provisions of Article 25(6) of Directive [95/46] notwithstanding?

- Or, alternatively, may and/or must the office holder conduct his or her own investigation of the matter in the light of factual developments in the meantime since that Commission decision was first published?

Many people were surprised when the ECJ ruled that the EU-US Safe Harbour decision was held invalid, and hence cancelled the measure providing a purported legal basis for a transfer permission channel to the US from the EU. The Court held that:

> '1 Article 25(6) of Directive 95/46/EC of the European Parliament and of the Council of 24 October 1995 on the protection of individuals with regard to the processing of personal data and on the free movement of such data as amended by Regulation (EC) No 1882/2003 of the European Parliament and of the Council of 29 September 2003, read in the light of Articles 7, 8 and 47 of the Charter of Fundamental Rights of the European Union, must be interpreted as meaning that a decision adopted pursuant to that provision, such as Commission Decision 2000/520/EC of 26 July 2000 pursuant to Directive 95/46 on the adequacy of the protection provided by the safe harbour privacy principles and related frequently asked questions issued by the US Department of Commerce, by which the European Commission finds that a third country ensures an adequate level of protection, does not prevent a supervisory authority of a Member State, within the meaning of Article 28 of that directive as amended, from examining the claim of a person concerning the protection of his rights and freedoms in regard to the processing of personal data relating to him which has been transferred from a Member State to that third country when that person contends that the law and practices in force in the third country do not ensure an adequate level of protection.
>
> 2. Decision 2000/520 is invalid.'

As one could expect, this caused international convulsions and head scratching with controller organisations as well as political policy makers as to what the decision meant, if or how international trade may continue, and what steps might the parties (ie EU and US) be able to negotiate anew in order to come up with an agreement which could take into account the problem issues at the core of the court's decision. Again, industry was put in a grave situation of uncertainty, and professional advisors were not immediately able to provide an instant remedy.

Problems also arose insofar as part of any solution rested at the US end. Essentially, critics were saying that the data of EU citizens was not being sufficiently protected in the US. This referred to safeguards as well as an ability for EU citizens to be able to litigate or otherwise protect their data in the US. Many observers felt that this would require certain positive changes to US law and procedure.

There was also a deluge of new commentary and discussion on the reason and impact of the solution, and some time further before the outlines of potential solutions would be expounded further upon. With a case of such importance, it would require careful study before policy makers would be confident to embark with any new measure. To some it would even present a Gordian Knot.[2]

PRIVACY SHIELD

17.03 The tumult of the strike down of the EU-US Safe Harbour arrangement decision eventually led the EU and US to negotiate and agree a further data transfer mechanism. This would be titled the EU-US Privacy Shield.[3] This again provided that personal data could be sent from the EU to companies in the US who signed up and adhered to a set of official data principles in the US.

It would be assumed that any and all lessons from what went wrong from the earlier Safe Harbour decision were learned and that officials both in the US and the EU knew what could and could not be done in terms of establishing a new international agreement that satisfies the EU data transfer regime.

Unfortunately for those putting the new arrangement in place, Mr Schrems still saw fault with how EU data was and was not being protected in the US. He complained again. In this instance Facebook was named in the case, which arised because Schrems complained that US companies in the EU were transferring certain personal data from the EU to the US. It was not necessarily picking on

---

2   Svantesson, 'Cross-Border Data Transfers after the CJEU's Safe Harbour Decision: A Tale of Gordian Knots' (2016) 41(1) *Alternative Law Journal* 39; Carrera and Guild, 'The End of Safe Harbor: What Future for EU-US Data Transfers' (2015) 22(5) *Maastricht Journal of European and Comparative Law* 651; Kuner, 'Reality and Illusion in EU Data Transfer Regulation Post Schrems' (2017) 18(4) *German Law Journal* 881; Padova, 'The Safe Harbour Is Invalid: What Tools Remain For Data Transfers And What Comes Next?' (2016) 6(2) *International Data Privacy Law* 139; Corrales Compagnucci, Minssen, Seitz and Aboy, 'Lost On The High Seas Without A Safe Harbor Or A Shield? Navigating Cross-Border Transfers In The Pharmaceutical Sector After Schrems II Invalidation Of The EU-US Privacy Shield' (2020) 4(3) *European Pharmaceutical Law Review* 153; Manny, 'Data Transfers From The EU To The U.S. After Schrems' (2016) 49(1) *Business Law Review*.

3   Decision 2000/520.

Facebook (now called Meta). The local court, again in Ireland, referred questions to the ECJ/CJEU. These quite detailed questions were as follows:

'(1) In circumstances in which personal data is transferred by a private company from a European Union (EU) Member State to a private company in a third country for a commercial purpose pursuant to [the SCC Decision] and may be further processed in the third country by its authorities for purposes of national security but also for purposes of law enforcement and the conduct of the foreign affairs of the third country, does EU law (including the Charter) apply to the transfer of the data notwithstanding the provisions of Article 4(2) TEU in relation to national security and the provisions of the first indent of Article 3(2) of Directive [95/46] in relation to public security, defence and State security?

(2)

(a) In determining whether there is a violation of the rights of an individual through the transfer of data from the [European Union] to a third country under the [SCC Decision] where it may be further processed for national security purposes, is the relevant comparator for the purposes of [Directive 95/46]:

(i) the Charter, the EU Treaty, the FEU Treaty, [Directive 95/46], the [European Convention for the Protection of Human Rights and Fundamental Freedoms, signed at Rome on 4 November 1950] (or any other provision of EU law); or

(ii) the national laws of one or more Member States?

(b) If the relevant comparator is (ii), are the practices in the context of national security in one or more Member States also to be included in the comparator?

(3) When assessing whether a third country ensures the level of protection required by EU law to personal data transferred to that country for the purposes of Article 26 of [Directive 95/46], ought the level of protection in the third country be assessed by reference to:

(a) the applicable rules in the third country resulting from its domestic law or international commitments, and the practice designed to ensure compliance with those rules, to include the professional rules and security measures which are complied with in the third country;

or

(b) the rules referred to in (a) together with such administrative, regulatory and compliance practices and policy safeguards, procedures, protocols, oversight mechanisms and non-judicial remedies as are in place in the third country?

(4) Given the facts found by the High Court in relation to US law, if personal data is transferred from the European Union to the United States under [the SCC Decision] does this violate the rights of individuals under Articles 7 and/or 8 of the Charter?

(5) Given the facts found by the High Court in relation to US law, if personal data is transferred from the European Union to the United States under [the SCC Decision]:

(a) does the level of protection afforded by the United States respect the essence of an individual's right to a judicial remedy for breach of his or her data privacy rights guaranteed by Article 47 of the Charter?

If the answer to Question 5(a) is in the affirmative:

(b) are the limitations imposed by US law on an individual's right to a judicial remedy in the context of US national security proportionate within the meaning of Article 52 of the Charter and do not exceed what is necessary in a democratic society for national security purposes?

(6)

(a) What is the level of protection required to be afforded to personal data transferred to a third country pursuant to standard contractual clauses adopted in accordance with a decision of the Commission under Article 26(4) [of Directive 95/46] in light of the provisions of [Directive 95/46] and in particular Articles 25 and 26 read in the light of the Charter?

(b) What are the matters to be taken into account in assessing whether the level of protection afforded to data transferred to a third country under [the SCC Decision] satisfies the requirements of [Directive 95/46] and the Charter?

(7) Does the fact that the standard contractual clauses apply as between the data exporter and the data importer and do not bind the national authorities of a third country who may require the data importer to make available to its security services for further processing the personal data transferred pursuant to the clauses provided for in [the SCC Decision] preclude the clauses from adducing adequate safeguards as envisaged by Article 26(2) of [Directive 95/46]?

(8) If a third country data importer is subject to surveillance laws that in the view of a data protection authority conflict with the [standard contractual clauses] or Article 25 and 26 of [Directive 95/46] and/or the Charter, is a data protection authority required to use its enforcement powers under Article 28(3) of [Directive 95/46] to suspend data flows or is the exercise of those powers limited to exceptional cases only, in light of recital 11 of [the SCC Decision], or can a data protection authority use its discretion not to suspend data flows?

(9)

(a) For the purposes of Article 25(6) of [Directive 95/46], does [the Privacy Shield Decision] constitute a finding of general application binding on data protection authorities and the courts of the Member States to the effect that the United States ensures an adequate level of protection within the meaning of Article 25(2) of [Directive 95/46] by reason of its domestic law or of the international commitments it has entered into?

(b) If it does not, what relevance, if any, does the Privacy Shield Decision have in the assessment conducted into the adequacy of the safeguards provided to data transferred to the United States which is transferred pursuant to the [SCC Decision]?

(10) Given the findings of the High Court in relation to US law, does the provision of the Privacy Shield ombudsperson under Annex A to Annex III to the Privacy Shield Decision when taken in conjunction with the existing regime in the United States ensure that the US provides a remedy to data subjects whose personal data is transferred to the United States under the [SCC Decision] that is compatible with Article 47 of the Charter]?

(11) Does the [SCC Decision] violate Articles 7, 8 and/or 47 of the Charter?'

The ECJ/CJEU held[4] that:

1. Article 2(1) and (2) of Regulation (EU) 2016/679 of the European Parliament and of the Council of 27 April 2016 on the protection of natural persons with regard to the processing of personal data and on the free movement of such data, and repealing Directive 95/46/EC (General Data Protection Regulation), must be interpreted as meaning that that regulation applies to the transfer of personal data for commercial purposes by an economic operator established in a Member State to another economic operator established in a third country, irrespective of whether, at the time of that transfer or thereafter, that data is liable to be processed by the authorities of the third country in question for the purposes of public security, defence and State security.

2. Article 46(1) and Article 46(2)(c) of Regulation 2016/679 must be interpreted as meaning that the appropriate safeguards, enforceable rights and effective legal remedies required by those provisions must ensure that data subjects whose personal data are transferred to a third country pursuant to standard data protection clauses are afforded a level of protection essentially equivalent to that guaranteed within the European Union by that regulation, read in the light of the Charter of Fundamental Rights of the European Union. To that end, the assessment of the level of protection afforded in the context of such a transfer must, in particular, take into consideration both the contractual clauses agreed between the controller or processor established in the European Union and the recipient of the transfer established in the third country concerned and, as regards any access by the public authorities of that third country to the personal data transferred, the relevant aspects of the legal system of that third country, in particular those set out, in a non-exhaustive manner, in Article 45(2) of that regulation.

---

4   *Data Protection Commissioner v Facebook Ireland Ltd, Maximillian Schrems*, Case C-311/18, ECJ/CJEU, 16 July 2020.

3. Article 58(2)(f) and (j) of Regulation 2016/679 must be interpreted as meaning that, unless there is a valid European Commission adequacy decision, the competent supervisory authority is required to suspend or prohibit a transfer of data to a third country pursuant to standard data protection clauses adopted by the Commission, if, in the view of that supervisory authority and in the light of all the circumstances of that transfer, those clauses are not or cannot be complied with in that third country and the protection of the data transferred that is required by EU law, in particular by Articles 45 and 46 of that regulation and by the Charter of Fundamental Rights, cannot be ensured by other means, where the controller or a processor has not itself suspended or put an end to the transfer.

4. Examination of Commission Decision 2010/87/EU of 5 February 2010 on standard contractual clauses for the transfer of personal data to processors established in third countries under Directive 95/46/EU of the European Parliament and of the Council, as amended by Commission Implementing Decision (EU) 2016/2297 of 16 December 2016 in the light of Articles 7, 8 and 47 of the Charter of Fundamental Rights has disclosed nothing to affect the validity of that decision.

5. Commission Implementing Decision (EU) 2016/1250 of 12 July 2016 pursuant to Directive 95/46/EC of the European Parliament and of the Council on the adequacy of the protection provided by the EU-US Privacy Shield is invalid.'

Again, therefore the best plans of the EU and the US to facilitate data transfers within EU data protection norms was held invalid. Uncertainty again clashed against certain expectations of the wider industry. Again, policy makers were left with red faces. It has been referred to as an 'earthquake' for business confidence and certainty. One law firm writes about the 'shock' it has caused to some. There is significant commentary, which is expected, given the import of the issues at stake.[5]

Data protection supervisory authorities have also been issuing guidance and commentary, but arguably for little comfort.

DATA PRIVACY FRAMEWORK

17.04   Just as we conclude the writing on this chapter, the US and EU have come to another agreement. A strike three in their efforts to facilitate EU-US data transfers now in the form of the GDPR. The EU and US had been negotiating for some time following the failure of the above two efforts.

On 25 March 2022, the Commission and the US announced that they have agreed in principle on a new Trans-Atlantic Data Privacy Framework.[6]

On 7 October 2022, President Biden signed an Executive Order on 'Enhancing Safeguards for United States Signals Intelligence Activities.' Along with the Regulations issued by the Attorney General, the Executive Order is intended to implement into US law the agreement in principle announced above in March.[7]

On that basis, the Commission will now prepare a draft adequacy decision and then launch its adoption procedure.[8] This looks like carrying on into 2023.

---

5   Zalnieriute, 'Data Transfers After Schrems II: The EU-US Disagreements Over Data Privacy And National Security' (2022) 55(1) *Vanderbilt Journal of Transnational Law* 48; Jordan, 'CJEU Déjà Vu: Facilitating International Data Transfers and Avoiding Internet Balkanization in the Wake of Schrems II by Enacting Targeted Reforms to US Surveillance Practices' (2022) 106(2) *Minnesota Law Review* 1073; Carlson, 'Behind The Curve: Schrems II And The Need For Increased U.S. Data Protections In A Global Economy' (2021) 47(1) *Journal of Corporation Law* 197; Bradford, Aboy and Liddell, 'Standard Contractual Clauses For Cross-Border Transfers Of Health Data After Schrems II' (2021) 8(1) *Journal of Law and the Biosciences* 36; McLaughlin, 'Schrem's Slippery Slope: Strengthening Governance Mechanisms To Rehabilitate EU-U.S. Cross-Border Data Transfers after Schrems II' (2021) 90(1) *Fordham Law Review* 217; Kuner, 'Reality And Illusion In EU Data Transfer Regulation Post Schrems' (2017) 18(4) *German Law Journal* 881; Minssen, Seitz, Aboy and Corrales Compagnucci, 'The EU-US Privacy Shield Regime For Cross-Border Transfers Of Personal Data Under The GDPR: What Are The Legal Challenges And How Might These Affect Cloud-Based Technologies, Big Data' (2020) 4(1) *European Pharmaceutical Law Review* 34; Manny, 'Data Transfers From The EU To The U.S. After Schrems' (2016) 49(1) *Business Law Review*; Corrales Compagnucci, Minssen, Seitz and Aboy, 'Lost On The High Seas Without A Safe Harbor Or A Shield? Navigating Cross-Border Transfers In The Pharmaceutical Sector After Schrems II Invalidation Of The EU-US Privacy Shield' (2020) 4(3) *European Pharmaceutical Law Review* 153.
6   'Commercial Sector: Ongoing Talks On A Successor Arrangement To The EU-US Privacy Shield' EC Commission, available at https://ec.europa.eu/info/law/law-topic/data-protection/international-dimension-data-protection/eu-us-data-transfers_en. Also Lima, 'Biden Issues Order Boosting Privacy Checks For Data Flows From Europe' *Washington Post*, 7 October 2022.
7   Ibid.
8   Ibid.

UK DATA TRANSFERS

17.05 The UK appears intent on arranging a series of new data transfer permission channels, at least as it relates to UK data being transferred to third countries and destinations internationally. It is too early to say at present what the final range of these methods will look like, nor to predict whether they may be challenged subsequently. The proposed new legislation referring to additional data rules (eg, Data Protection Bill 2022/2023) and separately referring to deletion of UK laws (eg, announcements referring to proposals to delete 2,400 laws with EU relevance) create a potential for data law litigation to commence. If this comes to pass, such data litigation could occur in the UK and or in the EU.

However, there may be other areas of data law which can also lead to potential litigation. EU data laws require that the data regulators and supervisory authorities must be independent. Unfortunately, there are certain aspects of current proposals which can be argued to undermine the very independence of the ICO as an independent data regulator. This would open opportunities for parties to seek to issue proceedings but separately also potentially require the EU Commission to review the adequacy decision – even before the scheduled review period.

CONCLUSION

17.06 It is too early to say which privacy groups or individuals will seek to challenge the new EU-US Data Privacy Framework. The most recent decision also opens the possibility of a national supervisory authority seeking to intervene on foot of an assessment that there may still be problems. However, it would be expected that challenges, if any, would take a number of years to fully present themselves during which time the new framework mechanism will continue in operation. Of course, at the time of writing the Commission assessment and decision has not yet been implemented, and interested parties as well as industry will be actively anticipating the final text of this decision. Obviously, as indicated above, the situation as regards new UK specific data transfer arrangements is a developing area. While there is already data transfer litigation in the EU, one can only speculate on if and when data transfer litigation might arise in the UK. If and when it does, a further issue will be the extent to which the existing EU jurisprudence may be argued and or influential for EU courts. Some litigants may also seek to adopt a strategy of issuing proceedings in relation to UK data transfer issues from within the EU. There is already precedence for this, in particular in terms of challenges to data transfers from the EU to the US. What can be said is that the greater the amount of data law change in the UK, and the more significant and divergent it is in terms of the EU, the potential also rises for data litigation or other contention to arise. One of the lessons is that UK and international businesses must remain alert to changes in the data transfer landscape.

CHAPTER 18

Standards and Vendors

INTRODUCTION

18.01   Some years ago, data protection law was less understood and appreciated as compared to its wide array of actors and the import of the types of personal data involved. Arguably the advent of the GDPR has done more to raise awareness of data protection than any other data law, document, or practice heretofore. The GDPR, as someone once said, was the law that was heard around the world.

At the same time that awareness at a public level and professional level has been raised massively, the need for advice, solutions, and compliance tools are also coming to the fore. This increased attention to compliance solutions and vendors is also relevant in the data transfer space.

STANDARDS

18.02   Companies need to be fully aware of relevant data protection laws. Increasingly, however, they also need to be aware of a wide and increasing array of direct and indirect standards. One example is the data law standards that exist in a third-party country when one is seeking to engage in data transfers with that third party jurisdiction.

Then in terms of companies within that country, most specifically an intended recipient company, one can consider the standards (such as policies, data law compliance, legal compliance, past data fines, etc).

There are a number of highly respected and well-known standards organisations in the technical sector. Some of these organisations have set out technical standards in relation to security and data security. These should be implemented by companies, and the extent to which such standards are not adhered to when relevant can lead to such events as data breaches, other failures, etc, and which can adversely affect personal data held. One example is the British Standards Institute or BSI.

There are a variety of other software and hardware standards setting organisations. These can be quite niche but no less important to those companies affected. Website design, for instance, relies on a variety of tools and standards. If the incorrect standards are used, there is increased risk of data breach or hacking.

Outside of these larger national and even international standards organisation there are a variety of industry bodies which also set standards. Some examples exist in the media and marketing industries.

The data protection regime also expressly refers to appropriateness of certificates, certification and codes of conduct. These are even promoted as a matter of data protection policy. There are therefore a variety of new avenues for standards to be introduced on an industry sector basis, and even across industries.

VENDOR SOLUTIONS

18.03   Perhaps in proportion to the increasing awareness of data protection laws, there is an increase in the number of third-party vendors, and third-party software solutions, being marketed to companies. Some of these third-party vendors are large and multinational, others are small, with a range of sizes in between. The types of solutions being offered to companies can be professed to be all encompassing compliance, to specific solution tools accomplishing particular tasks, to awareness tools, and training tools. A large range of consultants also offer their services to companies to assist in identifying risk, and eliminating the risks identified.

INTERNAL SOLUTIONS

18.04   Companies also implement their own processes, solutions, and standards. Companies will have, or at least should have, a large variety of reviews, officers, handbooks, policies and related documents in place to deal with the data which they hold.

These are separate from any services provided by third parties. Of course, these can interact and compliment each other.

CONCLUSION

18.05   This book is directed to legal professionals in the first part, but is also relevant and of assistance to companies and other interested parties. As mentioned above, data protection has become far more noticed and appreciated over recent years. In law firms, a number of years ago, issues of data protection may have been viewed as niche and an add on to some other area of law. Today, rather, it is a fully acknowledged expert specialism, and not just in larger law firms. It is well recognised now at the Bar.

Tradition and history are also relevant from another perspective. Some time ago law and the defined legal questions that lawyers would deal with would be clearly delineated. Today, however, data protection lawyers will be aware of a burgeoning service provider and solutions provider industry directed to data compliance in companies. To the extent that this new sector exists, lawyers must be aware of it, even interact with it, even speak at it, but more importantly be aware of the information and inputs that some of their clients will no doubt be receiving from this new sector. Some of these may be security and data security products, but the range is much wider and lawyers cannot ignore the need to be at least aware of what is happening on the other side of their clients.

Some may view it as competition, but lawyers must be alert to highlight bad solutions and risks arising. Numerous other issues arise. Just having a particular data security product per se does not make a company compliant with data protection laws. Many bad products exist which may say, or otherwise cause a customer to believe, that a given data transfer by a company to a third country, or a given hosting solution, is legally compliant. But in the particular situation it may be completely non compliant and illegal. The company has been exposed, as have the customers of the company whose data is illegally transferred. Increasingly lawyers are proactive and not just waiting for their client to accidentally find out that a grave error has occurred.

In some ways, the role and tasks of a data lawyer have become more difficult. While one's expertise should not be expected to extend to coding, for example, the range of data related technologies and issues that come to exist in the modern world call on data lawyers to have a much wider range of read knowledge than previously. The increasing range of how personal data may be transferred or otherwise collected across borders is just one such area. It is easy to think of company A wishing to transfer database X on a disc or email to company B in a different country. But in reality the range of activities are more complex and varied. The use of the internet can involve data collections and data transfers. Another example highlighted recently relates to data transfers and data collections occurring when a doctor operates remotely over the internet on a patient in a different country.[1] It may seem like blurring boundaries or creating new grey areas, but a data lawyer's knowledge sphere must be wide indeed, while of course remaining conscious that one is still expected to be providing legal answers (alone). It is no small task to be sure. It is also complicated when the policy of business, technology, and law do not always see eye to eye, as in the case of (some) data transfers.[2]

---

1   See Konicki, Wasmuht-Perroud, Aaron and Caplan, A, 'Virtual Surgical Planning And Data Ownership: Navigating The Provider-Patient-Vendor Relationship' (2022) 36(5) *Bioethics* 494. Also Bradford, Aboy and Liddell, 'Standard Contractual Clauses For Cross-Border Transfers Of Health Data After Schrems II' (2021) 8(1) *Journal of Law and the Biosciences* 36; Corrales Compagnucci, Minssen, Seitz and Aboy, 'Lost On The High Seas Without A Safe Harbor Or A Shield? Navigating Cross-Border Transfers In The Pharmaceutical Sector After Schrems II Invalidation Of The EU-US Privacy Shield' (2020) 4(3) *European Pharmaceutical Law Review* 153; Minssen, Seitz, Aboy and Corrales Compagnucci, 'The EU-US Privacy Shield Regime For Cross-Border Transfers Of Personal Data Under The GDPR: What Are The Legal Challenges And How Might These Affect Cloud-Based Technologies, Big Data, And AI In The Medical Sector?' (2020) 4(1) *European Pharmaceutical Law Review* 34.
2   Yakovleva, 'Personal Data Transfers in International Trade and EU Law: A Tale of Two "Necessities"' (2020) 21(6) *Journal of World Investment & Trade* 881; Mitchell and Hepburn, 'Don't Fence Me In: Reforming Trade and Investment Law to Better Facilitate Cross-Border Data Transfer' (2017) 19(1) *Yale Journal of Law & Technology* 182.

PART E

RULE FOCUS

CHAPTER 19

Adequacy Rule

INTRODUCTION

19.01   Adequacy is one of the solutions to the problem of data transfers to other countries.[1] However, there is an assessment process. Indeed, as in the example of the EU adequacy process there is a need for a country to apply to be assessed. A detailed process then ensues.

Brexit presented a significant problem for policy makers and to businesses. The question was whether millions of commercial relationships and transactions between the UK and the EU would have to stop as they would no longer be permitted.

In other instances, third party countries wonder whether they can commence these transactions in their own countries, and consider how their laws stack up to EU standards.

TRANSFERS RESTRICTED

19.02   Transfers (outside EU/EEA) are prohibited per se. The focus is directed upon the privacy protection elsewhere and the dangers of uncontrolled transfers of personal data. In addition to the GDPR there are also local law restrictions such as the UK GDPR, and even the prior Data Protection Act 1998 (DPA 1998) which stated previously that 'Personal data shall not be transferred to a country or territory outside the European Economic Area [EEA] unless that country or territory ensures an adequate level of protection for the rights and freedoms of Data Subjects in relation to the processing of personal data.'

Data protection compliance practice for organisations means that they will have to include a compliance assessment as well as an assessment of the risks associated with transfers of personal data outside of the jurisdiction. This applies to transfers from parent to subsidiary or to a branch office in the same way as a transfer to an unrelated company or entity. However, different exemptions can apply in different scenarios.

---

1   Gonzalo Domenech, 'Adequacy Decisions in European Law Related to International Data Transfers and Control Mechanisms Applied by the Member States' (2019) 11(1) *Cuadernos de Derecho Transnacional* 350.

ADEQUATE PROTECTION CHANNEL

19.03   If the recipient country has already been deemed by the UK or EU to already have an adequate level of protection for personal data, then the transfer is permitted.

A transfer can occur where there has been a positive Community finding in relation to the type of transfer proposed. A Community finding means a finding that a country or territory outside the EU/EEA does, or does not, ensure an adequate level of protection.

Therefore, if there has been a positive community finding in relation to a named country outside of the jurisdiction, this means that that country is deemed to have a level of protection in its laws comparable to the UK and EU data protection regime. This then makes it possible for organisations to make transfers to that specific country.

The EU Commission provides a list of Commission decisions on the adequacy of the protection of personal data in named third countries.[2] The EU Commission has thus far recognised that Andorra, Canada (commercial organisations), Faroe Islands, Israel, Japan, Switzerland, Argentina, Guernsey, Isle of Man, Jersey, New Zealand, Uruguay, the EU-US Privacy Shield rules (if signed up and adhered to), and the transfer of air passenger name record to the United States Bureau of Customs and Border Protection (as specified) as providing adequate protection for personal data. This list will expand over time, most recently the UK..

If the recipient country's protection for personal data is not adequate, or not ascertainable, but it is intended that transfers are still commercially desired, the organisation should ascertain if the transfer comes within one of the other excepted categories. Transfers of personal data from the UK to outside of the EU/EEA jurisdiction cannot occur unless it falls within one of the transfer exemptions.

The exemptions from the transfer restrictions, if there is a UK equivalent to the EU regime are:

- the data subject has given consent;

- the transfer is necessary for performance of contract between data subject and controller;

- the transfer is necessary for taking steps at the request of the data subject with a view to entering into a contract with the controller;

- the transfer is necessary for the conclusion of a contract between the controller and a person other than the data subject that is entered into at the request of the data subject and is in the interests of the data subject;

2   At http://ec.europa.eu/justice/data-protection/international-transfers/adequacy/index_en.htm.

- the transfer is necessary for the performance of such a contract;

- the transfer is required or authorised under any enactment or instrument imposing an international obligation on the UK;

- the transfer is necessary for reasons of substantial public interest;

- the transfer is necessary for purposes of or in connection with legal proceedings or prospective legal proceedings;

- the transfer is necessary in order to prevent injury or damage to the health of the data subject or serious loss of or damage to the property of the data subject or otherwise to protect vital interests;

- subject to certain conditions the transfer is only part of personal data on a register established by or under an enactment;

- the transfer has been authorised by a supervisory authority where the controller adduces adequate safeguards;

- the transfer is made to a country that has been determined by the EU Commission as having 'adequate levels of [data] protection' ie a Community finding (see above);

- the transfer is made to a US entity that has signed up to the EU-US 'Safe Harbour' arrangements [as updated];

- EU Commission contract provisions: the model contracts (the EU has set out model contracts which if incorporated into the data exporter – data importer/recipient relationship can act as an exemption thus permitting the transfer to occur.

In determining whether a third country ensures an adequate level of protection factors taken into account includes:

- 'any security measures taken in respect of the data in that country or territory';

- the transfer is necessary for obtaining legal advice or in connection with legal proceedings or prospective proceedings;

- (subject to certain conditions) it is necessary in order to prevent injury or damage to the health or property of the data subject, or in order to protect their vital interests;

- the transfer is required or authorised by law;

- the ICO has authorised the transfer where the controller has given or adduced adequate safeguards; or

- the contract relating to the transfer of the data embodies appropriate contract clauses as specified in a 'Community finding.'

Other potential exempted categories are where:

- the transfers are substantially in the public interest;

- the transfers are made in connection with any (legal) claim;

- the transfers are in the vital interests of the data subject;

- there are public protections;

- the transfer is necessary for the performance of a contract. (This will depend on the nature of the goods or services provided under the contract. The transfer must be necessary for the benefit of the transferee and not just convenient for the organisation).

ADEQUACY CONSIDERATION

19.04   A transfer of personal data to a third country or an international organisation may take place where the Commission has decided that the third country, a territory or one or more specified sectors within that third country, or the international organisation in question ensures an adequate level of protection. Such transfer shall not require any specific authorisation.[3]

When assessing the adequacy of the level of protection, the Commission shall, in particular, take account of the following elements:

- the rule of law, respect for human rights and fundamental freedoms, relevant legislation, both general and sectoral, including concerning public security, defence, national security and criminal law and the access of public authorities to personal data, as well as the implementation of such legislation, data protection rules, professional rules and security measures, including rules for onward transfer of personal data to another third country or international organisation, which are complied with in that country or international organisation, case law, as well as effective and enforceable data subject rights and effective administrative and judicial redress for the data subjects whose personal data are being transferred;

- the existence and effective functioning of one or more independent supervisory authorities in the third country or to which an international organisation is subject, with responsibility for ensuring and enforcing compliance with the data protection rules, including adequate enforcement powers, for assisting and advising the data subjects in exercising their rights and for co-operation with the supervisory authorities of the states; and

- the international commitments the third country or international organisation concerned has entered into, or other obligations arising from legally binding conventions or instruments as well as from its participation in multilateral or regional systems, in particular in relation to the protection of personal data.[4]

---

3   GDPR, Art 45(1).
4   Ibid, 45(2).

The Commission, after assessing the adequacy of the level of protection, may decide, by means of implementing act, that a third country, a territory or one or more specified sectors within a third country, or an international organisation ensures an adequate level of protection within the meaning of Article 45(3). The implementing act shall provide for a mechanism for a periodic review, at least every four years, which shall take into account all relevant developments in the third country or international organisation. The implementing act shall specify its territorial and sectorial application and, where applicable, identify the supervisory authority or authorities referred to in Article 45(2)(b). The implementing act shall be adopted in accordance with the examination procedure referred to in Article 93(2).[5]

The Commission shall, on an on-going basis, monitor developments in third countries and international organisations that could affect the functioning of decisions adopted pursuant to paragraph 3 and decisions adopted on the basis of Article 25(6) of the EU Data Protection Directive 1995 (DPD).[6]

The Commission shall, where available information reveals, in particular following the review referred to in Article 45(3), that a third country, a territory or one or more specified sectors within a third country, or an international organisation no longer ensures an adequate level of protection within the meaning of Article 45(2), to the extent necessary, repeal, amend or suspend the decision referred to in Article 45(3) without retro-active effect. Those implementing acts shall be adopted in accordance with the examination procedure referred to in Article 87(2), or, in cases of extreme urgency, in accordance with the procedure referred to in Article 93(2).[7] On duly justified imperative grounds of urgency, the Commission shall adopt immediately applicable implementing acts in accordance with the procedure referred to in Article 93(3).[8]

The Commission shall enter into consultations with the third country or international organisation with a view to remedying the situation giving rise to the decision made pursuant to Article 45(5).[9]

A decision pursuant to paragraph 5 is without prejudice to transfers of personal data to the third country, territory or one or more specified sectors within that third country, or the international organisation in question pursuant to Articles 46 to 49.[10]

The Commission shall publish in the Official Journal of the EU and on its website a list of those third countries, territories and specified sectors within a third

---

5   Ibid, 45(3).
6   Ibid, 45(4).
7   Ibid, 45(5).
8   Ibid.
9   Ibid, 45(6).
10 Ibid, 45(7).

country and international organisations for which it has decided that an adequate level of protection is or is no longer ensured.[11]

Decisions adopted by the Commission on the basis of Article 25(6) of the DPD 1995 shall remain in force until amended, replaced or repealed by a Commission Decision adopted in accordance with Article 45(3) or (5).[12]

(Also note Chapter 20 with regard to Brexit adequacy decision issues.)

UK ADEQUACY DECISION

19.05   Earlier chapters highlight how one of the biggest concerns prior to Brexit related to the business and official need for the EU-UK data transfer to be able to continue under some form of mechanism. It was already identified that the optimum mechanism might be the existing model of an EU adequacy decision for a third country, which the UK was shortly to be. But a lot of commentary, even official commentary, called into question whether such a decision could be made to facilitate the UK. There was also commentary suggesting that even if such a decision could in fact be made (which was not perceived as certain), it could not be done as quickly as it ultimately transpired.

To the relief of UK politicians and businesses, a quite swift adequacy decision in favour of the UK was made by the EU Commission. Some were no doubt a little surprised that this transpired to be the case.

It should not be overlooked, however, that all adequacy decisions are for a fixed time period and must be reviewed at the end of the period to determine if the grounds still exist for it to be continued for another fixed period.

Separate to this, if material facts arise which suggest that the previous basis for granting the adequacy decision have adversely changed, the Commission may have to review, suspend, or even cancel an adequacy decision during its currency and in advance of any fixed term review.

The government announced on 28 June 2021 that 'Personal data can continue to flow freely between Europe and the UK following agreement by the European Union to adopt "data adequacy" decisions.' It officially welcomed the decision stating that

> 'The UK government welcomes the move, which rightly recognises the country's high data protection standards. Formal adoption of the decisions under the EU General Data Protection Regulation (GDPR) and Law Enforcement Directive (LED) allows personal data to flow freely from the EU and wider European Economic Area (EEA) to the UK. The decisions mean that UK businesses and organisations can continue to receive personal

---

11   Ibid, 45(8).
12   Ibid, 45(9).

data from the EU and EEA without having to put additional arrangements in place with European counterparts.'

It adds that 'This free flow of personal data supports trade, innovation and investment, assists with law enforcement agencies tackling crime, and supports the delivery of critical public services sharing personal data as well as facilitating health and scientific research.'[13]

In terms of UK data transfers to the EU, the government statement states that 'The UK, which now operates a fully independent data policy, has already recognised the EU and EEA member states as 'adequate', as part of its commitment to establish a smooth transition for the UK's departure from the bloc.'[14]

The decision on the adequate protection of personal data by the UK GDPR was issued on 28 June 2021. It provides that,

> 'Article 1
>
> (1) For the purposes of Article 45 of Regulation (EU) 2016/679, the United Kingdom ensures an adequate level of protection for personal data transferred within the scope of Regulation (EU) 2016/679 from the European Union to the United Kingdom.'

Article 3 of the decision points out that

> 'The Commission shall continuously monitor the application of the legal framework upon which this Decision is based, including the conditions under which onward transfers are carried out, individual rights are exercised and United Kingdom public authorities have access to data transferred on the basis of this Decision, with a view to assessing whether the United Kingdom continues to ensure an adequate level of protection within the meaning of Article 1.'

Article 4 provides that 'This Decision shall expire on 27 June 2025, unless extended in accordance with the procedure referred to in Article 93(2) of Regulation (EU) 2016/679.'

---

13 'EU Adopts "Adequacy" Decisions Allowing Data to Continue Flowing Freely to the UK,' Government Press Release, 28 June 2021.
14 Ibid.

CHAPTER 20

UK Adequacy Decision, Consultation, and Change

INTRODUCTION

20.01   Reform of UK data laws as a result of Brexit, and now as a result of proposed political changes, has meant that the worry and uncertainty for industry continues. As if there were not enough issues to deal with, new official proposals were announced in September 2021 to make some quite wide ranging and significant changes to UK data protection law. These changes include changes to the legal rules in relation to the data transfer rules. The changes are announced in a consultation document, requesting responses to questions and proposed data protection law changes. The data protection law consultation document is entitled *Data: A new direction* (Consultation). It was issued by the Department for Digital, Culture, Media & Sport (DCMS) on 10 September 2021.

UK ADEQUACY

20.02   In July 2021 the EU Commission made a decision deciding that UK data protection law was sufficient to allow an adequacy decision for the purposes of the GDPR and to permit EU-UK data transfers under the adequacy transfer channel.[1] This solves the Brexit headache of the default data transfer ban kicking in. Article 1 provides that '[f]or the purposes of Article 45 of Regulation (EU) 2016/679, the United Kingdom ensures an adequate level of protection for personal data transferred within the scope of Regulation (EU) 2016/679 from the European Union to the United Kingdom.' It also provides that '[t]his decision does not cover personal data that is transferred for purposes of United Kingdom immigration control or that otherwise falls within the scope of the exemption from certain data subject rights for purposes of the maintenance of effective immigration control pursuant to paragraph 4(1) of Schedule 2 to the DPA 2018.'

---

1   European Commission, Brussels, 28.6.2021, C(2021) 4800 final, COMMISSION IMPLEMENTING DECISION of 28.6.2021 pursuant to Regulation (EU) 2016/679 of the European Parliament and of the Council on the adequate protection of personal data by the United Kingdom (Text with EEA relevance).

CONSULTATION

20.03   Despite the success of the UK adequacy decision referred to above, which some felt was not assured and others felt even if successful would take much longer than ultimately transpired, a new round of uncertainty and change arises. This comes from an official consultation process and new legislation proposed resulting from that consultation.

The Ministerial foreword to the consultation is made by the Rt Hon Oliver Dowden CBE MP, Secretary of State for Digital, Culture, Media and Sport. It states that:

> 'Data is now one of the most important resources in the world'. It also states that the 'reforms outlined in this consultation will:
>
> - strengthen our position as a science superpower, simplifying data use by researchers and developers of AI and other cutting-edge technologies
>
> - build on the unprecedented and life-saving use of data to tackle the COVID-19 pandemic
>
> - secure the UK's status as a global hub for the free and responsible flow of personal data -complementing our ambitious agenda for new trade deals and data partnerships with some of the world's fastest growing economies
>
> - reinforce the responsibility of businesses to keep personal information safe, while empowering them to grow and innovate
>
> - ensure that the ICO remains a world-leading regulator, enabling people to use data responsibly to achieve economic and social goals.'[2]

More specifically the changes are categorised over the following self-described areas and issues, namely:

- reducing barriers to responsible innovation;

- reducing burdens on businesses and delivering better outcomes for people;

- boosting trade and reducing barriers to data flows;

- delivering better public services;

- reform of the Information Commissioner's Office.

Some of these relate to a wide variety of data protection law and policy issues. One of these categories refers to data transfer issues and many changes thereto.

Some might suggest that many of the proposes changes are directed more to economic policy than to necessitated changes in the data protection field. In addition, some might point out that at least at this headline level the changes being referred to are suggestive of reducing corporate interest barriers and

---

2   *Data: A New Direction*, consultation, Department for Digital, Culture, Media & Sport (10 September 2021).

reducing data protection law standards. There is no headline category proposed, for example, where risks or even new risks are identified for individuals and for which the consultation is querying whether new protections need to be introduced and or whether some specific data protection rules may need to be strengthened. To that extent, the consultation will be open to criticism by some that it is skewed in favour of economics and corporate activity, as opposed to being balanced and considering trade *plus* individual rights.

WIDE ARRAY OF CHANGES

20.04   Given the large number of questions, and the wide number of areas referred to, it is reasonable to say that the overall consultation is wide and significant. This is the opposite of a small, limited, narrow, tailored, and specific number of changes.

Readers will have to assess for themselves whether such wide-ranging potential changes are narrow and targeted. One might assume that the greater the changes the greater the chances are that there is increased potential for divergence from the actual GDPR.

The greater are the changes, if any, from the GDPR in the new amended UK data protection law, the greater pressure on the current EU adequacy decisions for data transfers with the UK. As with all adequacy decisions they are reviewed from time to time. There is also capacity for the EU to urgently review an adequacy decision where significant changes occur which may have enhanced risks to individuals and their data. There is a risk to the UK that changes resulting from the review may be deemed significant and ultimately deemed to be so divergent that the EU may suspend and or cancel the UK adequacy decision.

This creates economic, trade, business, and legal risks for the UK and the UK economy if the adequacy decision is even suspended never mind cancelled.

Many of the questions are also styled as, *do you agree that* …, and gauges responses according to a scale of strongly agree to strongly disagree. While there are always difficulties in designing questions and options for responses and feedback, the model of *do you agree that* …, in this instance could be suggested by some as to create a risk that the suggested basis behind the question is of course correct, or of course there is a problem. Once there is a problem in mind, it leads to thinking of a solution to the problem. It makes it easier for people to agree with what seems, and is presented, as being the case. In effect, there is a potential bias effect in parts of the consultation.

Arguably a more neutral way of asking these questions may have been to ask, *do you agree or disagree that* …, and to assess layered responses.

That is not to suggest that there is a motivation behind the consultation of seeking responses which will support a previously determined line of intended change.

However, there is at least some scope for that criticism to at least be made. Readers should consider for themselves whether there is some element of, or risk of appearance of, fishing for answers to support the making of preferred policy changes to UK data protection law and or to deliberately make divergent changes from a level of equivalence with EU law standards.

European critics may worry that the consultation process is an effort at least in part to create a justification for making already intended changes to UK data protection laws in order to undercut the EU and attract international business on the basis that there are less stringent data rules to be complied with in the UK (whether actual or perceived).

One issue for readers to consider is that while the questions refer to perceived problem type areas, or areas of intended change, there are in general no specific texts provided as to what the text would look like for making such changes. Alternatively, there is no separate texts of alternative change options for respondents to consider.

As a general comment on law changes, sometimes there can be a need for urgent change after a new law is enacted (or in this case set of related laws). Typically some typographical error or unforeseen consequence of a particular clause has occurred. In some of these instances, but by no means all, the legislature returns to pass an amending correctional law. This amending law is very short, and very narrow in the change it is making.

Outside of these narrow legislative correctional interventions, political and legal policymakers most often follow the time honoured approach of waiting many, many years before making changes to recently enacted laws. This is the longstanding practice in the UK and across the world.

The consultation in this instance suggests that not only is more than narrow corrective change being anticipated, but a large number of consequential and policy changes are being considered. This is by its nature out of the ordinary. After all, many years of detailed discussions and even negotiations occurred in the lead up to the final agreed version of the GDPR. There was also detailed consideration of the now current UK data protection laws. No suggestion is made that an error occurred in the GDPR text or the text of the current UK data protection laws, and which require a correction. Rather the proposed change appeared to be more political and or policy driven. Critics may suggest they are strategy and political driven, but that is for readers and respondents to assess for themselves.

A large number of proposed changes are highlighted in the many questions set out in the consultation. While the consultation process is largely completed, it remains to be seen whether this will result on some areas being left alone and other areas targeted for change based on the responses. Some changes are suggested as being favoured and meant to be included in the proposed new Data Protection Bill 2022/2023, while some other proposed changes are suggested as favoured but still undergoing further research and review. (This is all separate to the wholesale changes proposed to 2,400 laws of EU relevance which has since been suggested).

A related issue is that the questions propose broad issues. Just because responses may say a particular subject focus presents an issue, does not mean that respondents also agree that a change should happen, nor what that specific change should be.

Some questions also refer to a particular subject area and related subject areas. A suggestion is made for respondents to agree that apparently related areas which appear in different locations, should be rearranged and all placed together. This may (or may not) make sense to do depending on local and wider specifics. Respondents may agree that a question phrased and presented in this way should be responded to affirmatively. Rearranging different provisions to appear together and nothing else may be one thing; but there is a risk that a policymaker may go further and make significant or wholesale changes to the text of the provisions in addition to merely rearranging where the provisions are located. Respondents may be presented with a single-change option, but a policymaker may take this to make a double-change. No suggestion is being made that there is any strategy, deliberation or calculation in so proceeding, but some readers may call to mind such a critique.

Those responding to the consultation and specific proposals were required by 19 November 2021. The government response to the consultation and responses were published in due course following closure of the consultation.[3]

CONSULTATION

20.05   The Consultation pitches 'innovative' data sharing options. It refers to 'Innovative Data Sharing Solutions' in section 1.7. These are referred to below.

Consultation: Data intermediaries

20.06   The consultation refers to data intermediaries. It asks,

Q1.7.1.	Do you think the government should have a role enabling the activity of responsible data intermediaries?
	Please explain your answer, with reference to the barriers and risks associated with the activities of different types of data intermediaries, and where there might be a case to provide cross-cutting support). Consider referring to the styles of government intervention identified by Policy Lab – e.g. the government's role as collaborator, steward, customer, provider, funder, regulator and legislator – to frame your answer.

---

3   *Data: A New Direction*, consultation, Department for Digital, Culture, Media & Sport (10 September 2021).

This raises a number of potential change areas to data protection law in the UK. These need to be considered in relation to the impact of data transfer rules, and how compliance will be affected, as well as how data rights may be affected. It is not known in advance of the text of exact proposed changes being made available, what the specific law changes may be.

The following question is set out in the consultation document for respondents.

Q.1.7.2.	What lawful grounds other than consent might be applicable to data intermediary activities, as well as the conferring of data processing rights and responsibilities to those data intermediaries, whereby organisations share personal data without it being requested by the data subject?
	Please explain your answer, and provide supporting evidence where possible, including on:
	If Article 6(1)(f) is relevant, i) what types of data intermediary activities might constitute a legitimate interest and how is the balancing test met and ii) what types of intermediary activity would not constitute a legitimate interest
	What role the government should take in codifying this activity, including any additional conditions that might be placed on certain kinds of data intermediaries to bring them within scope of legitimate interest
	Whether you consider a government approved accreditation scheme for intermediaries would be useful

This raises a number of potential change areas to data protection law in the UK. These need to be considered in relation to the impact of data transfer rules, and how compliance will be affected, as well as how data rights may be affected. It is not known in advance of the text of the exact proposed changes being made available, or what the specific law changes may be.

Consultation: Further questions

20.07 The consultation then asks some further questions at paragraph 1.8.

The following question is set out in the consultation document for respondents.

Q1.8.1.	*In your view, which, if any, of the proposals in 'Reducing barriers to responsible innovation' would impact on people who identify with the protected characteristics under the Equality Act 2010 (i.e. age, disability, gender reassignment, marriage and civil partnership, pregnancy and maternity, race, religion or belief, sex and sexual orientation)?*

This raises a number of potential change areas to data protection law in the UK. These need to be considered in relation to the impact of data transfer rules, and how compliance will be affected, as well as how data rights may be affected. It is not known in advance of the text of exact proposed changes being made available, what the specific law changes may be.

The following question is set out in the consultation document for respondents.

Q1.8.2.	*In addition to any of the reforms already proposed in 'Reducing barriers to responsible innovation' (or elsewhere in the consultation), what reforms do you think would be helpful to reduce barriers to responsible innovation?*

This raises a number of potential change areas to data protection law in the UK. All questions highlight different unique areas, while the changes to each area can be quite significant and impactful of themselves and as compared to changes in other areas. These need to be considered in relation to the impact of data transfer rules, and how compliance will be affected, as well as how data rights may be affected. It is not known in advance of the text of exact proposed changes being made available, what the specific law changes may be.

Chapter 2 refers in part to reducing burdens on businesses, however, there is no equivalence whereby burdens and the reduction of burdens on individuals are considered in the same manner.

Using the phrase '**Reducing burdens on businesses and delivering better outcomes for people**' (original bold emphasis) could also be taken as suggesting that reducing burdens on business automatically equates with there being better outcomes for individuals. This is not something that is always the case. It is much more nuanced. Indeed, a lack of regulation or lax regulation can contribute to or lead to bad outcomes for individuals and society.

Consultation: Adequacy and boosting data transfers

20.08   The consultation refers in its chapter 3 to boosting trade and reducing barriers to data flows.

The consultation refers to 'Adequacy' in section 3.2.

In particular it then refers to a risk-based approach to adequacy regulations. It states,

> 'The government will use a four stage procedure to ensure that UK citizens and consumers can have confidence in the adequacy regulations that are made. These four stages are:
>
> a.   *Gatekeeping stage*: consideration of whether to commence an adequacy assessment in respect of a country, by reference to policy

factors, including high standards of data protection and the UK's strategic interests

b. *Assessment stage*: collection and analysis of information relating to the level of data protection in another country; this will look at questions based on key principles of the safeguards in the UK GDPR, while recognising that countries protect personal data in different ways

c. *Recommendation stage*: officials will make a recommendation to the Secretary of State for Digital, Culture, Media and Sport, who will, after consulting the Information Commissioner and any others considered appropriate, decide whether to make a determination of adequacy in respect of a specific country

d. *Procedural stage*: making relevant regulations – and laying these in Parliament – to give legal effect to an adequacy determination' [para 245].

The following question is set out in the consultation document for respondents.

Q3.2.1.	*To what extent do you agree that the UK's future approach to adequacy decisions should be risk-based and focused on outcomes?*

This raises a number of potential change areas to data protection law in the UK. These need to be considered in relation to the impact of data transfer rules, and how compliance will be affected, as well as how data rights may be affected. It is not known in advance of the text of exact proposed changes being made available, what the specific law changes may be.

The consultation refers to creating a scalable, flexible adequacy regime. The consultation states that,

> **'The government intends therefore to relax the requirement to review adequacy regulations every four years'** (original bold emphasis) [para 250].

The following question is set out in the consultation document for respondents.

Q3.2.2.	*To what extent do you agree that the government should consider making adequacy regulations for groups of countries, regions and multilateral frameworks?*

This raises a number of potential change areas to data protection law in the UK. These need to be considered in relation to the impact of data transfer rules, and how compliance will be affected, as well as how data rights may be affected. It is not known in advance of the text of exact proposed changes being made available, what the specific law changes may be.

The following question is set out in the consultation document for respondents.

Q3.2.3.	*To what extent do you agree with the proposal to strengthen ongoing monitoring of adequacy regulations and relax the requirement to review adequacy regulations every four years?*

This raises a number of potential change areas to data protection law in the UK. These need to be considered in relation to the impact of data transfer rules, and how compliance will be affected, as well as how data rights may be affected. It is not known in advance of the text of exact proposed changes being made available, what the specific law changes may be.

The consultation refers to redress requirements. The consultation states that,

> '... **the government proposes to amend the legislation to be clear that both administrative and judicial redress are acceptable as long as the redress mechanism is effective**' (original bold emphasis) [para 254].

Just before, the consultation states,

> 'The current text of the UK GDPR is not clear about whether the redress that data subjects are entitled to ought to be administrative or judicial. Judicial redress generally refers to a remedy in a court or tribunal, whereas administrative redress could be provided through other means, such as through a national regulator or ombudsperson. In the UK, for example, redress sought through the ICO would be considered administrative' [para 252].

The following question is set out in the consultation document for respondents.

Q3.2.4.	*To what extent do you agree that redress requirements for international data transfers may be satisfied by either administrative or judicial redress mechanisms, provided such mechanisms are effective?*

This raises a number of potential change areas to data protection law in the UK. These need to be considered in relation to the impact of data transfer rules, and how compliance will be affected, as well as how data rights may be affected. It is not known in advance of the text of exact proposed changes being made available, what the specific law changes may be.

Consultation: Alternative and alternative transfer mechanisms

20.09   The consultation refers to the 'Reform of the Accountability Framework' in section 3.3. The consultation states that,

> 'The government intends to explore legislative change to ensure that the suite of alternative transfer mechanisms available to UK

organisations in the UK GDPR is clear, flexible and provides the necessary protections for personal data. Its ambition is to develop the regime for international transfer mechanisms in three broad ways:

a. *Proportionality*: the safeguards applied during international transfers should be based on clear principles and proportionate to the risks facing data subjects in practice. When making an international data transfer, organisations must currently carry out case-by-case assessments to ensure that the alternative transfer mechanism provides the necessary protections and that there are enforceable data subject rights and effective redress, accounting for laws and practices in the recipient country and any supplementary measures which may be required. There is large variation between different countries' data protection regimes. Addressing risk can be challenging and time-consuming for organisations. Deciding what safeguards are necessary to transfer data without a significant degree of technical expertise can create large burdens for the small organisations without a significant degree of technical expertise.

   The government intends to clarify the legislation in order to facilitate more detailed, practical support for organisations on determining and addressing risks. This will help to create a more proportionate regime that both appropriately protects personal data and supports organisations to use alternative mechanisms with more confidence and ease

b. *Flexibility and future-proofing*: the international data protection landscape and the ways that organisations use data will continue to change rapidly. Article 46 (2) of the UK GDPR includes a set of alternative transfer mechanisms that is exhaustive and constrained in form, and may not be sufficiently adaptable for the purposes of UK organisations and their international partners in the future. The limitations of a fixed set of transfer options become evident when considering possible future developments in the data protection landscape or particularly complex interdependent relationships, such as international networks of collaborating researchers.

   The government intends to explore amendments to the international transfers regime to give organisations greater flexibility in their use of transfer mechanisms. These changes will complement the work already underway by the ICO to support organisations to take greater advantage of the existing options for tailored transfer mechanisms, like Binding Corporate Rules, Codes of Conduct and Certification Schemes.

c. *Interoperability*: the UK's international transfer regime should have a flexible design which allows it to adapt, not only to businesses' specific transfer activities but also to mechanisms for international transfers developed by other countries or groups. New transfer mechanisms and new data protection practices are likely to develop as more countries and multilateral fora develop international transfer regimes. A regime that improves interoperability with such regimes will provide an advantage to UK businesses and consumers.

   The government wants the UK regime to have the capacity to be compatible with any potential new international transfer regimes regardless of the mechanisms they use to transfer data, as long as they can provide the necessary protections for data subjects' (original bold emphasis) [para 257].

Consultation: Proportionality of appropriate safeguards

20.10   The consultation refers to proportionality of appropriate safeguards. The consultation states,

> 'To help organisations to determine the most appropriate safeguards for a particular personal data transfer, the government proposes to reinforce the importance of proportionality when using alternative transfer mechanisms' (original bold emphasis) [para 259].

The following question is set out in the consultation document for respondents.

Q3.3.1.	*To what extent do you agree with the proposal to reinforce the importance of proportionality when assessing risks for alternative transfer mechanisms?*

This raises a number of potential change areas to data protection law in the UK. These need to be considered in relation to the impact of data transfer rules, and how compliance will be affected, as well as how data rights may be affected. It is not known in advance of the text of exact proposed changes being made available, what the specific law changes may be.

The following question is set out in the consultation document for respondents.

Q3.3.2.	*What support or guidance would help organisations assess and mitigate the risks in relation to international transfers of personal data under alternative transfer mechanisms, and how might that support be most appropriately provided?*

This raises a number of potential change areas to data protection law in the UK. These need to be considered in relation to the impact of data transfer rules, and how compliance will be affected, as well as how data rights may be affected. It is not known in advance of the text of exact proposed changes being made available, what the specific law changes may be.

Consultation: Reverse transfers exemption

20.11   The consultation refers to a reverse transfers exemption. The consultation states,

> 'The government proposes to exempt 'reverse transfers' from the scope of the UK international transfer regime' (original bold emphasis) [para 260].

The following question is set out in the consultation document for respondents.

Q3.3.3.	*To what extent do you agree that the proposal to exempt 'reverse transfers' from the scope of the UK international transfer regime would reduce unnecessary burdens on organisations, without undermining data protection standards?*

This raises a number of potential change areas to data protection law in the UK. These need to be considered in relation to the impact of data transfer rules, and how compliance will be affected, as well as how data rights may be affected. It is not known in advance of the text of exact proposed changes being made available, what the specific law changes may be.

Consultation: Adaptable transfer mechanisms

20.12 The consultation refers to adaptable transfer mechanisms (ATMs). The consultation states that,

> '**The government is considering whether to empower organisations to create or identify their own alternative transfer mechanisms in addition to those listed in Article 46 of the UK GDPR**' (original bold emphasis) [para 261].

The following question is set out in the consultation document for respondents.

Q3.3.4.	*To what extent do you agree that empowering organisations to create or identify their own alternative transfer mechanisms that provide appropriate safeguards will address unnecessary limitations of the current set of alternative transfer mechanisms?*

This raises a number of potential change areas to data protection law in the UK. These need to be considered in relation to the impact of data transfer rules, and how compliance will be affected, as well as how data rights may be affected. It is not known in advance of the text of exact proposed changes being made available, what the specific law changes may be.

The following question is set out in the consultation document for respondents.

Q3.3.5	*What guidance or other support should be made available in order to secure sufficient confidence in organisations' decisions about whether an alternative transfer mechanism, or other legal protections not explicitly provided for in UK legislation, provide appropriate safeguards?*

This raises a number of potential change areas to data protection law in the UK. These need to be considered in relation to the impact of data transfer rules, and how compliance will be affected, as well as how data rights may be affected. It is not known in advance of the text of exact proposed changes being made available, what the specific law changes may be.

The following question is set out in the consultation document for respondents.

Q3.3.6.	*Should organisations be permitted to make international transfers that rely on protections provided for in another country's legislation, subject to an assessment that such protections offer appropriate safeguards?*

This raises a number of potential change areas to data protection law in the UK. These need to be considered in relation to the impact of data transfer rules, and how compliance will be affected, as well as how data rights may be affected. It is not known in advance of the text of exact proposed changes being made available, what the specific law changes may be.

Consultation: New alternative transfer mechanisms power

20.13   The consultation refers to a power to create new alternative transfer mechanisms. The consultation states that,

> '**The government proposes creating a new power for the Secretary of State to formally recognise new alternative transfer mechanisms**' (original bold emphasis) [para 265].

The following question is set out in the consultation document for respondents.

Q3.3.7.	To what extent do you agree that the proposal to create a new power for the Secretary of State to formally recognise new alternative transfer mechanisms would increase the flexibility of the UK's regime?

This raises a number of potential change areas to data protection law in the UK. These need to be considered in relation to the impact of data transfer rules, and how compliance will be affected, as well as how data rights may be affected. It is not known in advance of the text of exact proposed changes being made available, what the specific law changes may be.

The following question is set out in the consultation document for respondents.

Q3.3.8.	Are there any mechanisms that could be supported that would benefit UK organisations if they were recognised by the Secretary of State?

This raises a number of potential change areas to data protection law in the UK. These need to be considered in relation to the impact of data transfer rules, and how compliance will be affected, as well as how data rights may be affected. It is not known in advance of the text of exact proposed changes being made available, what the specific law changes may be.

Consultation: Certification schemes

20.14   The consultation refers to 'Alternative Schemes' in section 3.4. The consultation states,

> '**The government is considering modifications to the framework for certification schemes to provide for a more globally interoperable**

market-driven system that better supports the use of certifications as an alternative transfer mechanism' (original bold emphasis) [para 266].

'**To facilitate compatibility with a wider range of personal data protection regimes, the government proposes to allow certification to be provided for by different approaches to accountability'** (original bold emphasis) [para 267].

'**To bolster their use internationally, the government is considering provisions that clarify that prospective certification bodies outside of the UK can be accredited to run UK approved international transfer schemes'** (original bold emphasis) [para 268].

The following question is set out in the consultation document for respondents.

Q3.4.1.	*To what extent do you agree with the approach the government is considering to allow certifications to be provided by different approaches to accountability, including privacy management programmes?*

This raises a number of potential change areas to data protection law in the UK. These need to be considered in relation to the impact of data transfer rules, and how compliance will be affected, as well as how data rights may be affected. It is not known in advance of the text of exact proposed changes being made available, what the specific law changes may be.

The following question is set out in the consultation document for respondents.

Q3.4.2.	*To what extent do you agree that allowing accreditation for non-UK bodies will provide advantages to UK-based organisations?*

This raises a number of potential change areas to data protection law in the UK. These need to be considered in relation to the impact of data transfer rules, and how compliance will be affected, as well as how data rights may be affected. It is not known in advance of the text of exact proposed changes being made available, what the specific law changes may be.

The following question is set out in the consultation document for respondents.

Q3.4.3.	*Do you see allowing accreditation for non-UK bodies as being potentially beneficial for you or your organisation?*
	Please explain the advantages and risks that you foresee for allowing accreditation of non-UK bodies.

This raises a number of potential change areas to data protection law in the UK. These need to be considered in relation to the impact of data transfer rules, and how compliance will be affected, as well as how data rights may be affected. It is not known in advance of the text of exact proposed changes being made available, what the specific law changes may be.

The following question is set out in the consultation document for respondents.

Q3.4.4.	*Are there any other changes to certifications that would improve them as an international transfer tool?*

This raises a number of potential change areas to data protection law in the UK. These need to be considered in relation to the impact of data transfer rules, and how compliance will be affected, as well as how data rights may be affected. It is not known in advance of the text of exact proposed changes being made available, what the specific law changes may be.

Consultation: Derogations

20.15   The consultation refers to 'Derogations' in section 3.5. It refers to repetitive use of derogations. The consultation states,

> '**The government proposes establishing a proportionate increase in flexibility for use of derogations by making explicit that repetitive use of derogations is permitted**' (original bold emphasis) [para 270].

The following question is set out in the consultation document for respondents.

Q3.5.1.	*To what extent do you agree that the proposal described in paragraph 270 represents a proportionate increase in flexibility that will benefit UK organisations without unduly undermining data protection standards?*

This raises a number of potential change areas to data protection law in the UK. These need to be considered in relation to the impact of data transfer rules, and how compliance will be affected, as well as how data rights may be affected. It is not known in advance of the text of exact proposed changes being made available, what the specific law changes may be.

GOVERNMENT RESPONSE TO CONSULTATION

20.16   The government response to the Consultation is a document entitled 'Consultation outcome, Data: A New Direction – Government Response to Consultation', dated or updated on 23 June 2022. This refers to the government's response position, but more importantly also contains the government's proposals for where it intends to legislate changes to the UK data protection regime. Some of these changes are suggested to be imminent while other are referred to be coming but after a period of further official examination of those particular issues.

While there are a large number of particular changes proposed in the consultation response and over a range of data protection issue areas, quite a significant number of these refer to direct data transfer issues. These are referred to below.

Chapter 3 of the government response is indicated to refer to '[b]oosting trade and reducing barriers to data flows.' It is indicated that in chapter 3 of the consultation, the government agrees that global networks of personal data flows are critical to the UK's prosperity and modern way of life. In this chapter, the government then sets out what it considers the importance of removing unnecessary barriers to cross border data flows, including by progressing an ambitious programme of adequacy assessments. Some may find this somewhat controversial. Time will also tell if such actuations transpire to be counterproductive, for example, in undermining the EU adequacy decision for the UK.

The government indicates that it intends to create an autonomous framework for international data transfers that reflects the UK's (new) independent approach to data protection, that (in the government's view will) help drive international commerce, trade and development and underpins modern day business transactions and financial institutions.

The UK government's approach is indicated to be driven by outcomes for individuals and organisations. (Some readers will note that the current UK data protection regime and also the EU data protection regime already considers and balances the interests of individuals and industry. A swift publication of the government's response might suggest that there is an official or political view that this balance does not already exist, nor has previously been taken into account in setting the data protection regime – which would appear to be an incorrect interpretation).

The government indicates that continuing to ensure high standards of data protection will remain at the core of the future international transfers regime.

However, the government indicates that '[r]eforms will allow the UK government and businesses to take an agile approach, recognising there are varying frameworks operating internationally that offer a high level of data protection to data subjects. Businesses and organisations will benefit from reduced burdens and clarity on how and where personal data can be transferred across borders.' Whether correct or not, some readers could be forgiven for taking this to imply a lessening of standards, or at least making things easier for industry – but without indicating there is any enhanced benefit, rights, or protection afforded to individuals.

It is suggested by the government that '[a] more agile approach to the international transfer regime will help domestic businesses to connect more easily with international markets, and attract investment from abroad by businesses that rightly have confidence in the responsible use of personal data within the UK.' It also states that '[i]ndividuals will reap the benefits of organisations, hospitals and universities being able to share personal data quickly, efficiently and responsibly for the public good.' This seems to be suggesting law changes which benefit controllers. There do not appear to be any balancing law changes benefiting individuals. Rather, any benefits, if any, are effectively indicated to be trickle down benefits indirectly coming from entity controllers, not the data protection regime laws and rules. The government response indicates that '[i]nternational data flows help people to stay emotionally and socially connected to friends, families and communities around the world.' This suggestion appears curious on a number of levels, including its location placement. It also appears to be in some way equating with social media or social networking. It is also disjointed and unrelated to the policy change referred to immediately beforehand in the response document.

The government response document refers to adequacy issues at paragraph 3.2. The government recognises, it is suggested, that organisations currently 'face challenges and uncertainty when transferring personal data internationally'. This is a broad sweeping statement without identifying specific transfer channels. It would be helpful if the specific challenges and specific uncertainty matters that the government has in mind were identified.

Then the government refers to the risk-based approach to adequacy (see question 3.2.1).

The government states that the proposed 'underpinning' of the UK's future approach to adequacy decisions will be so called 'principles of risk assessment and proportionality'.

Here the government indicates that around half of respondents agreed with this proposal. Thus half or more did not. The government states that respondents thought that the proposal represented a pragmatic approach, with some articulating that the UK should be flexible and not prescriptive when making adequacy decisions. This could mean quite a number of things, and differing approaches. Having said that, it does not suggest altering a default data transfer ban approach as the starting point. It is indicated at least that many respondents (without saying how many) made clear that an outcome-based approach should not come at the expense of data protection standards.

The government indicates that it will move forward data transfer reforms that 'better enable' the UK to approach adequacy assessments with a focus on 'risk-based decision-making and outcomes', and 'continuing to support the UK's commitments relating to data flows'. Of course, the data protection regime already permits and enables data transfers – without the need for further change to do so. The reformed UK data regime will, the government indicates, retain the same broad standard that a country needs to meet in order to be found adequate, meaning that 'individuals'' data will continue to be well-protected by a regime that ensures high data protection standards.'

It then seems to suggest a focus on data transfer channels from the UK to other international countries (other than the EU Member States). It states that '[w]here countries meet those high data protection standards, the law will recognise that the DCMS Secretary of State may also consider the desirability of facilitating international data flows when making adequacy decisions.' This clearly suggests a new regime, administered by the DCMS, whereby UK adequacy decisions can be made in favour of third countries so as to permit data transfers from the UK to the identified country. It does not identify the examination, criteria, and application processes associated with such proposed UK made adequacy decisions. In the first instance, one might assume that such UK based adequacy decisions would contemplate and favour those third countries which currently have favourable adequacy decisions from the EU. Questions might be asked, if not eyebrows raised, if an expansive list of countries pass (or enter) a new UK adequacy decision process which are countries outside the list of countries successfully benefitting from the EU adequacy decisions. This will be an interesting aspect of the new changes to monitor.

The government indicates that it is 'respectful of countries' sovereign rights, and the different cultural and legal traditions that can contribute to high standards of data protection'. The reformed UK data protection regime is suggested by the government to recognise the 'contexts in which other countries operate', and take into account the 'different factors that play a part in protecting personal data' (whatever that may mean).

Adequacy for groups of countries, regions and multilateral frameworks is referred to in question 3.2.2. This is an issue already in terms of Canada and the EU, where differential adequacy is provided for. While it may not be an issue as yet, this holds at least some potential for differential consideration of different parts of the UK, for example, Scotland or Northern Ireland. This is naturally a highly political issue.

The government refers to it having consulted on whether to make adequacy regulations for groups of countries, regions and multilateral frameworks. The EU has not made any of these individual suggestions itself, so this would suggest a potential wide expansion of data transfer rules or channels if pioneered in the UK. The EU operates in individual assessments. The government indicates that a majority of respondents agreed with 'this approach'. Support was indicated to be based on the 'greater interoperability that this approach would provide' – presumably interoperability in this context meaning more data transfers. Conversely, it is acknowledged, that there were some concerns that this could be of limited use as adequacy decisions will still need to consider the laws of each country, as recognised in the consultation document. Indeed, an adequacy decision is based on a process whereby the laws and norms of the jurisdiction that have applied to be assessed for adequacy are researched and examined by the examining transferor country.

The government states that it will consider the implications of using this approach in the future, which may indicate this may not be in the first wave of new data law changes. It is said that this is especially so as the government seeks to prioritise work on multilateral solutions (which suggests the opposed to bilateral solutions) for data flows. The government does not intend to make any immediate data law legislative changes on this point.

The next section of the response refers to relaxing the requirement to review adequacy regulations every four years (question 3.2.3). The EU reviews each adequacy decision every four years.

The government proposed to invest in the ongoing monitoring of adequacy regulations and relax the requirement to review adequacy regulations every four years. It is noted that the EU also engages in ongoing monitoring in addition to full reviews every four years, even if arguably soft monitoring. It seems in this instance the government is suggesting dropping the more in depth four year reviews altogether. There were mixed views on this proposal, the government states, with some respondents believing that this would be both a 'more pragmatic and more effective approach', while other respondents cited concerns that the change could present 'risks to data protection standards'.

The government notes that adequacy regulations must be scrutinised in the face of constant developments to the legal landscapes of adequate countries. In addition, the government recognises the balance of views, and assesses that, *if* used appropriately, 'ongoing monitoring can safeguard data subjects more effectively than intermittent review points'. As ever, therefore, the devil may be in the detail. If the general theme of 'reducing red tape and facilitating data transfers, is followed, some readers may wonder how well "ongoing monitoring"' may be provided for and funded. It would also be interesting to see what role the ICO and the DCMA respectively might have in such a process. The response continues thar '[a] well-functioning, rigorous and ongoing monitoring process removes the need for a formal review.' In theory it may indeed do so, but the rub lies in what level of monitoring occurs. The government states that it intends to proceed with relaxing the requirement to review adequacy regulations every four years. It does not, however, detail what type of ongoing monitoring might replace it – which seems counter intuitive.

Redress requirements are referred to next in the government response to the consultation (question 3.2.4). The government proposed 'clarifying that when assessing another country for adequacy, it is acceptable for that country to provide either administrative or judicial redress for UK data subjects, as long as the redress mechanism is effective.' Around half of respondents are indicated to have agreed with this proposal. The most common view was that the effectiveness of redress is more important than its form. This should not be considered in isolation however, as assessment and consideration of the general data laws and norms that exist in the given country should be assessed with great importance. In addition, merely providing access to courts per a bilateral agreement may have less effect if there is no range of effective data rights recognised in the target jurisdiction. Even if a redress mechanism is effective, if there is no right recognised to be pursued with a data regulator or court, the reference to such a mechanism would be a mere pro forma exercise. An effective redress mechanism must rest upon robust data rights. It is otherwise practically ineffective even if technically existing on paper. The government indicates that it intends to proceed with this proposal. Under the reformed data protection regime, the government states that it will not specify the *form* in which redress should be provided. Instead, when conducting adequacy assessments, the government will consider the effectiveness of redress mechanisms available. While it is not expressly stated – nor acknowledged – by the government, redress and rights go hand in hand.

Alternative transfer mechanisms (or ATMs) are referred to in paragraph 3.3 of the response document. These ATMs are indicated to provide a route for cross border data transfers of personal data to countries that are *not* subject to an adequacy decision. Many organisations, the response correctly notes, send data all over the world and often have complex infrastructure to support such data sharing. As the book comments, any given controller may have to consider operating many data transfer channels simultaneously (and of course associated compliance).

Proportionality of appropriate safeguards is also referred to in government response document (questions 3.3.1, 3.3.2). To 'facilitate' safe and effective international data sharing, the government proposed changes to 'reinforce' the importance of 'proportionality' when assessing risk for ATMs. The government called for views on support or guidance that could help organisations assess and mitigate risks in relation to international transfers of personal data when using so called ATMs.

The response indicates that the majority of respondents agreed with this proposal, noting the challenges organisations have faced in assessing the risks of international transfers using ATMs. Respondents who disagreed cited concerns around a perceived risk of degrading data protection standards. Some readers might even question the need to refer to 'perceived' at all as a result of the tone or intention of some of the questions, proposals, and intended changes. Respondents are referred to as having showed strong support for more clarity and guidance on the requirements for ATMs.

The government announces that it will proceed with reforms to 'ensure that data exporters can act pragmatically and proportionally when using' ATMs, whilst still maintaining a high standard of protection for data subjects. A critical reader might query what daylight might exist between current standards of protection for data subjects and some future change to high standards of protection for data subjects. If there is to be daylight, and especially if it is large and significant, that will tell a lot in terms of policy intentions, political expediency, and moving the bar on existing balance and proportionality, skewing the weight of it one way.

Reverse transfers are also referred to (question 3.3.3). The government proposed to remove 'reverse transfers' from the scope of the international data transfer regime. There were mixed responses regarding this proposal. Those in support agreed that it could 'reduce unnecessary and disproportionate burdens on organisations' without corresponding risks to data protection. However, there were mixed views on the 'extent' of the 'positive impact' anticipated by respondents. (This seems to refer to positive impacts only on one side of the equation). Those who disagreed with the proposed reform refer to the potential risks to data subject rights. It was also noted that this reform will be complex and may not lead to a reduction in complexity for data controllers. The government agrees with this appraisal and as a result will not pursue this particular legislative reform.

ATMs are also further referred to (in questions 3.3.4, 3.3.5, 3.3.6). The government proposed to allow organisations to 'create' or identify their 'own' transfer mechanism. Most respondents disagreed with this proposal. They felt that this reform would be too difficult to use and may generate uncertainty about what is required for safeguarding transfers. For instance, it may create an unending list of data transfer channels. Some expressed concern that the proposal may risk data protection standards. Respondents who supported the proposal believed it would help organisations overcome complex and specific transfer requirements in some situations. Given the absence of clear use cases for this proposal, the government has decided that it will not pursue this approach.

A power to create ATMs is also considered (in questions 3.3.7, 3.3.8). The government proposed creating a new power for the DCMS Secretary of State to formally recognise new ATMs. This would allow the Secretary of State to create new UK mechanisms for transferring data overseas or recognise in UK law other international data transfer mechanisms (if they achieve the outcomes required by UK law). There were mixed views on this proposal. There was support for the opportunities for interoperability and future proofing. Concerns were raised about the potential risk that new transfer mechanisms would not maintain data protection standards.

The government recognises the mixed views on this issue. However, the government assesses that this reform will help to future proof the UK's approach to international data transfers by allowing the UK to respond rapidly to international developments. Some readers might consider this to be legislating a solution that has not yet been presented as a problem. The government intends to proceed with this reform to 'ensure' that new mechanisms must meet the same high data protection standards as the other ATMs. Similar daylight queries may arise as mentioned above.

UK certification schemes are referred to at paragraph 3.4. Certification schemes are referred to as 'voluntary, market-driven frameworks of context-specific rules that, under the UK GDPR, can be used to demonstrate a high standard of compliance and to provide appropriate safeguards for international transfers'. Of course, there is also data regulator involvement, which is not mentioned. These certification schemes are, the document indicates, characteristically framed at the sectoral or industry level, defining data protection rules and practices covering specific products, processes and services within the context of that sector, industry or similar group.

However, the response indicates that certification schemes are complex measures that require significant time and resources to design, implement and maintain, and demonstrate accountability for. Of course getting it right can take time, especially with the initial set up. The government considered modifications to the framework for certification schemes, to provide for a more globally interoperable market-driven system that 'better supports' the use of certifications as an ATM.

Amending the certification schemes to increase 'interoperability' is considered (in questions 3.4.1, 3.4.2). To facilitate 'compatibility' with a wider range of personal data protection regimes, the government proposed two changes. First, to allow certification to be provided for by different approaches to accountability, such as privacy management programmes. Second, to clarify that certification bodies outside the UK can be accredited to run UK approved international transfer schemes. There were mixed views on both of these proposals. Respondents noted that the reforms could benefit UK businesses by facilitating easier personal data transfers. Other respondents were less sure that these proposals would benefit them or their organisation directly. There is no reference to the perspective for individuals. Supporting 'interoperability' is important for organisations, the government suggests. However, there remains potential within the current approach to use certifications more extensively. That of course is correct. In fact, the initiation process for certification mechanisms often rests with the industry side. It is also unclear, at this time the government says, whether the proposed reforms are the best way to deliver greater interoperability. The government states that it will consider other approaches to meeting this goal.

Derogations are also referred to at paragraph 3.5 by the government. The consultation sets out that the current overarching approach to the use of derogations will be maintained. They should be used only in situations where they are necessary and where neither adequacy nor other safeguards are appropriate. As outlined in this section of the consultation, technical changes may help to clarify the restrictions on using derogations. These are being considered by the government.

Repetitive use of derogations are also referred to (in question 3.5.1). The government proposed establishing a 'proportionate increase in flexibility' for the use of derogations, by making explicit that repetitive use of derogations is permitted. There was some opposition to this proposal, with respondents expressing concerns that it may 'negatively impact data subject rights'. There was minimal support, with respondents agreeing that it would represent a proportionate increase in flexibility for transfers. The government confirmed that it would not pursue this reform.

Further questions are also referred to in the response and consultation (paragraph 3.6). The government asked for views on whether any of the proposals would impact on anyone with protected characteristics. There were no specific concerns related to the impact any proposals would have on those with protected characteristics, nor were there significant issues raised by respondents in relation to the questions and topics in this chapter. The consultation posed some open ended questions at the end of this chapter for respondents to provide any other comments on the proposed reforms.

Respondents highlighted the importance of protecting people's personal data when these reforms come into force, particularly those with protected characteristics. 'The protection of people's personal data is already at the heart of the UK's data regime and will continue to be as the government embarks on its reform agenda.' This remains to be seen.

Annex A to the consultation response sets out a list of consultation proposals for changing UK data protection data transfer laws and other data protection laws. This is referred to below.

Question	Proposal	Next steps
3.3.7	To reform the DCMS Secretary of State's adequacy making power.	A – The government plans to proceed with this proposal
3.2.2	Making adequacy regulations for groups of countries, regions and multilateral frameworks	B – The government will continue to consider this approach
3.2.3	To remove the requirement for the DCMS Secretary of State to conduct a review adequacy decisions every 4 years	A – The government plans to proceed with this proposal
3.3.7	Clarifying that either judicial or administrative redress is acceptable for international transfers	A – The government plans to proceed with this proposal
3.3.3	Exempt "reverse transfers" from the scope of the UK ITR	C – The government does not plan to proceed with this proposal
3.3.4	Empowering organisations to create their own ATMs	C – The government does not plan to proceed with this proposal
3.3.1, 3.3.8	Creating a new power for the DCMS Secretary of State to formally recognise new ATMs	A – The government plans to proceed with this proposal
3.2.3	Reinforcing the importance of proportionality when using ATMs	A – The government plans to proceed with this proposal
3.4.1	Allowing certification for international transfers to be provided for by different approaches to accountability	C – The government does not plan to proceed with this proposal
3.4.1	Clarifying that prospective certification bodies outside the UK can be accredited to run UK-approved international transfer schemes	C – The government does not plan to proceed with this proposal

CHANGES

20.17   Despite the government's response document to the consultation barely having landed it is clear that the government was working swiftly as it soon issued a Proposed Bill, Data Protection and Digital Information Bill 2022 to reform UK data protection law.[4]

Section 21 of the bill refers to transfers of personal data to third countries and international organisations. It provides that:

'(1)   Schedule 5 amends Chapter 5 of the UK GDPR (general processing and transfers of personal data to third countries and international organisations).

(2)   Schedule 6 amends Chapter 5 of Part 3 of the 2018 Act (law enforcement processing and transfers of personal data to third countries and international organisations).

(3)   Schedule 7 contains consequential and transitional provision.'

Schedule 5 refers to Section 21, which relates to transfers of personal data to third countries etc: general processing. The schedule contains the following amendments, namely:

'Introduction

1   Chapter 5 of the UK GDPR (transfers of personal data to third countries or international organisations) is amended as follows.

General principles for transfers

2(1) Omit Article 44 (transfers of personal data to third countries etc: general principles for transfers).

(2)   After that Article insert—

"Article 44A

General principles for transfers

1.   A controller or processor may transfer personal data to a third country or an international organisation only if—

(a)   the condition in paragraph 2 is met, and

(b)   the transfer is carried out in compliance with the other provisions of this Regulation.

2.   The condition is met if the transfer—

(a)   is approved by regulations under Article 45A that are in force at the time of the transfer,

(b)   is made subject to appropriate safeguards (see Article 46), or

---

4   Bill 143 2022-23 (as introduced).

(c)   is made in reliance on a derogation for special situations (see Article 49).

3.   A transfer may not be made in reliance on paragraph 2(b) or (c) if, or to the extent that, it would breach a restriction in regulations under Article 49A."

Transfers approved by regulations

3   Omit Article 45 (transfers on the basis of an adequacy decision).

4   After that Article insert—

"Article 45A

Transfers approved by regulations

1.   For the purposes of Article 44A, the Secretary of State may by regulations approve transfers of personal data to—

(a)   a third country, or

(b)   an international organisation.

2.   The Secretary of State may only make regulations under this Article approving transfers to a third country or international organisation if the Secretary of State considers that the data protection test is met in relation to the transfers (see Article 45B).

3.   In making regulations under this Article, the Secretary of State may have regard to any matter which the Secretary of State considers relevant, including the desirability of facilitating transfers of personal data to and from the United Kingdom.

4.   Regulations under this Article may, among other things—

(a)   make provision in relation to a third country or international organisation specified in the regulations or a description of country or organisation;

(b)   approve all transfers of personal data to a third country or international organisation or only transfers specified or described in the regulations;

(c)   identify a transfer of personal data by any means, including by reference to—

(i)   a sector or geographic area within a third country,

(ii)   the controller or processor,

(iii)   the recipient of the personal data,

(iv)   the personal data transferred,

(v)   the means by which the transfer is made, or

(vi)   relevant legislation, schemes, lists or other arrangements or documents, as they have effect from time to time;

> (d)   confer a discretion on a person.

5.   Regulations under this Article are subject to the negative resolution procedure.

Article 45B

The data protection test

1.   For the purposes of Article 45A, the data protection test is met in relation to transfers of personal data to a third country or international organisation if the standard of the protection provided for data subjects with regard to general processing of personal data in the country or by the organisation is not materially lower than the standard of the protection provided for data subjects by or under—

> (a)   this Regulation,
>
> (b)   Part 2 of the 2018 Act, and
>
> (c)   Parts 5 to 7 of that Act, so far as relevant to general processing

2.   In considering whether the data protection test is met in relation to transfers of personal data to a third country or international organisation, the Secretary of State must consider, among other things—

> (a)   respect for the rule of law and for human rights in the country or by the organisation,
>
> (b)   the existence, and powers, of an authority responsible for enforcing the protection of data subjects with regard to the processing of personal data in the country or by the organisation,
>
> (c)   arrangements for judicial or non-judicial redress for data subjects in connection with such processing,
>
> (d)   rules about the transfer of personal data from the country or by the organisation to other countries or international organisations,
>
> (e)   relevant international obligations of the country or organisation,
>
> and
>
> (f)   the constitution, traditions and culture[5] of the country or organisation.

---

5   Note one article referring to data culture issues, namely, Coley, 'International Data Transfers: The Effect of Divergent Cultural Views in Privacy Causes Déjà vu' (2017) 68(5) *Hastings Law Journal* 1111.

3. In paragraphs 1 and 2—

   (a) the references to the protection provided for data subjects are to that protection taken as a whole,

   (b) the references to general processing are to processing to which this Regulation applies or equivalent types of processing in the third country or by the international organisation (as appropriate), and

   (c) the references to processing of personal data in the third country or by the international organisation are references only to the processing of personal data transferred from the United Kingdom.

4. When the data protection test is applied only to certain transfers to a third country or international organisation that are specified or described, or to be specified or described, in regulations (in accordance with Article 45A(4)(b))—

   (a) the references in paragraphs 1 to 3 to personal data are to be read as references only to personal data likely to be the subject of such transfers, and

   (b) the reference in paragraph 2(d) to the transfer of personal data to other countries or international organisations is to be read as a including the transfer of personal data within the third country or international organisation."

Transfers approved by regulations: monitoring

5 After Article 45B (inserted by paragraph 4) insert—

"Article 45C

Transfers approved by regulations: monitoring

1. The Secretary of State must, on an ongoing basis, monitor developments in third countries and international organisations that could affect decisions to make regulations under Article 45A or to amend or revoke such regulations.

2. Where the Secretary of State becomes aware that the data protection test is no longer met in relation to transfers approved, or of a description approved, in regulations under Article 45A, the Secretary of State must, to the extent necessary, amend or revoke the regulations.

3. Where regulations under Article 45A are amended or revoked in accordance with paragraph 2, the Secretary of State must enter into consultations with the third country or international organisation concerned with a view to improving the protection provided to data subjects with regard to the processing of personal data in the country or by the organisation.

4.   The Secretary of State must publish—

(a)   a list of the third countries and international organisations, and the descriptions of such countries and organisations, which are for the time being approved by regulations under Article 45A as places or persons to which personal data may be transferred, and

(b)   a list of the third countries and international organisations, and the descriptions of such countries and organisations, which have been but are no longer approved by such regulations.

5.   In the case of regulations under Article 45A which approve only certain transfers to a third country or international organisation specified or described in the regulations (in accordance with Article 45A(4)(b)), the lists published under paragraph 4 must specify or describe the relevant transfers."

Transfers subject to appropriate safeguards

6   (1)   Article 46 (transfers subject to appropriate safeguards) is amended as follows.

(2)   Omit paragraph 1.

(3)   After that paragraph insert—

"1A. A transfer of personal data to a third country or an international organisation by a controller or processor is made subject to appropriate safeguards only—

(a)   in a case in which—

(i)   safeguards are provided in connection with the transfer as described in paragraph 2 or 3 or regulations made under Article 47A(4), and

(ii)   the controller or processor, acting reasonably and proportionately, considers that the data protection test is met in relation to the transfer or that type of transfer (see paragraph 6), or

(b)   in a case in which—

(i)   safeguards are provided in accordance with paragraph 2(a) by an instrument that is intended to be relied on in connection with the transfer or that type of transfer, and

(ii)   each public body that is a party to the instrument, acting reasonably and proportionately, considers that the data protection test is met in relation to the transfers, or types of transfer, intended to be made in reliance on the instrument (see paragraph 6)."

(4) In paragraph 2—

    (a) in the words before point (a)—

        (i) omit "appropriate", and

        (ii) for "paragraph 1" substitute "paragraph 1A(a)",

    (b) in point (a), for "public authorities or bodies" substitute "a public body and another relevant person or persons",

    (c) in point (b), after "rules" insert "approved",

    (d) in point (c), for "section 17C of the 2018 Act" substitute "Article 47A(1)",

    (e) in point (e), for "appropriate safeguards" substitute "safeguards provided by the code", and

    (f) in point (f), "appropriate safeguards" substitute "safeguards provided by the mechanism".

(5) In paragraph 3, in the words before point (a)—

    (a) omit "appropriate",

    (b) for "paragraph 1" substitute "paragraph 1A(a)",

    (c) omit ", in particular,", and

    (d) in point (b), for "public authorities or bodies" substitute "a public body and another relevant person or persons".

(6) At the end insert—

    "6. For the purposes of this Article, the data protection test is met in relation to a transfer, or a type of transfer, of personal data if, after the transfer, the standard of the protection provided for the data subject with regard to that personal data by the safeguards required under paragraph 1A, and (where relevant) by other means, would not be materially lower than the standard of the protection provided for the data subject with regard to the personal data by or under—

        (a) this Regulation,

        (b) Part 2 of the 2018 Act, and

        (c) Parts 5 to 7 of that Act, so far as relevant to processing to which this Regulation applies.

7. For the purposes of paragraph 1A(a)(ii) and (b)(ii), what is reasonable and proportionate is to be determined by reference to all the circumstances, or likely circumstances, of the transfer or type of transfer, including the nature and volume of the personal data transferred.

8. In this Article—

(a) references to the protection provided for the data subject are to that protection taken as a whole;

(b) "relevant person" means a public body or another person exercising functions of a public nature."

7   In the heading of Article 47 (binding corporate rules) at the beginning insert "Transfers subject to appropriate safeguards:".

8   After Article 47 insert—

"Article 47A

Transfers subject to appropriate safeguards: further provision

1.   The Secretary of State may by regulations specify standard data protection clauses which the Secretary of State considers are capable of securing that the data protection test set out in Article 46 is met in relation to transfers of personal data generally or in relation to a type of transfer specified in the regulations.

2.   The Secretary of State must keep under review the standard data protection clauses specified in regulations under paragraph 1 that are for the time being in force.

3.   Regulations under paragraph 1 are subject to the negative resolution procedure.

4.   The Secretary of State may by regulations make provision about further safeguards that may be relied on for the purposes of Article 46(1A)(a).

5.   The Secretary of State may only make regulations under paragraph 4 if the Secretary of State considers that the further safeguards are capable of securing that the data protection test set out in Article 46 is met in relation to transfers of personal data generally or in relation to a type of transfer specified in the regulations.

6.   Regulations under paragraph 4 may (among other things)—

(a) make provision by adopting safeguards prepared or published by another person;

(b) make provision about ways of providing safeguards which require authorisation from the Commissioner;

(c) amend Article 46 by—

(i) adding ways of providing safeguards, or

(ii) varying or omitting ways of providing safeguards which were added by regulations under this Article.

7.   Regulations under paragraph 4 are subject to the affirmative resolution procedure."

Derogations for specific circumstances

9 (1) Article 49 (derogations for specific situations) is amended as follows.

(2) In paragraph 1, in the first subparagraph—

(a) for "adequacy regulations under section 17A of the 2018 Act, or of appropriate safeguards pursuant to Article 46, including binding corporate rules" substitute "approval by regulations under Article 45A and of compliance with Article 46 (appropriate safeguards)",

and

(b) in point (a), for "an adequacy decision" substitute "approval by regulations under Article 45A".

(3) In paragraph 1, in the second subparagraph, for "a provision in Article 45" substitute "Article 45A".

(4) In paragraph 4, for "section 18(1) of the 2018 Act" substitute "paragraph 4A".

(5) After paragraph 4 insert—

"4A. The Secretary of State may by regulations specify for the purposes of point (d) of paragraph 1—

(a) circumstances in which a transfer of personal data to a third country or international organisation is to be taken to be necessary for important reasons of public interest, and

(b) circumstances in which a transfer of personal data to a third country or international organisation which is not required by an enactment is not to be taken to be necessary for important reasons of public interest."

(6) Omit paragraph 5A.

(7) After paragraph 6 insert—

"7. Regulations under this Article—

(a) are subject to the made affirmative resolution procedure where the Secretary of State has made an urgency statement in respect of them;

(b) otherwise, are subject to the affirmative resolution procedure.

8. For the purposes of this Article, an urgency statement is a reasoned statement that the Secretary of State considers it desirable for the regulations to come into force without delay."

Public interest restrictions

10   After Article 49 insert—

"Article 49A

1.   The Secretary of State may by regulations restrict the transfer of a category of personal data to a third country or international organisation where—

(a)   the transfer is not approved by regulations under Article 45A for the time being in force, and

(b)   the Secretary of State considers the restriction to be necessary for important reasons of public interest.

2.   Regulations under this Article—

(a)   are subject to the made affirmative resolution procedure where the Secretary of State has made an urgency statement in respect of them;

(b)   otherwise, are subject to the affirmative resolution procedure.

3.   For the purposes of this Article, an urgency statement is a reasoned statement that the Secretary of State considers it desirable for the regulations to come into force without delay.'''

This Bill was introduced in 2022 and will progress further during 2023. As with any proposed legal measure, amendments may occur during the parliamentary process. It is also clear from other legal proposals such as the Online Safety Bill proposal, that it can never be assured in advance how quickly any given legal proposal will take before it is enacted. What is clear is that this portends further uncertainly during this process for organisations. Even once the Bill becomes law, with whatever changes occur in the interim, organisations will need a period of adjustment to the new arrangements and the specific impact upon their own individual's data transfer channels.

CHAPTER 21

Approved Contracts

INTRODUCTION

21.01 The consultation and response indicates that government policy recognises a need for new UK data transfer standard contracts, much like the EU model. However, some of the consultation responses from the government seem to indicate the possibility that there may be an even wider UK model contract regime than the EU precursor. There are now not just new UK contracts for the first time, but also newly updated model contracts from the EU that businesses must also consider.

CREATING ADEQUACY THROUGH CONTRACT

21.02 One of the data transfer permission channels relates to transfers permitted as a result of adopting the EU model contracts into the legal relationship between the data exporter and the data importer/recipient.

Transfers of data to a third country may be made even though there is no adequate protection in place in the third country, if the controller secures the necessary level of protection through contractual obligations.

These contractual protections are the model contract clauses emanating from the Commission. The Commission has issued what it considers to be adequate clauses which are incorporated into the contract relationship of the data exporter and data importer as then provide an adequate level of consent.

Obtaining consent of pre-existing customers may pose a problem so in some cases may not be possible or practical. For example, it may not be possible to retrospectively change existing contracts and terms.

However, going forward it may be possible to include 'transfer' issues in any data protection compliance and related models.

NEW EU STANDARD CONTRACT CLAUSES

21.03 One of the other transfer exemptions from the default transfer ban under the GDPR which is relevant in relation to streaming one data transfer from the EU to the UK is what is known as the Commission's endorsed standard contractual clause to govern such transfers.

The Commission recently endorsed a second generation of such clauses. The Commission states:

> 'According to the General Data Protection Regulation (GDPR), contractual clauses ensuring appropriate data protection safeguards can be used as a ground for data transfers from the EU to third countries. This includes model contract clauses – so-called standard contractual clauses (SCCs) – that have been "pre-approved" by the European Commission.
>
> On 4 June 2021, the Commission issued modernised standard contractual clauses under the GDPR for data transfers from controllers or processors in the EU/EEA (or otherwise subject to the GDPR) to controllers or processors established outside the EU/EEA (and not subject to the GDPR):
>
> These modernised SCCs replace the three sets of SCCs that were adopted under the previous Data Protection Directive 95/46. Since 27 September 2021, it is no longer possible to conclude contracts incorporating these earlier sets of SCCs.
>
> Until 27 December 2022, controllers and processors can continue to rely on those earlier SCCs for contracts that were concluded before 27 September 2021, provided that the processing operations that are the subject matter of the contract remain unchanged.'[1]

The following innovations are referred to in the new generation of the standard contractual clauses:

* update in line with the GDPR;

* one single entry-point covering a broad range of transfer scenarios, instead of separate sets of clauses;

* more flexibility for complex processing chains, through a 'modular approach' and by offering the possibility for more than two parties to join and use the clauses;

* practical toolbox to comply with the *Schrems II* judgment; ie an overview of the different steps companies have to take to comply with the *Schrems II* judgment as well as examples of possible 'supplementary measures', such as encryption, that companies may take if necessary.[2]

The European Commission adopted

> 'two sets of standard contractual clauses, one for use between controllers and processors and one for the transfer of personal data to third countries. They reflect new requirements under the General Data Protection Regulation (GDPR) and take into account the Schrems II judgement of the Court of Justice, ensuring a high level of data protection for citizens. These new tools will offer more legal predictability to European businesses and help,

---

1   'Standard Contractual Clauses For International Transfers, Modernised Standard Contractual Clauses For The Transfer Of Personal Data To Third Countries,' EU Commission, JUSTICE AND CONSUMERS, 4 June 2021.
2   'European Commission Adopts New Tools For Safe Exchanges Of Personal Data,' EU Commission, Press Release, 4 June 2021.

in particular, SMEs to ensure compliance with requirements for safe data transfers, while allowing data to move freely across borders, without legal barriers.'[3]

There are therefore two types of standard contracts for a business to be aware of. The activities of the business and its relationship with the counterparty in the EU will influence which is the appropriate contract that the business will need to consider implementing.

The EU has enacted two new model contracts regimes, one for controller to processor contracts; and contracts and transfers to international third countries (see following chapters).

NEED FOR UK MODEL CONTRACTS

21.04 Given that Brexit has occurred, businesses will have been keen to have the UK promote its own set of model contracts which entities can execute on a bilateral basis to ensure a lawful mechanism for data transfers to occur. Previously, the EU had promoted its own set of model contracts for controller-to-controller situations, and separately for controller to processor situations.

These were and are important in terms of an alternative, or even back up permission mechanism, in the event of problems with the adequacy model arising.

Given the finalisation of Brexit, these prior EU model contracts are now, at least directly, a UK data law guaranteed data transfer mechanism. (That said they can be indirectly relevant where an EU company requests a UK counterparty to sign up on a bilateral basis). There was and will be a need, therefore, for the UK to have its own UK version or concept of the prior EU model contracts. However, given the UK political imperative to appear different from anything EU based, review is needed of how the recently announced model contracts mimic or diverge from the EU versions. Added attention is also needed as the EU has since updated its own version of the prior model contracts.

3   Ibid.

CHAPTER 22

Controller to Processor Contracts

INTRODUCTION

22.01 Controller-to-processor contracts refer to the types of contract models issued or endorsed by official authorities which are deemed to be sufficient under data laws to permit a controller in a jurisdiction to transfer data to a processor in a separate jurisdiction and which jurisdiction may not be officially deemed to have a similar or identical level of data protections as exist in the controller's jurisdiction. The best example historically is the model contracts or standard contracts issued by the EU Commission to enable recipient processors in non-EU third countries to undertake activities involving personal data with entities in the EU.

These entities can sometimes be related within the same international corporate business group (eg, payroll processing carried out in a non-EU country for an EU company in the same group). There can also be examples where the entities are unrelated but the processor is carrying out some very specific, defined, and contracted activities for and on behalf of the controller.

These model contracts or standard contract clauses as originated in the EU data protection regime were recognised under EU data laws (including the GDPR) and act as a derogation from the default data transfer ban.

The EU controller to processor contracts (as now recently updated) are relevant to the extent that a processor company in the UK wishes to deal with an EU controller company. However, the UK has also deemed it beneficial, if not necessary, to establish its own rules for UK controllers and international processors.

NEW EU STANDARD CONTRACT CLAUSES

22.02 One of the other transfer exemptions from the default transfer ban under the GDPR which is relevant in relation to streaming one data transfer from the EU to the UK is what is known as the Commission endorsed standard contractual clauses to govern such transfers.

The Commission recently endorsed a second generation of such clauses. The Commission states:

> 'According to the General Data Protection Regulation (GDPR), contractual clauses ensuring appropriate data protection safeguards can be used as a

ground for data transfers from the EU to third countries. This includes model contract clauses – so-called standard contractual clauses (SCCs) – that have been "pre-approved" by the European Commission.

On 4 June 2021, the Commission issued modernised standard contractual clauses under the GDPR for data transfers from controllers or processors in the EU/EEA (or otherwise subject to the GDPR) to controllers or processors established outside the EU/EEA (and not subject to the GDPR):

These modernised SCCs replace the three sets of SCCs that were adopted under the previous Data Protection Directive 95/46. Since 27 September 2021, it is no longer possible to conclude contracts incorporating these earlier sets of SCCs.

Until 27 December 2022, controllers and processors can continue to rely on those earlier SCCs for contracts that were concluded before 27 September 2021, provided that the processing operations that are the subject matter of the contract remain unchanged.'[1]

The following innovations are referred to in the new generation of the standard contractual clauses:

• update in line with the GDPR;

• one single entry-point covering a broad range of transfer scenarios, instead of separate sets of clauses;

• more flexibility for complex processing chains, through a 'modular approach' and by offering the possibility for more than two parties to join and use the clauses;

• practical toolbox to comply with the *Schrems II* judgment; ie an overview of the different steps companies have to take to comply with the *Schrems II* judgment as well as examples of possible 'supplementary measures', such as encryption, that companies may take if necessary.[2]

The European Commission adopted 'two sets of standard contractual clauses, one for use between controllers and processors and one for the transfer of personal data to third countries. They reflect new requirements under the GDPR and take into account the *Schrems II* judgement of the Court of Justice, ensuring a high level of data protection for citizens. These new tools will offer more legal predictability to European businesses and help, in particular, SMEs to ensure compliance with requirements for safe data transfers, while allowing data to move freely across borders, without legal barriers.'[3]

---

1   'Standard Contractual Clauses For International Transfers, Modernised Standard Contractual Clauses For The Transfer Of Personal Data To Third Countries,' EU Commission, JUSTICE AND CONSUMERS, 4 June 2021.
2   'European Commission Adopts New Tools For Safe Exchanges Of Personal Data,' EU Commission, Press Release, 4 June 2021.
3   'European Commission Adopts New Tools For Safe Exchanges Of Personal Data,' EU Commission, Press Release, 4 June 2021.

There are therefore two types of standard contract for a business to be aware of. The activities of the business and its relationship with the counterparty in the EU will influence which is the appropriate contract that the business will need to consider implementing.

CONTROLLER TO PROCESSOR CONTRACTS

22.03   The decision states that:

'The standard contractual clauses as set out in the Annex fulfil the requirements for contracts between controllers and processors in Article 28(3) and (4) of Regulation (EU) 2016/679 and of Article 29(3) and (4) of Regulation (EU) 2018/1725.' (Article 1)

'The standard contractual clauses as set out in the Annex may be used in contracts between a controller and a processor who processes personal data on behalf of the controller.' (Article 2)

The Annex to the decision states in relation to purpose and scope that:

'The purpose of these Standard Contractual Clauses (the Clauses) is to ensure compliance with [choose relevant option: OPTION 1: Article 28(3) and (4) of Regulation (EU) 2016/679 of the European Parliament and of the Council of 27 April 2016 on the protection of natural persons with regard to the processing of personal data and on the free movement of such data, and repealing Directive 95/46/EC (General Data Protection Regulation)] / [OPTION 2: Article 29(3) and (4) of Regulation (EU) 2018/1725 of the European Parliament and of the Council of 23 October 2018 on the protection of natural persons with regard to the processing of personal data by the Union institutions, bodies, offices and agencies and on the free movement of such data, and repealing Regulation (EC) No 45/2001 and Decision No 1247/2002/EC].'

The Contracts and Transfers to International Third Countries decision also refers to controller and processor issues. The new rules for international data transfers requires review of both the Commission decision document pursuant to the GDPR, and the related contract clauses document. The decision is the Commission Implementing Decision on standard contractual clauses for the transfer of personal data to third countries pursuant to Regulation (EU) 2016/679.[4] The decision itself states that: 'The standard contractual clauses set out in the Annex are now considered to 'provide appropriate safeguards within the meaning of Article 46(1) and (2)(c) of Regulation (EU) 2016/679 for the transfer by a controller or processor of personal data processed subject to that Regulation (data exporter) to a controller or (sub-)processor whose processing of the data

---

4   Commission Implementing Decision (EU) 2021/914 of 4 June 2021 on standard contractual clauses for the transfer of personal data to third countries pursuant to Regulation (EU) 2016/679 of the European Parliament and of the Council (Text with EEA relevance), C/2021/3972, [2021] OJ L199, 31–61.

is not subject to that Regulation (data importer);'[5] and 'The standard contractual clauses also set out the rights and obligations of controllers and processors with respect to the matters referred to in Article 28(3) and (4) of Regulation (EU) 2016/679, as regards the transfer of personal data from a controller to a processor, or from a processor to a sub-processor.'[6]

UK CONTROLLER TO PROCESSOR CONTRACTS

22.04   The UK has now established its own rules in terms of seeking to set out official contracts or contract terms which businesses can consider implementing into their own bilateral relationships and which if incorporated might be sufficient to permit otherwise non permitted data transfers, in this instance from UK controllers to foreign processors.

Obviously, compare and contrast exercises will occur in due course to see if there are comparisons or divergences between the UK models and the EU models, and to consider what this may mean in a particular proposed data transfer situation.

Parliament was presented with these new rules referred to as the International Data Transfer Agreement (IDTA) and International Data Transfer Addendum (UK Addendum) on 2 February 2022 and became law from 21 March 2022. The documents were issued under section 119A of the Data Protection Act 2018.

The International Data Transfer Agreement contains the following provisions,

- parties and signatures;
- transfer Details;
- transferred data;
- security requirements;
- commercial clauses;
- mandatory clauses;
- data rights;
- breaches;
- claims;
- meanings.

Both controller and processor are referred to as defined in the UK GDPR.

Section 6.7.2 provides that 'a Party acts as Processor and the inconsistent or conflicting terms of the Linked Agreement are obligations on that Party expressly

---

5   Art 1(1).
6   Art 1(2).

required by Article 28 UK GDPR, in which case those terms will override the inconsistent or conflicting terms of the IDTA in relation to Processing by that Party as Processor.'

The International Data Transfer Addendum (UK Addendum) acts as an addendum to the EU standard contractual clauses, thus maintaining a direct express relevance under EU data laws to the UK standard contracts. It refers to,

- parties;

- selected SCCs, modules and selected clauses;

- appendix information;

- ending this Addendum when the approved Addendum changes;

- mandatory clauses;

- incorporation of and changes to the EU SCCs;

- amendments to this Addendum;

- alternative Part 2 mandatory clauses.

These new provisions are important where data transfer situations arise and depending on where the entities are controllers or processors, and whether data is general or special (ie sensitive).

It will take some time for these contracts to bed in and to be fully assessed and critically scrutinised.

In terms of processors, regard will have to be had not just to the contract provisions, and associated or linked documentation, but also the UK GDPR (and even the GDPR itself) in terms of careful understanding of the obligations of processors and the obligations of controllers engaging processors, and not forgetting that the new UK rules endorse the EU models in the sense of being, in part, viewed as an addendum to the EU contracts. Any problems of conflicts which may exist will be something which becomes more apparent from a practical implementation viewpoint rather than an immediate textual analysis.

One further issue to note is that as originally envisaged in the EU model, and not without some contention itself, is that there must exist rights and mechanisms for individuals to get access to legal remedies. Post Brexit, this will at least in the first instance apply to UK courts and recipient country courts.

CHAPTER 23

Controller to Controller Contracts

INTRODUCTION

23.01   Data transfers in an international sense would appear to occur in more significant numbers between controllers. Businesses are constantly seeking to engage and do business with one another, even when one of the parties is located in some other jurisdiction. Personal data may also be caught up in these dealings.

It is necessary for each of the parties to be responsible for assessing how any personal data may be transferred where this may be desirable or necessary in order to facilitate the business activities.

The new EU model contracts and the new UK contract provisions each seek to facilitate such activities. These are each contemplated to apply where there may be no other channel mechanism available to permit such data transfers where a default transfer ban may exist.

Bear in mind also that while part of the rationale is to facilitate business activities there is also a large rationale resting on the individual interest and business interest in ensuring that such transfers should safeguard the data in question. The former aspect refers to data rights, safeguards, process, contracts, and data security. The later refers to the fact that there is a large business case for being able to say that data rules and data security applies, both specifically and more generally. Consumers will be more confident in international commerce and data transfers where they are assured that their rights and data security are an important part of the process.

These new data transfer permission mechanisms, however, are not pure box-ticking exercises. While there is an element of user-friendly design and form format involved in how these standard data transfer contracts are set out, there is still a lot of responsibility placed on the counter parties. The controllers must assess the data in question, assess what the activities are, what the intended purposes of the processing will be, the legal entities, the data security, etc. Certain sections in the form contracts must be inserted, and sometimes ticked, but very important parts also require a detailed diligence process be activated in order to arrive at the appropriate answers that must be inserted. If that was not sufficient to ensure that the controller take the process with all seriousness, the contracts also make clear that liability and legal redress issues must also be considered.

Given that each of these contract models are new, we do not yet have examples of companies breaching the contracts and the intention behind them. However, businesses should be assured that in time if they are found to be signing these model contracts but not properly implementing them and abiding by the conditions set out, a data regulator may investigate. In appropriate circumstances a data fine may also be imposed. Such investigations and fines are not without precedent under the data transfer regime internationally.

NEW EU STANDARD CONTRACT CLAUSES

23.02 There is as a principle a default data transfer ban on transfers to third party jurisdictions which have lower standards of protection for personal data. The primary example is under the GDPR, which is relevant in relation to stream one data transfers from the EU to the UK. However, one of the mechanisms to overcome the default ban exists where the Commission approves standard contractual clauses to govern such transfers and these are implemented between the respective parties to the transfer.

The Commission has now issued a new second generation of these transfer contracts. The Commission has stated that:

> 'According to the General Data Protection Regulation (GDPR), contractual clauses ensuring appropriate data protection safeguards can be used as a ground for data transfers from the EU to third countries. This includes model contract clauses – so-called standard contractual clauses (SCCs) – that have been "pre-approved" by the European Commission.

> On 4 June 2021, the Commission issued modernised standard contractual clauses under the GDPR for data transfers from controllers or processors in the EU/EEA (or otherwise subject to the GDPR) to controllers or processors established outside the EU/EEA (and not subject to the GDPR):

> These modernised SCCs replace the three sets of SCCs that were adopted under the previous Data Protection Directive 95/46. Since 27 September 2021, it is no longer possible to conclude contracts incorporating these earlier sets of SCCs.

> Until 27 December 2022, controllers and processors can continue to rely on those earlier SCCs for contracts that were concluded before 27 September 2021, provided that the processing operations that are the subject matter of the contract remain unchanged.'[1]

A number of changes and innovations are included in the new generation of the standard contractual clauses. These include:

- updates to conform with the new GDPR (given that the earlier model contracts were issued prior to the GDPR;

- seeking to provide one single entry-point covering a broad range of transfer scenarios (instead of separate sets of clauses);

---

1   'Standard Contractual Clauses For International Transfers, Modernised Standard Contractual Clauses For The Transfer Of Personal Data To Third Countries,' EU Commission, JUSTICE AND CONSUMERS, 4 June 2021.

- seeking more flexibility for complex processing chains, through a 'modular approach' and by offering the possibility for more than two parties to join and use the clauses (where the older clauses were envisages as having only two counter parties);

- a so called practical toolbox to comply with the *Schrems II* judgment;

- an overview of the different steps companies have to take to comply with the *Schrems II* judgment as well as examples of possible 'supplementary measures', such as encryption, that companies may take if necessary.[2]

The EU Commission adopted two sets of standard contractual clauses.

One set is for use between controllers and processors.

A separate set is for the transfer of personal data to third countries.

They reflect new requirements under the GDPR and take into account the *Schrems II* judgement of the Court of Justice (CJEU), to ensure a high level of data protection for citizens.

Officials believe that the new tools will offer more legal certainty to businesses and help SMEs to ensure compliance with requirements for safe data transfers, while allowing data to move freely across borders, without undue legal barriers.[3]

There are therefore two types of standard contract for a business to be aware of.

The activities of the business and its relationship with the counterparty in the EU will influence which is the appropriate contract that the business will need to consider implementing.

CONTRACTS AND TRANSFERS TO INTERNATIONAL THIRD COUNTRIES

23.03   The new rules for international data transfers requires review of both the Commission decision document pursuant to the GDPR, and the related contract clauses document.

The decision is the Commission Implementing Decision on standard contractual clauses for the transfer of personal data to third countries pursuant to Regulation (EU) 2016/679.[4]

---

2   'European Commission Adopts New Tools For Safe Exchanges Of Personal Data,' EU Commission, Press Release, 4 June 2021.
3   'European Commission Adopts New Tools For Safe Exchanges Of Personal Data,' EU Commission, Press Release, 4 June 2021.
4   Commission Implementing Decision (EU) 2021/914 of 4 June 2021 on standard contractual clauses for the transfer of personal data to third countries pursuant to Regulation (EU) 2016/679 of the European Parliament and of the Council (Text with EEA relevance), C/2021/3972, [2021] OJ L199, 31–61

The decision states that:

> 'The standard contractual clauses set out in the Annex are now considered to 'provide appropriate safeguards' within the meaning of Article 46(1) and (2) (c) of Regulation (EU) 2016/679 for the transfer by a controller or processor of personal data processed subject to that Regulation (data exporter) to a controller or (sub-)processor whose processing of the data is not subject to that Regulation (data importer).'[5]

> 'The standard contractual clauses also set out the rights and obligations of controllers and processors with respect to the matters referred to in Article 28(3) and (4) of Regulation (EU) 2016/679, as regards the transfer of personal data from a controller to a processor, or from a processor to a sub-processor.'[6]

UK CONTRACTS AND TRANSFERS TO INTERNATIONAL THIRD COUNTRIES

23.04 The UK appears intent on arranging a series of new data transfer permission channels, at least as it relates to UK data being transferred to third countries and destinations internationally. It is too early to say at present what the final range of these methods will look like, nor to predict whether they may be challenged subsequently.

There is already commentary on at least some aspects of the new consultancy and Bill proposals for facilitating the UK to international data transfers, most specifically UK model contracts or standard contractual clauses[7] – which we would hope will be in part substantially similar to the new UK updated contracts. It is also important to bear in mind that the government appears to be favouring a variety of new data transfer permission channels. Attention is also needed to see if and how many of these may be different to the EU permission channels. The ICO also established its own consultation process of proposals for UK standard contractual clauses during 2021–2022.

The ICO website currently advises that:

> 'On 2 February 2022, the Secretary of State laid before Parliament the international data transfer agreement (IDTA), the international data transfer addendum to the European Commission's standard contractual clauses for international data transfers (Addendum) and a document setting out transitional provisions. This final step followed the consultation the ICO ran in 2021. The documents were issued under Section 119A of the Data Protection Act 2018 and following Parliamentary approval came into force on 21 March 2022.

5   Article 1(1).
6   Article 1(2).
7   Hutt and Boardman, 'New UK Standard Contractual Clauses for Personal Data Transfers' (2022) 39(7) *Computer & Internet Lawyer* 12; De Boel, Dhont and Fol, 'New Model Clauses For Personal Data Transfers Outside the UK' (2022) 39(6) *Computer & Internet Lawyer* 12.

Exporters can use the IDTA or the Addendum as a transfer tool to comply with Article 46 of the UK GDPR when making restricted transfers.

The IDTA and Addendum replaced standard contractual clauses for international transfers. They take into account the binding judgement of the European Court of Justice, in the case commonly referred to as "Schrems II".

These documents are immediately of use to organisations transferring personal data outside of the UK:

International data transfer agreement (PDF)

International data transfer agreement (Word document)

International data transfer addendum to the European Commission's standard contractual clauses for international data transfers (PDF)

International data transfer addendum to the European Commission's standard contractual clauses for international data transfers (Word document)

Transitional provisions

The IDTA and Addendum form part of the wider UK package to assist international transfers. This includes independently supporting the Government's approach to adequacy assessments of third countries.

We consulted on our approach to international transfers under UK GDPR from 11 August 2021 to 11 October 2021. When finalising the documents we considered the detailed responses we received and will be publishing these soon.

In our Guide to UK GDPR we have added clarification as to what is a restricted transfer. We are developing additional tools to provide support and guidance to organisations. These will be published soon.

Clause by clause guidance to the IDTA and Addendum.

Guidance on how to use the IDTA.

Guidance on transfer risk assessments.

Further clarifications on our international transfers guidance.'[8]

It appears that the ICO and government have decided to use the EU contracts as the starting point which is reassuring. The issue will be the extent to which variations may arise. As with these types of contracts, they relate to transfers between one entity to another, and are not country-wide permissions.

This new International Data Transfer Agreement and contract clause is dated 21 March 2022. It states that '[t]his IDTA has been issued by the Information Commissioner for Parties making Restricted Transfers. The Information Commissioner considers that it provides Appropriate Safeguards for Restricted

---

8   *International Data Transfer Agreement and Guidance*, ICO, at https://ico.org.uk/for-organisations/guide-to-data-protection/guide-to-the-general-data-protection-regulation-gdpr/international-data-transfer-agreement-and-guidance/.

Transfers when it is entered into as a legally binding contract.' It contains sections on:

- Parties and signatures;

- Transfer Details;

- Security Requirements;

- Extra Protection Clauses;

- Commercial Clauses;

- Mandatory Clauses (including how safeguards apply; governing law; rights);

- Alternative Part 4 Mandatory Clauses.

Users will need to become very familiar with the internal mechanics and also when to use such contracts.

UK CONTROLLER-TO-CONTROLLER CONTRACTS

23.05 The new EU model contracts will clearly be important to businesses, and across different data transfer channels. Now, in addition, the new UK transfer contract rules will also be important for businesses. They are each official model contracts or contract clauses which businesses can consider implementing in their own bilateral or even multilateral relationships which if incorporated into the formal business relationships may permit otherwise non permitted data transfers to occur, for example from UK controllers to foreign controllers.

The government presented the new UK contract rules on 2 February 2022. They are entitled as the: (1) International Data Transfer Agreement (IDTA); and (2) International Data Transfer Addendum (UK Addendum). These contract models became law in the UK from 21 March 2022. They were issued under Section 119A of the current Data Protection Act 2018.

The International Data Transfer Agreement contains provisions dealing with a variety of issues. These include provisions dealing with: the parties and signatures of the parties; the start date of the agreement; the respective parties' details; key contacts within each of the respective party organisations; the importer data subject contact; and signatures confirming each party agrees to be bound by this IDTA.

There are then provisions dealing with some of the specifics of the data transfers for each specific agreement and transaction, in particular: the data transfer details; details of the UK data laws that governs the IDTA; the primary place for legal claims or disputes to be filed by the parties; the legal status of the exporter; the legal status of the importer; whether and how the UK GDPR applies to the importer.

It also refers to the separate linked agreement.

Additional details referred to and to be specified include: the term period; ending the IDTA before the end of the term; ending the IDTA when the approved IDTA changes; whether the importer will make further transfers of the transferred data; specific restrictions when the importer may transfer on the transferred data; review dates; details of the important transferred data.

Where there are special categories of personal data and criminal convictions and offences data, this must be identified and specified.

The agreement must also specify: the relevant data subjects; purpose; security requirements; security of transmission; security of storage; security of processing; organisational security measures; technical security minimum requirements; updates to the security requirements; extra protection clauses; extra technical security protections; extra organizational protections; extra contractual protections; commercial clauses; mandatory clauses; information that helps you to understand this IDTA; IDTA and linked agreements; legal meaning of words; provided all the information required; how to sign the IDTA; changing this IDTA; understanding this IDTA.

Data security is always important. The agreement must specify: how the IDTA provides appropriate safeguard; appropriate safeguards; reviews to ensure the appropriate safeguards continue; and what happens if there is an importer personal data breach.

Additional provisions include: reference to ICO; exporter; exporter's obligations; importer; general importer obligations; importer's obligations if it is subject to the UK data protection laws; importer's obligations to comply with key data protection principles; transferring on the transferred data; importer's responsibility if it authorises others to perform its obligations; rights of individuals; right to a copy of the IDTA; right to Information about the Importer and its processing; how relevant data subjects can exercise their data subject right; how relevant data subjects can exercise their data subject rights– if the importer is the exporter's processor or sub-processor; rights of relevant data subjects are subject to the exemptions in the UK data protection laws; how to give third parties access to transferred data under local laws; access requests and direct access; giving notice; giving notice; breaches of the IDTA; breaches of the IDTA by the importer; breaches of the IDTA by the exporter; ending the IDTA; how to end this IDTA without there being a breach; How to end this IDTA if there is a breach; What must the parties do when the IDTA ends; how to bring a legal claim under this IDTA; liability; how relevant data subjects and the ICO may bring legal claims; courts legal claims can be brought in; arbitration; legal glossary; and alternative Part 4 mandatory clauses.

Controllers are referred to as being defined in the UK GDPR.

Section 11 refers to the exporter's obligations, as follows:

191

'11.1 The Exporter agrees that UK Data Protection Laws apply to its Processing of the Transferred Data, including transferring it to the Importer.

11.2 The Exporter must:

    11.2.1 comply with the UK Data Protection Laws in transferring the Transferred Data to the Importer;

    11.2.2 comply with the Linked Agreement as it relates to its transferring the Transferred Data to the Importer; and

    11.2.3 carry out reasonable checks on the Importer's ability to comply with this IDTA, and take appropriate action including under Section 9.2, Section 29 or Section 30, if at any time it no longer considers that the Importer is able to comply with this IDTA or to provide Appropriate Safeguards.

11.3 The Exporter must comply with all its obligations in the IDTA, including any in the Security Requirements, and any Extra Protection Clauses and any Commercial Clauses.

11.4 The Exporter must co-operate with reasonable requests of the Importer to pass on notices or other information to and from Relevant Data Subjects or any Third Party Controller where it is not reasonably practical for the Importer to do so. The Exporter may pass these on via a third party if it is reasonable to do so.

11.5 The Exporter must co-operate with and provide reasonable assistance to the Importer, so that the Importer is able to comply with its obligations to the Relevant Data Subjects under Local Law and this IDTA.

Importer obligations are referred to in section 12. These refer as follows:

12.1 The Importer must:

    12.1.1 only Process the Transferred Data for the Purpose;

    12.1.2 comply with all its obligations in the IDTA, including in the Security Requirements, any Extra Protection Clauses and any Commercial Clauses;

    12.1.3 comply with all its obligations in the Linked Agreement which relate to its Processing of the Transferred Data;

    12.1.4 keep a written record of its Processing of the Transferred Data, which demonstrate its compliance with this IDTA, and provide this written record if asked to do so by the Exporter;

    12.1.5 if the Linked Agreement includes rights for the Exporter to obtain information or carry out an audit, provide the Exporter with the same rights in relation to this IDTA; and

    12.1.6 if the ICO requests, provide the ICO with the information it would be required on request to provide to the Exporter under this Section

12.1 (including the written record of its Processing, and the results of audits and inspections).

12.2 The Importer must co-operate with and provide reasonable assistance to the Exporter and any Third Party Controller, so that the Exporter and any Third Party Controller are able to comply with their obligations under UK Data Protection Laws and this IDTA.'

The International Data Transfer Addendum (UK Addendum) acts as an addendum to the EU standard contractual clauses. It therefore maintains an express connection between the UK data law contracts and the EU standard contracts. It refers to: parties; parties' details; key contact; signature; selected SCCs, modules and selected clauses; addendum EU SCCs; appendix information; ending this addendum when the approved addendum changes; mandatory clauses; entering into this addendum; interpretation of this addendum; hierarchy; incorporation of and changes to the EU SCCs; amendments to this addendum; and alternative Part 2 mandatory clauses.

These new provisions are important where data transfer situations arise and depending on where the entities are controllers, and whether data is general or special (ie sensitive).

It will take some time for these contracts to be assessed in practice, to include practicality as well as compliance.

CHAPTER 24

Binding Corporate Rules

INTRODUCTION

24.01 Binding corporate rules or BCRs are one of the data transfer permission channels referred to under the GDPR. A BCR is defined as 'personal data protection policies which are adhered to by a controller or processor established on the territory of a Member State for transfers or a set of transfers of personal data to a controller or processor in one or more third countries within a group of undertakings, or group of enterprises engaged in a joint economic activity'.[1] Although defining it as a policy is somewhat to underscore the full extent of such a policy and the multitude of sub components encompassed within it. To the uninitiated it might also appear at first glance something which might apply to every type of controller, whereas in reality it is specifically designed or geared towards large multinational companies whom have offices in many different countries and share data across these disperse jurisdictional locations. It is also worth pointed out that these arrangements are mostly focused in internal group data transfers, as opposed to some of the other permission channels.

BCR DATA TRANSFER PERMISSION CHANNEL

24.02 The Commission and the WP29[2] (now the EDPB) developed a policy of recognising adequate protection of the policies of multinational organisations transferring personal data that satisfy the determined binding corporate rules (BCR).[3] This relates to transfers internally between companies within a related group of large multinational companies. It therefore, differs from the model contract clauses above which generally relate to non-related companies, rather than group companies.

Organisations which have contracts, policies and procedures which satisfy the BCR and are accepted as having so after a review process with the Commission

---

1   GDPR, Art 4(20).
2   WP29, Recommendation 1/2007 on the Standard Application for Approval of Binding Corporate Rules for the Transfer of Personal Data; Working Document setting up a table with the elements and principles to be found in Binding Corporate Rules, WP153 (2008); Working Document Setting up a framework for the structure of Binding Corporate Rules, WP154 (2008); Working Document on Frequently Asked Questions (FAQs) related to Binding Corporate Rules, WP155 (2008).
3   See http://ec.europa.eu/justice/data-protection/international-transfers/binding-corporate-rules/index_en.htm; Moerel, *Binding Corporate Rules, Corporate Self-Regulation of Global Data Transfers* (OUP, 2012).

or one of the national data protection supervisory authorities can transfer personal data outside of the EU within the group organisation.

WP29 has issued the following documents in relation to the BCR. These include:

- Working Document on Transfers of personal data to third countries: Applying Article 26 (2) of the EU Data Protection Directive to Binding Corporate Rules for International Data Transfers (WP74).

- Model Checklist, Application for approval of Binding Corporate Rules (WP102).

- Working Document Setting Forth a Co-Operation Procedure for Issuing Common Opinions on Adequate Safeguards Resulting From Binding Corporate Rules (WP107).

- Working Document Establishing a Model Checklist Application for Approval of Binding Corporate Rules (WP108).

- Recommendation on the Standard Application for Approval of Binding Corporate Rules for the Transfer of Personal Data.

- Working Document setting up a table with the elements and principles to be found in Binding Corporate Rules (WP153).

- Working Document Setting up a framework for the structure of Binding Corporate Rules (WP154).

- Working Document on Frequently Asked Questions (FAQs) related to Binding Corporate Rules.

Note that the WP39 is now replaced by the EDPB (even though Brexit issues now intervene).

The BCR[4] appear to be increasingly popular to large multinational organisations in relation to their data processing and data transfer compliance obligations. While perhaps still small in number the approved number of BCRs are significant as they encompass large multinational group companies, and hence large sets of personal data. The official guidance and general commentary on BCRs is growing too.[5] The ICO also refers to the BCR rules in it guidance.

---

4   See also Moerel, *Binding Corporate Rules, Corporate Self-Regulation and Global Data Transfers* (OUP, 2012).

5   Wilkes, 'Binding Corporate Rules, the Accenture Experience' (2008) 2(5) *International In-House Counsel Journal* 726; Bender and Ponemon, 'Binding Corporate Rules For Cross-Border Data Transfer' (2006) 3(2) *Rutgers Journal of Law and Urban Policy* 154; Moerel, *Binding Corporate Rules: Corporate Self-Regulation of Global Data Transfers* (Lokke Moerel, 2012); Szoke, 'Progressive Changes in Hungarian Data Protection Law: Introducing Binding Corporate Rules and Recording of Data Breaches' (2016) 2(2) *European Data Protection Law Review* (EDPL) 227; Makso, 'Exporting The Policy – International Data Transfer And The Role of Binding Corporate Rules For Ensuring Adequate Safeguards' (2016) 2 *Pecs Journal of International and European Law* 79; Bannerman, 'Colt Introduces GDPR-Compliant Binding Corporate Rules' *Capacity Magazine* (12/6/2021) 1.

It is envisaged that the popularity of the BCR option for exemption from the data protection regime transfer restrictions will increase. However, the review process with the Commission or one of the national data protection supervisory authorities (such as the ICO) can take some time given the complexity involved. It is entitled the Guide to Binding Corporate Rules. It provides that:

> 'The concept of using Binding Corporate Rules (BCRs) to provide adequate safeguards for making restricted transfers was developed under EU law and continues to be part of UK law under the UK GDPR, specifically, Article 47.
>
> You can make a restricted transfer within an international organisation if both you and the receiver have signed up to approved BCRs. UK BCRs are approved by the Commissioner under Article 58.3(j).
>
> BCRs are intended for use by multinational corporate groups, groups of undertakings or a group of enterprises engaged in a joint economic activity such as franchises, joint ventures or professional partnerships.'[6]

Note that it now refers to the UK GDPR and no longer the GDPR directly. As was previously the case, a large company will need to actively engage with the ICO in terms of having a new proposed BCR policy officially accepted. One issue will be the recognition of UK BCRs in the EU and vice versa. Extending beyond that, mutual recognition issues arise when BCRs are approved by third party data regulators in other third countries.

BCR RULES

24.03 The competent supervisory authority shall approve BCRs in accordance with the consistency mechanism set out in Article 63, provided that they:

- are legally binding and apply to and are enforced by every member concerned of the group of undertakings or groups of enterprises engaged in a joint economic activity, including their employees;

- expressly confer enforceable rights on data subjects with regard to the processing of their personal data;

- fulfil the requirements laid down in Article 47(2) (Article 47(1)).

The binding corporate rules shall specify at least:

- the structure and contact details of the concerned group of undertakings or group of enterprises engaged in a joint economic activity and of each of its members;

- the data transfers or set of transfers, including the categories of personal data, the type of processing and its purposes, the type of data subjects affected and the identification of the third country or countries in question;

---

6   *Guide to Binding Corporate Rules*, ICO, available at https://ico.org.uk/for-organisations/guide-to-binding-corporate-rules/.

- their legally binding nature, both internally and externally;

- the application of the general data protection principles, in particular purpose limitation, data minimisation, limited storage periods, data quality, data protection by design and by default (DPbD), legal basis for the processing, processing of special categories of personal data, measures to ensure data security, and the requirements in respect of onward transfers to bodies not bound by the binding corporate rules [d];

- the rights of data subjects in regard to processing and the means to exercise these rights, including the right not to be subject to decisions based solely on automated processing, including profiling in accordance with Article 22, the right to lodge a complaint before the competent supervisory authority and before the competent courts of the states in accordance with Article 79, and to obtain redress and, where appropriate, compensation for a breach of the binding corporate rules [e];

- the acceptance by the controller or processor established on the territory of a state of liability for any breaches of the binding corporate rules by any member concerned not established in the EU; the controller or the processor shall be exempted from this liability, in whole or in part, only if it proves that that member is not responsible for the event giving rise to the damage [f];

- how the information on the binding corporate rules, in particular on the provisions referred to in this Article 47(2)(d), (e) and (f) is provided to the data subjects in addition to Articles 13 and 14;

- the tasks of any DPO designated in accordance with Article 37 or any other person or entity in charge of the monitoring compliance with the binding corporate rules within the group of undertakings, or group of enterprises engaged in a joint economic activity, as well as monitoring the training and complaint handling;

- the complaint procedures;

- the mechanisms within the group of undertakings, or group of enterprises engaged in a joint economic activity, for ensuring the verification of compliance with the binding corporate rules. Such mechanisms shall include data protection audits and methods for ensuring corrective actions to protect the rights of the data subject. Results of such verification should be communicated to the person or entity referred under point (h) and to the board of the controlling undertaking or of the group of enterprises engaged in a joint economic activity, and should be available upon request to the competent supervisory authority [i];

- the mechanisms for reporting and recording changes to the rules and reporting these changes to the supervisory authority;

- the co-operation mechanism with the supervisory authority to ensure compliance by any member of the group of undertakings, or group of enterprises engaged in a joint economic activity, in particular by making available to the supervisory authority the results of verifications of the measures referred to in this Article 47(2)(j);

- the mechanisms for reporting to the competent supervisory authority any legal requirements to which a member of the group of undertakings, or group of enterprises engaged in a joint economic activity is subject in a third country which are likely to have a substantial adverse effect on the guarantees provided by the binding corporate rules; and

- the appropriate data protection training to personnel having permanent or regular access to personal data (Article 47(2)).

There may be future changes and requirements too. The Commission may specify the format and procedures for the exchange of information between controllers, processors and supervisory authorities for binding corporate rules. Those implementing acts shall be adopted in accordance with the examination procedure set out in Article 93(2) (Article 48(3)).

UK BCRS

24.04   The ICO has issued guidance in relation to BCRs. This will also need to be considered post Brexit and organisations will also need to assess when and if these may begin to differ from those as provided for under the earlier EU data protection regime as applied in the UK.

CHAPTER 25

Individual Data Regulator Approvals and Safeguards

INTRODUCTION

25.01   The main data transfer permission channel is the new EU-UK data transfer adequacy decision channel. It is also arguably the easiest for companies as there is no technical required process on the part of the individual company. However, not every potential data transfer will easily fit within this channel. Therefore, in many cases a company will also need to consider permission mechanisms for its other data transfer channels. Data regulators, such as the ICO, can sometimes play a role in permitting specific data transfers.

ICO TRANSFER PERMISSION CHANNELS

25.02   If the transfer does not fall withing the EU-UK adequacy decision channel and the recipient country's protection for personal data is not adequate, or even not ascertainable (in a timely manner) as may sometimes be the case, the company should ascertain if the transfer comes within one of the other permission channel categories. Data transfers of personal data from the UK to third counties outside of the EU/EEA jurisdiction cannot occur unless it falls within one of the other data transfer channels.

One of the permission channels to allow data transfers is where 'the transfer has been *authorised by a supervisory authority where the Controller adduces adequate safeguards*' (emphasis added).[1] This is as specified in the GDPR, so

---

1   The exemptions from the transfer restrictions, if there is a UK equivalent to the EU regime are: the data subject has given consent; the transfer is necessary for performance of contract between data subject and controller; the transfer is necessary for taking steps at the request of the data subject with a view to entering into a contract with the controller; the transfer is necessary for the conclusion of a contract between the controller and a person other than the data subject that is entered into at the request of the data subject and is in the interests of the data subject; the transfer is necessary for the performance of such a contract; the transfer is required or authorised under any enactment or instrument imposing international obligation on UK; the transfer is necessary for reasons of substantial public interest; the transfer is necessary for purposes of or in connection with legal proceedings or prospective legal proceedings; the transfer is necessary in order to prevent injury or damage to the health of the data subject or serious loss of or damage to the property of the data subject or otherwise to protect vital interests; subject to certain conditions the transfer is only part of personal data on a register established by or under an enactment; the transfer has been authorised by a supervisory authority where the controller adduces adequate safeguards; the transfer is made to a country that has been determined by the

companies will need to ascertain the phraseology and any amendments in the UK GDPR (or related legislation). However, for present purposes, a company could consider engaging with the ICO in the UK to ascertain if and how it may seek permission from the ICO to make a specific type of data transfer.

Particular criteria or factors are outlined for determining whether a third country ensures an adequate level of protection.[2] The company may wish to refer to the local laws and protection in the destination country. One of the factors is whether the supervisory authority has authorised the transfer where the controller has given or adduced adequate safeguards. Thus, it will be important for the company to be able to refer to how adequate safeguards are to be adduced. This may encompass contracts and even technical safeguards. Data security safeguards may also be relevant to consider. One might assume that the nature of the particular data in question, as well as the intended processing activities in the destination country may be relevant. Another issue to consider is whether it is intended to send the data to one or more recipients in the destination country.

INTERNATIONAL COOPERATION

25.03 In relation to third countries and international organisations, the EU data rules provide that the Commission and supervisory authorities shall take appropriate steps to develop international co-operation mechanisms to facilitate the effective enforcement of legislation for the protection of personal data. They must also in addition provide international mutual assistance in the enforcement of legislation for the protection of personal data, including through notification, complaint referral, investigative assistance and information exchange, subject to appropriate safeguards for the protection of personal data and other fundamental rights and freedoms. There is also an obligation to engage relevant stakeholders in discussion and activities aimed at furthering international co-operation in the enforcement of legislation for the protection of personal data; and to promote the exchange and documentation of personal data protection legislation and practice, including on jurisdictional conflicts with third countries.[3] The issue of

EU Commission as having 'adequate levels of [data] protection' ie a Community finding; the transfer is made to a US entity that has signed up to the EU-US 'Safe Harbour' arrangements (although less have signed up than originally envisaged); EU Commission contract provisions: the model contracts (the EU has set out model contracts which if incorporated into the data exporter – data importer/recipient relationship can act as an exemption thus permitting the transfer to occur.

2   The factors to be taken into account, at least in an EU context, include: 'any security measures taken in respect of the data in that country or territory'; the transfer is necessary for obtaining legal advice or in connection with legal proceedings or prospective proceedings; (subject to certain conditions) it is necessary in order to prevent injury or damage to the health or property of the data subject, or in order to protect his or her vital interests; the transfer is required or authorised by law; the supervisory authority has authorised the transfer where the Controller has given or adduced adequate safeguards; or the contract relating to the transfer of the data embodies appropriate contract clauses as specified in a 'Community finding.'

3   GDPR, Art 50.

international cooperation and international agreements is a developing area in the UK and will need to be considered on an ongoing basis by companies.

RESTRICTIONS

25.04   EU or state law to which the controller or processor is subject may restrict by way of a legislative measure the scope of the obligations and rights,[4] when such a restriction respects the essence of the fundamental rights and freedoms and is a necessary and proportionate measure in a democratic society to safeguard.[5] These range from such issues as security, defence, etc.[6] Any such legislative measures must take account of specific considerations.[7] Therefore, companies will also need to consider on an ongoing basis whether any such restrictions have been specified in the UK, and if so, what the implications may be.

CONCLUSION

25.05   There are obviously moving developments occurring in this area. Ultimately, however, it is possible the ICO approval route may not be an optimum avenue as it is an individualised process. As an application type format, it will require time, costs, and resources to be expended. It also could take some time to complete.

---

4   Provided for in Arts 12 to 22 and Art 34, as well as Art 5 in so far as its provisions correspond to the rights and obligations provided for in Arts 12 to 20.

5   Chapter III, Section 5 of the new GDPR refers to restrictions.

6   GDPR, Art 23(1). The full list is: national security [a]; defence [b]; public security [c]; the prevention, investigation, detection or prosecution of criminal offences or the execution of criminal penalties, including the safeguarding against and the prevention of threats to public security [d]; other important objectives of general public interests of EU or of a state, in particular an important economic or financial interest of EU or of a state, including monetary, budgetary and taxation matters, public health and social security [e]; the protection of judicial independence and judicial proceedings; the prevention, investigation, detection and prosecution of breaches of ethics for regulated professions [g]; a monitoring, inspection or regulatory function connected, even occasionally, to the exercise of official authority in cases referred to in (a) to (e) and (g); the protection of the data subject or the rights and freedoms of others; the enforcement of civil law claims.

7   GDPR, Art 23(2). Such as: the purposes of the processing or categories of processing; the categories of personal data; the scope of the restrictions introduced; the safeguards to prevent abuse or unlawful access or transfer; the specification of the controller or categories of controllers; the storage periods and the applicable safeguards taking into account the nature, scope and purposes of the processing or categories of processing; the risks for the rights and freedoms of data subjects; and the right of data subjects to be informed about the restriction, unless this may be prejudicial to the purpose of the restriction.

SCHEDULES

SCHEDULES

SCHEDULE 1

GDPR

Regulation (EU) 2016/679 of the European Parliament and of the Council of 27 April 2016 on the protection of natural persons with regard to the processing of personal data and on the free movement of such data, and repealing Directive 95/46/EC (General Data Protection Regulation) (OJ L 119, 4.5.2016, pp. 1–88).

Successive amendments to Regulation (EU) 2016/679

Article 44

General principle for transfers

Any transfer of personal data which are undergoing processing or are intended for processing after transfer to a third country or to an international organisation shall take place only if, subject to the other provisions of this Regulation, the conditions laid down in this Chapter are complied with by the controller and processor, including for onward transfers of personal data from the third country or an international organisation to another third country or to another international organisation. All provisions in this Chapter shall be applied in order to ensure that the level of protection of natural persons guaranteed by this Regulation is not undermined.

Article 45

Transfers on the basis of an adequacy decision

1. A transfer of personal data to a third country or an international organisation may take place where the Commission has decided that the third country, a territory or one or more specified sectors within that third country, or the international organisation in question ensures an adequate level of protection. Such a transfer shall not require any specific authorisation.

2. When assessing the adequacy of the level of protection, the Commission shall, in particular, take account of the following elements:

   (a) the rule of law, respect for human rights and fundamental freedoms, relevant legislation, both general and sectoral, including concerning public security, defence, national security and criminal law and the access of public authorities to personal data, as well as the implementation of such legislation, data protection rules, professional rules and security measures, including rules for the onward transfer of personal data to another third country or international organisation which are complied with in that country or international organisation, case-law, as well as effective and enforceable data subject rights and effective administrative and judicial redress for the data subjects whose personal data are being transferred;

(b) the existence and effective functioning of one or more independent supervisory authorities in the third country or to which an international organisation is subject, with responsibility for ensuring and enforcing compliance with the data protection rules, including adequate enforcement powers, for assisting and advising the data subjects in exercising their rights and for cooperation with the supervisory authorities of the Member States; and

(c) the international commitments the third country or international organisation concerned has entered into, or other obligations arising from legally binding conventions or instruments as well as from its participation in multilateral or regional systems, in particular in relation to the protection of personal data.

3. The Commission, after assessing the adequacy of the level of protection, may decide, by means of implementing act, that a third country, a territory or one or more specified sectors within a third country, or an international organisation ensures an adequate level of protection within the meaning of paragraph 2 of this Article. The implementing act shall provide for a mechanism for a periodic review, at least every four years, which shall take into account all relevant developments in the third country or international organisation. The implementing act shall specify its territorial and sectoral application and, where applicable, identify the supervisory authority or authorities referred to in point (b) of paragraph 2 of this Article. The implementing act shall be adopted in accordance with the examination procedure referred to in Article 93(2).

4. The Commission shall, on an ongoing basis, monitor developments in third countries and international organisations that could affect the functioning of decisions adopted pursuant to paragraph 3 of this Article and decisions adopted on the basis of Article 25(6) of Directive 95/46/EC.

5. The Commission shall, where available information reveals, in particular following the review referred to in paragraph 3 of this Article, that a third country, a territory or one or more specified sectors within a third country, or an international organisation no longer ensures an adequate level of protection within the meaning of paragraph 2 of this Article, to the extent necessary, repeal, amend or suspend the decision referred to in paragraph 3 of this Article by means of implementing acts without retroactive effect. Those implementing acts shall be adopted in accordance with the examination procedure referred to in Article 93(2).

On duly justified imperative grounds of urgency, the Commission shall adopt immediately applicable implementing acts in accordance with the procedure referred to in Article 93(3).

6.   The Commission shall enter into consultations with the third country or international organisation with a view to remedying the situation giving rise to the decision made pursuant to paragraph 5.

7.   A decision pursuant to paragraph 5 of this Article is without prejudice to transfers of personal data to the third country, a territory or one or more specified sectors within that third country, or the international organisation in question pursuant to Articles 46 to 49.

8.   The Commission shall publish in the Official Journal of the European Union and on its website a list of the third countries, territories and specified sectors within a third country and international organisations for which it has decided that an adequate level of protection is or is no longer ensured.

9.   Decisions adopted by the Commission on the basis of Article 25(6) of Directive 95/46/EC shall remain in force until amended, replaced or repealed by a Commission Decision adopted in accordance with paragraph 3 or 5 of this Article.

Article 46

Transfers subject to appropriate safeguards

1.   In the absence of a decision pursuant to Article 45(3), a controller or processor may transfer personal data to a third country or an international organisation only if the controller or processor has provided appropriate safeguards, and on condition that enforceable data subject rights and effective legal remedies for data subjects are available.

2.   The appropriate safeguards referred to in paragraph 1 may be provided for, without requiring any specific authorisation from a supervisory authority, by:

      (a)   a legally binding and enforceable instrument between public authorities or bodies;

      (b)   binding corporate rules in accordance with Article 47;

      (c)   standard data protection clauses adopted by the Commission in accordance with the examination procedure referred to in Article 93(2);

      (d)   standard data protection clauses adopted by a supervisory authority and approved by the Commission pursuant to the examination procedure referred to in Article 93(2);

      (e)   an approved code of conduct pursuant to Article 40 together with binding and enforceable commitments of the controller or processor in the third country to apply the appropriate safeguards, including as regards data subjects' rights; or

      (f)   an approved certification mechanism pursuant to Article 42 together with binding and enforceable commitments of the controller or processor in the third country to apply the appropriate safeguards, including as regards data subjects' rights.

3.   Subject to the authorisation from the competent supervisory authority, the appropriate safeguards referred to in paragraph 1 may also be provided for, in particular, by:

(a)   contractual clauses between the controller or processor and the controller, processor or the recipient of the personal data in the third country or international organisation; or

(b)   provisions to be inserted into administrative arrangements between public authorities or bodies which include enforceable and effective data subject rights.

4.   The supervisory authority shall apply the consistency mechanism referred to in Article 63 in the cases referred to in paragraph 3 of this Article.

5.   Authorisations by a Member State or supervisory authority on the basis of Article 26(2) of Directive 95/46/EC shall remain valid until amended, replaced or repealed, if necessary, by that supervisory authority. Decisions adopted by the Commission on the basis of Article 26(4) of Directive 95/46/EC shall remain in force until amended, replaced or repealed, if necessary, by a Commission Decision adopted in accordance with paragraph 2 of this Article.

Article 47

Binding corporate rules

1.   The competent supervisory authority shall approve binding corporate rules in accordance with the consistency mechanism set out in Article 63, provided that they:

(a)   are legally binding and apply to and are enforced by every member concerned of the group of undertakings, or group of enterprises engaged in a joint economic activity, including their employees;

(b)   expressly confer enforceable rights on data subjects with regard to the processing of their personal data; and

(c)   fulfil the requirements laid down in paragraph 2.

2.   The binding corporate rules referred to in paragraph 1 shall specify at least:

(a)   the structure and contact details of the group of undertakings, or group of enterprises engaged in a joint economic activity and of each of its members;

(b)   the data transfers or set of transfers, including the categories of personal data, the type of processing and its purposes, the type of data subjects affected and the identification of the third country or countries in question;

(c)   their legally binding nature, both internally and externally;

(d)   the application of the general data protection principles, in particular purpose limitation, data minimisation, limited storage periods, data quality, data protection by design and by default, legal basis for processing, processing of special categories of personal data, measures to ensure data security, and the requirements in respect of onward transfers to bodies not bound by the binding corporate rules;

(e) the rights of data subjects in regard to processing and the means to exercise those rights, including the right not to be subject to decisions based solely on automated processing, including profiling in accordance with Article 22, the right to lodge a complaint with the competent supervisory authority and before the competent courts of the Member States in accordance with Article 79, and to obtain redress and, where appropriate, compensation for a breach of the binding corporate rules;

(f) the acceptance by the controller or processor established on the territory of a Member State of liability for any breaches of the binding corporate rules by any member concerned not established in the Union; the controller or the processor shall be exempt from that liability, in whole or in part, only if it proves that that member is not responsible for the event giving rise to the damage;

(g) how the information on the binding corporate rules, in particular on the provisions referred to in points (d), (e) and (f) of this paragraph is provided to the data subjects in addition to Articles 13 and 14;

(h) the tasks of any data protection officer designated in accordance with Article 37 or any other person or entity in charge of the monitoring compliance with the binding corporate rules within the group of undertakings, or group of enterprises engaged in a joint economic activity, as well as monitoring training and complaint-handling;

(i) the complaint procedures;

(j) the mechanisms within the group of undertakings, or group of enterprises engaged in a joint economic activity for ensuring the verification of compliance with the binding corporate rules. Such mechanisms shall include data protection audits and methods for ensuring corrective actions to protect the rights of the data subject. Results of such verification should be communicated to the person or entity referred to in point (h) and to the board of the controlling undertaking of a group of undertakings, or of the group of enterprises engaged in a joint economic activity, and should be available upon request to the competent supervisory authority;

(k) the mechanisms for reporting and recording changes to the rules and reporting those changes to the supervisory authority;

(l) the cooperation mechanism with the supervisory authority to ensure compliance by any member of the group of undertakings, or group of enterprises engaged in a joint economic activity, in particular by making available to the supervisory authority the results of verifications of the measures referred to in point (j);

(m) the mechanisms for reporting to the competent supervisory authority any legal requirements to which a member of the group of undertakings, or group of enterprises engaged in a joint economic activity is subject in a third country which are likely to have a substantial adverse effect on the guarantees provided by the binding corporate rules; and

(n) the appropriate data protection training to personnel having permanent or regular access to personal data.

3. The Commission may specify the format and procedures for the exchange of information between controllers, processors and supervisory authorities for binding corporate rules within the meaning of this Article. Those implementing acts shall be adopted in accordance with the examination procedure set out in Article 93(2).

Article 48

Transfers or disclosures not authorised by Union law

Any judgment of a court or tribunal and any decision of an administrative authority of a third country requiring a controller or processor to transfer or disclose personal data may only be recognised or enforceable in any manner if based on an international agreement, such as a mutual legal assistance treaty, in force between the requesting third country and the Union or a Member State, without prejudice to other grounds for transfer pursuant to this Chapter.

Article 49

Derogations for specific situations

1. In the absence of an adequacy decision pursuant to Article 45(3), or of appropriate safeguards pursuant to Article 46, including binding corporate rules, a transfer or a set of transfers of personal data to a third country or an international organisation shall take place only on one of the following conditions:

(a) the data subject has explicitly consented to the proposed transfer, after having been informed of the possible risks of such transfers for the data subject due to the absence of an adequacy decision and appropriate safeguards;

(b) the transfer is necessary for the performance of a contract between the data subject and the controller or the implementation of pre-contractual measures taken at the data subject's request;

(c) the transfer is necessary for the conclusion or performance of a contract concluded in the interest of the data subject between the controller and another natural or legal person;

(d) the transfer is necessary for important reasons of public interest;

(e) the transfer is necessary for the establishment, exercise or defence of legal claims;

(f) the transfer is necessary in order to protect the vital interests of the data subject or of other persons, where the data subject is physically or legally incapable of giving consent;

(g) the transfer is made from a register which according to Union or Member State law is intended to provide information to the public and which is open to consultation either by the public in general or by any person who can demonstrate a legitimate interest, but only to the extent that the conditions laid down by Union or Member State law for consultation are fulfilled in the particular case.

Where a transfer could not be based on a provision in Article 45 or 46, including the provisions on binding corporate rules, and none of the derogations for a specific situation referred to in the first subparagraph of this paragraph is applicable, a transfer to a third country or an international organisation may take place only if the transfer is not repetitive, concerns only a limited number of data subjects, is necessary for the purposes of compelling legitimate interests pursued by the controller which are not overridden by the interests or rights and freedoms of the data subject, and the controller has assessed all the circumstances surrounding the data transfer and has on the basis of that assessment provided suitable safeguards with regard to the protection of personal data. The controller shall inform the supervisory authority of the transfer. The controller shall, in addition to providing the information referred to in Articles 13 and 14, inform the data subject of the transfer and on the compelling legitimate interests pursued.

2. A transfer pursuant to point (g) of the first subparagraph of paragraph 1 shall not involve the entirety of the personal data or entire categories of the personal data contained in the register. Where the register is intended for consultation by persons having a legitimate interest, the transfer shall be made only at the request of those persons or if they are to be the recipients.

3. Points (a), (b) and (c) of the first subparagraph of paragraph 1 and the second subparagraph thereof shall not apply to activities carried out by public authorities in the exercise of their public powers.

4. The public interest referred to in point (d) of the first subparagraph of paragraph 1 shall be recognised in Union law or in the law of the Member State to which the controller is subject.

5. In the absence of an adequacy decision, Union or Member State law may, for important reasons of public interest, expressly set limits to the transfer of specific categories of personal data to a third country or an international organisation. Member States shall notify such provisions to the Commission.

6. The controller or processor shall document the assessment as well as the suitable safeguards referred to in the second subparagraph of paragraph 1 of this Article in the records referred to in Article 30.

SCHEDULE 2

UK GDPR

Article 44

General principle for transfers[1]

Any transfer of personal data which are undergoing processing or are intended for processing after transfer to a third country or to an international organisation shall take place only if, subject to the other provisions of this Regulation, the conditions laid down in this Chapter are complied with by the controller and processor, including for onward transfers of personal data from the third country or an international organisation to another third country or to another international organisation. All provisions in this Chapter shall be applied in order to ensure that the level of protection of natural persons guaranteed by this Regulation is not undermined.

Article 45

Transfers on the basis of an adequacy decision[2]

1. A transfer of personal data to a third country or an international organisation may take place where the Commission has decided that the third country, a territory or one or more specified sectors within that third country, or the international organisation in question ensures an adequate level of protection **where it is based on adequacy regulations (see section 17A of the 2018 Act).**[3] Such a transfer shall not require any specific authorisation.

2. When assessing the adequacy of the level of protection, the Commission **"for the purposes of sections 17A and 17B of the 2018 Act, the Secretary of State"**[4] shall, in particular, take account of the following elements:

    (a) the rule of law, respect for human rights and fundamental freedoms, relevant legislation, both general and sectoral, including concerning public security, defence, national security and criminal law and the access of public authorities to personal data, as well as the

---

1   The potentially most relevant Recitals to this Article are Recitals 101, and 102.
2   The potentially most relevant Recitals to this Article are Recitals 103, 104, 105, 106, and 107.
3   Data Protection, Privacy and Electronic Communications (Amendments etc) (EU Exit) Regulations 2019 (2019 No. 419), Regulation 38(2) in Article 45(1), deletes '"where the Commission' to the end of the first sentence" and inserts '"where it is based on adequacy regulations (see section 17A of the 2018 Act)'.
4   Data Protection, Privacy and Electronic Communications (Amendments etc) (EU Exit) Regulations 2019 (2019 No. 419), Regulation 38(3)(a) in Article 45(2), deletes ',the Commission' and inserts 'for the purposes of sections 17A and 17B(**12**) of the 2018 Act, the Secretary of State'.

implementation of such legislation, data protection rules, professional rules and security measures, including rules for the onward transfer of personal data to another third country or international organisation which are complied with in that country or international organisation, case-law, as well as effective and enforceable data subject rights and effective administrative and judicial redress for the data subjects whose personal data are being transferred;

(b) the existence and effective functioning of one or more independent supervisory authorities in the third country or to which an international organisation is subject, with responsibility for ensuring and enforcing compliance with the data protection rules, including adequate enforcement powers, for assisting and advising the data subjects in exercising their rights and for cooperation with the supervisory authorities of the Member States **the Commissioner**[5]; and

(c) the international commitments the third country or international organisation concerned has entered into, or other obligations arising from legally binding conventions or instruments as well as from its participation in multilateral or regional systems, in particular in relation to the protection of personal data.

3. The Commission, after assessing the adequacy of the level of protection, may decide, by means of implementing act, that a third country, a territory or one or more specified sectors within a third country, or an international organisation ensures an adequate level of protection within the meaning of paragraph 2 of this Article. The implementing act shall provide for a mechanism for a periodic review, at least every four years, which shall take into account all relevant developments in the third country or international organisation. The implementing act shall specify its territorial and sectoral application and, where applicable, identify the supervisory authority or authorities referred to in point (b) of paragraph 2 of this Article. The implementing act shall be adopted in accordance with the examination procedure referred to in Article 93(2).[6]

4. The Commission shall, on an ongoing basis, monitor developments in third countries and international organisations that could affect the functioning of decisions adopted pursuant to paragraph 3 of this Article and decisions adopted on the basis of Article 25(6) of Directive 95/46/EC.[7]

---

5 Data Protection, Privacy and Electronic Communications (Amendments etc) (EU Exit) Regulations 2019 (2019 No. 419), Regulation 38(3)(b) in Article 45(2), deletes 'the supervisory authorities of the Member States' and inserts 'the Commissioner'.

6 Data Protection, Privacy and Electronic Communications (Amendments etc) (EU Exit) Regulations 2019 (2019 No. 419), Regulation 38(4) in Article 45(3)-(6), deletes 'paragraphs 3, 4, 5 and 6'.

7 Data Protection, Privacy and Electronic Communications (Amendments etc) (EU Exit) Regulations 2019 (2019 No. 419), Regulation 38(4) in Article 45(3)-(6), deletes 'paragraphs 3, 4, 5 and 6'.

5. The Commission shall, where available information reveals, in particular following the review referred to in paragraph 3 of this Article, that a third country, a territory or one or more specified sectors within a third country, or an international organisation no longer ensures an adequate level of protection within the meaning of paragraph 2 of this Article, to the extent necessary, repeal, amend or suspend the decision referred to in paragraph 3 of this Article by means of implementing acts without retro-active effect. Those implementing acts shall be adopted in accordance with the examination procedure referred to in Article 93(2).

    On duly justified imperative grounds of urgency, the Commission shall adopt immediately applicable implementing acts in accordance with the procedure referred to in Article 93(3).[8]

6. The Commission shall enter into consultations with the third country or international organisation with a view to remedying the situation giving rise to the decision made pursuant to paragraph 5.[9]

7. A decision pursuant to paragraph 5 of this Article **The amendment or revocation of regulations under section 17A of the 2018 Act**[10] is without prejudice to transfers of personal data to the third country, a territory or one or more specified sectors within that third country, or the international organisation in question pursuant to Articles 46 to 49.

8. The Commission shall publish in the *Official Journal of the European Union* and on its website a list of the third countries, territories and specified sectors within a third country and international organisations for which it has decided that an adequate level of protection is or is no longer ensured.[11]

9. Decisions adopted by the Commission on the basis of Article 25(6) of Directive 95/46/EC shall remain in force until amended, replaced or repealed by a Commission Decision adopted in accordance with paragraph 3 or 5 of this Article.[12]

---

8   Data Protection, Privacy and Electronic Communications (Amendments etc) (EU Exit) Regulations 2019 (2019 No. 419), Regulation 38(4) in Article 45(3)-(6), deletes 'paragraphs 3, 4, 5 and 6'.
9   Data Protection, Privacy and Electronic Communications (Amendments etc) (EU Exit) Regulations 2019 (2019 No. 419), Regulation 38(4) in Article 45(3)-(6), deletes 'paragraphs 3, 4, 5 and 6'.
10 Data Protection, Privacy and Electronic Communications (Amendments etc) (EU Exit) Regulations 2019 (2019 No. 419), Regulation 38(5) in Article 45(7), deletes 'A decision pursuant to paragraph 5 of this Article' and inserts 'The amendment or revocation of regulations under section 17A of the 2018 Act'.
11 Data Protection, Privacy and Electronic Communications (Amendments etc) (EU Exit) Regulations 2019 (2019 No. 419), Regulation 38(6) in Article 45(7), deletes 'paragraphs 8 and 9'.
12 Data Protection, Privacy and Electronic Communications (Amendments etc) (EU Exit) Regulations 2019 (2019 No. 419), Regulation 38(6) in Article 45(7), deletes 'paragraphs 8 and 9'.

Article 46

Transfers subject to appropriate safeguards[13]

1. In the absence of a decision pursuant to Article 45(3) **adequacy regulations under section 17A of the 2018 Act**[14], a controller or processor may transfer personal data to a third country or an international organisation only if the controller or processor has provided appropriate safeguards, and on condition that enforceable data subject rights and effective legal remedies for data subjects are available.

2. The appropriate safeguards referred to in paragraph 1 may be provided for, without requiring any specific authorisation from a supervisory authority **the Commissioner**[15], by:

    (a) a legally binding and enforceable instrument between public authorities or bodies;

    (b) binding corporate rules in accordance with Article 47;

    (c) standard data protection clauses adopted by the Commission in accordance with the examination procedure referred to in Article 93(2); **(c) standard data protection clauses specified in regulations made by the Secretary of State under section 17C(13) of the 2018 Act and for the time being in force;**[16]

    (d) standard data protection clauses adopted by a supervisory authority and approved by the Commission pursuant to the examination procedure referred to in Article 93(2); **(d) standard data protection clauses specified in a document issued (and not withdrawn) by the Commissioner under section 119A(14) of the 2018 Act and for the time being in force;**[17]

    (e) an approved code of conduct pursuant to Article 40 together with binding and enforceable commitments of the controller or processor in the third country to apply the appropriate safeguards, including as regards data subjects' rights; or

---

13 The potentially most relevant Recitals to this Article are Recitals 108, and 109.
14 Data Protection, Privacy and Electronic Communications (Amendments etc) (EU Exit) Regulations 2019 (2019 No. 419), Regulation 39(2) in Article 46(1), deletes 'a decision pursuant to Article 45(3)' and inserts 'adequacy regulations under section 17A of the 2018 Act'.
15 Data Protection, Privacy and Electronic Communications (Amendments etc) (EU Exit) Regulations 2019 (2019 No. 419), Regulation 39(3)(a) in Article 46(2), deletes 'a supervisory authority' and inserts 'the Commissioner'.
16 Data Protection, Privacy and Electronic Communications (Amendments etc) (EU Exit) Regulations 2019 (2019 No. 419), Regulation 39(3)(b) in Article 46(2), deletes 'paragraph (c)' and inserts '(c) standard data protection clauses specified in regulations made by the Secretary of State under section 17C(13) of the 2018 Act and for the time being in force;'.
17 Data Protection, Privacy and Electronic Communications (Amendments etc) (EU Exit) Regulations 2019 (2019 No. 419), Regulation 39(3)(c) in Article 46(2), deletes 'paragraph (d)' and inserts '(d) standard data protection clauses specified in a document issued (and not withdrawn) by the Commissioner under section 119A of the 2018 Act and for the time being in force;'.

(f)   an approved certification mechanism pursuant to Article 42 together with binding and enforceable commitments of the controller or processor in the third country to apply the appropriate safeguards, including as regards data subjects' rights.

3.   Subject to the authorisation from the competent supervisory authority **With authorisation from the Commissioner,**[18] the appropriate safeguards referred to in paragraph 1 may also be provided for, in particular, by:

(a)   contractual clauses between the controller or processor and the controller, processor or the recipient of the personal data in the third country or international organisation; or

(b)   provisions to be inserted into administrative arrangements between public authorities or bodies which include enforceable and effective data subject rights.

4.   The supervisory authority shall apply the consistency mechanism referred to in Article 63 in the cases referred to in paragraph 3 of this Article.[19]

5.   Authorisations by a Member State or supervisory authority on the basis of Article 26(2) of Directive 95/46/EC shall remain valid until amended, replaced or repealed, if necessary, by that supervisory authority. Decisions adopted by the Commission on the basis of Article 26(4) of Directive 95/46/EC shall remain in force until amended, replaced or repealed, if necessary, by a Commission Decision adopted in accordance with paragraph 2 of this Article.[20]

Article 47

Binding corporate rules[21]

1.   The competent supervisory authority **The Commission**[22] shall approve binding corporate rules in accordance with the consistency mechanism set out in Article 63,[23] provided that they:

---

18   Data Protection, Privacy and Electronic Communications (Amendments etc) (EU Exit) Regulations 2019 (2019 No. 419), Regulation 39(4) in Article 46(3), deletes 'Subject to the authorisation from the competent supervisory authority" and inserts "With authorisation from the Commissioner'.

19   Data Protection, Privacy and Electronic Communications (Amendments etc) (EU Exit) Regulations 2019 (2019 No. 419), Regulation 39(5) in Article 46(4)-(5), deletes 'paragraphs 4 and 5'.

20   Data Protection, Privacy and Electronic Communications (Amendments etc) (EU Exit) Regulations 2019 (2019 No. 419), Regulation 39(5) in Article 46(4)-(5), deletes 'paragraphs 4 and 5'.

21   The potentially most relevant Recitals to this Article are Recital 110.

22   Data Protection, Privacy and Electronic Communications (Amendments etc) (EU Exit) Regulations 2019 (2019 No. 419), Regulation 40(2) in Article 47(1)(a), deletes 'The competent supervisory authority' and inserts 'The Commissioner'.

23   Data Protection, Privacy and Electronic Communications (Amendments etc) (EU Exit) Regulations 2019 (2019 No. 419), Regulation 40(2) in Article 47(1)(b), deletes 'in accordance with the consistency mechanism set out in Article 63'.

(a) are legally binding and apply to and are enforced by every member concerned of the group of undertakings, or group of enterprises engaged in a joint economic activity, including their employees;

(b) expressly confer enforceable rights on data subjects with regard to the processing of their personal data; and

(c) fulfil the requirements laid down in paragraph 2.

2. The binding corporate rules referred to in paragraph 1 shall specify at least:

(a) the structure and contact details of the group of undertakings, or group of enterprises engaged in a joint economic activity and of each of its members;

(b) the data transfers or set of transfers, including the categories of personal data, the type of processing and its purposes, the type of data subjects affected and the identification of the third country or countries in question;

(c) their legally binding nature, both internally and externally;

(d) the application of the general data protection principles, in particular purpose limitation, data minimisation, limited storage periods, data quality, data protection by design and by default, legal basis for processing, processing of special categories of personal data, measures to ensure data security, and the requirements in respect of onward transfers to bodies not bound by the binding corporate rules;

(e) the rights of data subjects in regard to processing and the means to exercise those rights, including the right not to be subject to decisions based solely on automated processing, including profiling in accordance with Article 22, the right to lodge a complaint with the competent supervisory authority and before the competent courts of the Member States in accordance with Article 79 **the Commissioner and before a court in accordance with Article 79 (see section 180 of the 2018 Act)**,[24] and to obtain redress and, where appropriate, compensation for a breach of the binding corporate rules;

(f) the acceptance by the controller or processor established on the territory of a Member State **established in the United Kingdom**[25] of liability for any breaches of the binding corporate rules by any member concerned not established in the Union **not established in the United**

---

24 Data Protection, Privacy and Electronic Communications (Amendments etc) (EU Exit) Regulations 2019 (2019 No. 419), Regulation 40(3) in Article 47(2)(e), deletes 'the competent supervisory authority and before the competent courts of the Member States in accordance with Article 79' and inserts 'the Commissioner and before a court in accordance with Article 79 (see section 180 of the 2018 Act)'.

25 Data Protection, Privacy and Electronic Communications (Amendments etc) (EU Exit) Regulations 2019 (2019 No. 419), Regulation 40(4)(a) in Article 47(2)(f), deletes 'established on the territory of a Member State' and inserts 'established in the United Kingdom'.

Kingdom[26]; the controller or the processor shall be exempt from that liability, in whole or in part, only if it proves that that member is not responsible for the event giving rise to the damage;

(g) how the information on the binding corporate rules, in particular on the provisions referred to in points (d), (e) and (f) of this paragraph is provided to the data subjects in addition to Articles 13 and 14;

(h) the tasks of any data protection officer designated in accordance with Article 37 or any other person or entity in charge of the monitoring compliance with the binding corporate rules within the group of undertakings, or group of enterprises engaged in a joint economic activity, as well as monitoring training and complaint-handling;

(i) the complaint procedures;

(j) the mechanisms within the group of undertakings, or group of enterprises engaged in a joint economic activity for ensuring the verification of compliance with the binding corporate rules. Such mechanisms shall include data protection audits and methods for ensuring corrective actions to protect the rights of the data subject. Results of such verification should be communicated to the person or entity referred to in point (h) and to the board of the controlling undertaking of a group of undertakings, or of the group of enterprises engaged in a joint economic activity, and should be available upon request to the competent supervisory authority **the Commissioner**;[27]

(k) the mechanisms for reporting and recording changes to the rules and reporting those changes to the supervisory authority **the Commissioner**;[28]

(l) the cooperation mechanism with the supervisory authority **the Commissioner**[29] to ensure compliance by any member of the group of undertakings, or group of enterprises engaged in a joint economic activity, in particular by making available to the supervisory authority **the Commissioner**[30] the results of verifications of the measures referred to in point (j);

---

26 Data Protection, Privacy and Electronic Communications (Amendments etc) (EU Exit) Regulations 2019 (2019 No. 419), Regulation 40(4)(b) in Article 47(2)(f), deletes 'not established in the Union' and inserts 'not established in the United Kingdom'.

27 Data Protection, Privacy and Electronic Communications (Amendments etc) (EU Exit) Regulations 2019 (2019 No. 419), Regulation 40(5) in Article 47(2)(j), deletes 'the competent supervisory authority' and inserts 'the Commissioner'.

28 Data Protection, Privacy and Electronic Communications (Amendments etc) (EU Exit) Regulations 2019 (2019 No. 419), Regulation 40(6) in Article 47(2)(k), deletes 'the supervisory authority' and inserts 'the Commissioner'.

29 Data Protection, Privacy and Electronic Communications (Amendments etc) (EU Exit) Regulations 2019 (2019 No. 419), Regulation 40(7) in Article 47(2)(l), deletes 'the supervisory authority' (in both places) and inserts 'the Commissioner'.

30 Data Protection, Privacy and Electronic Communications (Amendments etc) (EU Exit) Regulations 2019 (2019 No. 419), Regulation 40(7) in Article 47(2)(l), deletes 'the supervisory authority' (in both places) and inserts 'the Commissioner'.

(m) the mechanisms for reporting to the competent supervisory authority **the Commissioner**[31] any legal requirements to which a member of the group of undertakings, or group of enterprises engaged in a joint economic activity is subject in a third country which are likely to have a substantial adverse effect on the guarantees provided by the binding corporate rules; and

(n) the appropriate data protection training to personnel having permanent or regular access to personal data.

3. The Commission may specify the format and procedures for the exchange of information between controllers, processors and supervisory authorities for binding corporate rules within the meaning of this Article. Those implementing acts shall be adopted in accordance with the examination procedure set out in Article 93(2).[32]

Article 48[33]

Transfers or disclosures not authorised by Union law

Any judgment of a court or tribunal and any decision of an administrative authority of a third country requiring a controller or processor to transfer or disclose personal data may only be recognised or enforceable in any manner if based on an international agreement, such as a mutual legal assistance treaty, in force between the requesting third country and the Union or a Member State, without prejudice to other grounds for transfer pursuant to this Chapter.

Article 49

Derogations for specific situations[34]

1. In the absence of an adequacy decision pursuant to Article 45(3) **adequacy regulations under section 17A of the 2018 Act,**[35] or of appropriate safeguards pursuant to Article 46, including binding corporate rules, a transfer or a set of transfers of personal data to a third country or an international organisation shall take place only on one of the following conditions:

---

31 Data Protection, Privacy and Electronic Communications (Amendments etc) (EU Exit) Regulations 2019 (2019 No. 419), Regulation 40(8) in Article 47(2)(m), deletes 'the competent supervisory authority' and inserts 'the Commissioner'.

32 Data Protection, Privacy and Electronic Communications (Amendments etc) (EU Exit) Regulations 2019 (2019 No. 419), Regulation 40(9) in Article 47(3), deletes 'paragraph 3'.

33 Data Protection, Privacy and Electronic Communications (Amendments etc) (EU Exit) Regulations 2019 (2019 No. 419), Regulation 41 at Article 48, deletes 'Article 48'. Article 48 is therefore deleted and does not apply in the UK.

34 The potentially most relevant Recitals to this Article are Recitals 111, 112, 113, 114, and 115.

35 Data Protection, Privacy and Electronic Communications (Amendments etc) (EU Exit) Regulations 2019 (2019 No. 419), Regulation 42(2)(a) in Article 49, in the opening words deletes 'an adequacy decision pursuant to Article 45(3)' and inserts 'adequacy regulations under section 17A of the 2018 Act'.

(a) the data subject has explicitly consented to the proposed transfer, after having been informed of the possible risks of such transfers for the data subject due to the absence of an adequacy decision and appropriate safeguards;

(b) the transfer is necessary for the performance of a contract between the data subject and the controller or the implementation of pre-contractual measures taken at the data subject's request;

(c) the transfer is necessary for the conclusion or performance of a contract concluded in the interest of the data subject between the controller and another natural or legal person;

(d) the transfer is necessary for important reasons of public interest;

(e) the transfer is necessary for the establishment, exercise or defence of legal claims;

(f) the transfer is necessary in order to protect the vital interests of the data subject or of other persons, where the data subject is physically or legally incapable of giving consent;

(g) the transfer is made from a register which according to Union or Member State law **domestic law**[36] is intended to provide information to the public and which is open to consultation either by the public in general or by any person who can demonstrate a legitimate interest, but only to the extent that the conditions laid down by Union or Member State law **domestic law**[37] for consultation are fulfilled in the particular case.

Where a transfer could not be based on a provision in Article 45 or 46, including the provisions on binding corporate rules, and none of the derogations for a specific situation referred to in the first subparagraph of this paragraph is applicable, a transfer to a third country or an international organisation may take place only if the transfer is not repetitive, concerns only a limited number of data subjects, is necessary for the purposes of compelling legitimate interests pursued by the controller which are not overridden by the interests or rights and freedoms of the data subject, and the controller has assessed all the circumstances surrounding the data transfer and has on the basis of that assessment provided suitable safeguards with regard to the protection of personal data. The controller shall inform the supervisory authority **the Commissioner**[38] of the transfer. The controller shall, in addition to providing the information referred to in Articles 13 and

36 Data Protection, Privacy and Electronic Communications (Amendments etc) (EU Exit) Regulations 2019 (2019 No. 419), Regulation 42(2)(b) in Article 49(1)(g), deletes 'Union or Member State law' (in both places) and inserts 'domestic law'.
37 Data Protection, Privacy and Electronic Communications (Amendments etc) (EU Exit) Regulations 2019 (2019 No. 419), Regulation 42(2)(b) in Article 49(1)(g), deletes 'Union or Member State law' (in both places) and inserts 'domestic law'.
38 Data Protection, Privacy and Electronic Communications (Amendments etc) (EU Exit) Regulations 2019 (2019 No. 419), Regulation 42(2)(c) in Article 49(1)(g) second subparagraph, deletes 'the supervisory authority' and inserts 'the Commissioner'.

14, inform the data subject of the transfer and on the compelling legitimate interests pursued.

2. A transfer pursuant to point (g) of the first subparagraph of paragraph 1 shall not involve the entirety of the personal data or entire categories of the personal data contained in the register. Where the register is intended for consultation by persons having a legitimate interest, the transfer shall be made only at the request of those persons or if they are to be the recipients.

3. Points (a), (b) and (c) of the first subparagraph of paragraph 1 and the second subparagraph thereof shall not apply to activities carried out by public authorities in the exercise of their public powers.

4. The public interest referred to in point (d) of the first subparagraph of paragraph 1 shall be recognised in Union law or in the law of the Member State to which the controller is subject **must be public interest that is recognised in domestic law (whether in regulations under section 18(1) of the 2018 Act or otherwise).**[39]

5. In the absence of an adequacy decision, Union or Member State law may, for important reasons of public interest, expressly set limits to the transfer of specific categories of personal data to a third country or an international organisation. Member States shall notify such provisions to the Commission.[40]

5A. This Article and Article 46 are subject to restrictions in regulations under section 18(2) of the 2018 Act.[41]

6. The controller or processor shall document the assessment as well as the suitable safeguards referred to in the second subparagraph of paragraph 1 of this Article in the records referred to in Article 30.

Article 50

International cooperation for the protection of personal data[42]

In relation to third countries and international organisations, the Commission and supervisory authorities **the Commissioner**[43] shall take appropriate steps to:

39 Data Protection, Privacy and Electronic Communications (Amendments etc) (EU Exit) Regulations 2019 (2019 No. 419), Regulation 42(3) in Article 49(4), deletes 'shall be recognised in Union law or in the law of the Member State to which the controller is subject' and inserts 'must be public interest that is recognised in domestic law (whether in regulations under section 18(1) of the 2018 Act or otherwise)'.

40 Data Protection, Privacy and Electronic Communications (Amendments etc) (EU Exit) Regulations 2019 (2019 No. 419), Regulation 42(4) in Article 49(5), deletes 'paragraph 5'.

41 Data Protection, Privacy and Electronic Communications (Amendments etc) (EU Exit) Regulations 2019 (2019 No. 419), Regulation 42(5) in Article 49, after Article 49(5), inserts '5A. This Article and Article 46 are subject to restrictions in regulations under section 18(2) of the 2018 Act.'.

42 The potentially most relevant Recitals to this Article are Recital 116.

43 Data Protection, Privacy and Electronic Communications (Amendments etc) (EU Exit) Regulations 2019 (2019 No. 419), Regulation 43 in Article 50, deletes 'the Commission and supervisory authorities' and inserts 'the Commissioner'.

(a) develop international cooperation mechanisms to facilitate the effective enforcement of legislation for the protection of personal data;

(b) provide international mutual assistance in the enforcement of legislation for the protection of personal data, including through notification, complaint referral, investigative assistance and information exchange, subject to appropriate safeguards for the protection of personal data and other fundamental rights and freedoms;

(c) engage relevant stakeholders in discussion and activities aimed at furthering international cooperation in the enforcement of legislation for the protection of personal data;

(d) promote the exchange and documentation of personal data protection legislation and practice, including on jurisdictional conflicts with third countries.

Data Protection Act 2018

Section 18 Transfers of personal data to third countries etc

(1) The Secretary of State may by regulations specify, for the purposes of Article 49(1)(d) of the GDPR—

  (a) circumstances in which a transfer of personal data to a third country or international organisation is to be taken to be necessary for important reasons of public interest, and

  (b) circumstances in which a transfer of personal data to a third country or international organisation which is not required by an enactment is not to be taken to be necessary for important reasons of public interest.

(2) The Secretary of State may by regulations restrict the transfer of a category of personal data to a third country or international organisation where—

  (a) the transfer is not authorised by an adequacy decision under Article 45(3) of the GDPR, and

  (b) the Secretary of State considers the restriction to be necessary for important reasons of public interest.

(3) Regulations under this section—

  (a) are subject to the made affirmative resolution procedure where the Secretary of State has made an urgency statement in respect of them;

  (b) are otherwise subject to the affirmative resolution procedure.

(4) For the purposes of this section, an urgency statement is a reasoned statement that the Secretary of State considers it desirable for the regulations to come into force without delay.

SCHEDULE 4

Government Response to Consultation

Consultation outcome
Data: a new direction - government response to consultation
Updated 23 June 2022

CHAPTER 3: BOOSTING TRADE AND REDUCING BARRIERS TO DATA FLOWS

3.1 Summary

In chapter 3 of the consultation, the government set out that global networks of personal data flows are critical to the UK's prosperity and modern way of life. In this chapter, the government sets out the importance of removing unnecessary barriers to cross-border data flows, including by progressing an ambitious programme of adequacy assessments.

The government intends to create an autonomous framework for international data transfers that reflects the UK's independent approach to data protection, that helps drive international commerce, trade and development and underpins modern day business transactions and financial institutions. The UK's approach will be driven by outcomes for individuals and organisations. Continuing to ensure high standards of data protection will remain at the core of the future international transfers regime. Reforms will allow the UK government and businesses to take an agile approach, recognising there are varying frameworks operating internationally that offer a high level of data protection to data subjects. Businesses and organisations will benefit from reduced burdens and clarity on how and where personal data can be transferred across borders.

A more agile approach to the international transfer regime will help domestic businesses to connect more easily with international markets, and attract investment from abroad by businesses that rightly have confidence in the responsible use of personal data within the UK. Individuals will reap the benefits of organisations, hospitals and universities being able to share personal data quickly, efficiently and responsibly for the public good. International data flows help people to stay emotionally and socially connected to friends, families and communities around the world.

3.2 Adequacy

The government recognises that organisations currently face challenges and uncertainty when transferring personal data internationally.

Risk-based approach to adequacy (question 3.2.1)

The government proposed underpinning the UK's future approach to adequacy decisions with principles of risk assessment and proportionality.

Around half of respondents agreed with this proposal. Respondents thought that the proposal represented a pragmatic approach, with some articulating that the UK should be flexible and not prescriptive when making adequacy decisions. Many respondents made clear that an outcomes-based approach should not come at the expense of data protection standards.

The government will take forward reforms that better enable the UK to approach adequacy assessments with a focus on risk-based decision-making and outcomes, and continuing to support the UK's commitments relating to data flows. The reformed regime will retain the same broad standard that a country needs to meet in order to be found adequate, meaning individuals' data will continue to be well-protected by a regime that ensures high data protection standards. Where countries meet those high data protection standards, the law will recognise that the DCMS Secretary of State may also consider the desirability of facilitating international data flows when making adequacy decisions.

The government is respectful of countries' sovereign rights, and the different cultural and legal traditions that can contribute to high standards of data protection. The reformed regime will recognise the contexts in which other countries operate, and take account of the different factors that play a part in protecting personal data.

Adequacy for groups of countries, regions and multilateral frameworks (question 3.2.2)

The government consulted on whether to make adequacy regulations for groups of countries, regions and multilateral frameworks. The majority of respondents agreed with this approach. Support was based on the greater interoperability that this approach would provide. Conversely there was some concern that this could be of limited use as adequacy decisions will still need to consider the laws of each country, as recognised in the consultation document.

The government will consider the implications of using this approach in the future, especially as it seeks to prioritise work on multilateral solutions for data flows, but does not intend to make any immediate legislative changes.

Relaxing the requirement to review adequacy regulations every 4 years (question 3.2.3)

The government also proposed investing in ongoing monitoring of adequacy regulations and relaxing the requirement to review adequacy regulations every 4 years. There were mixed views on this proposal, with some respondents believing that this would be both a more pragmatic and more effective approach, while others cited concerns that the change could present risks to data protection standards.

Adequacy regulations must be scrutinised in the face of constant developments to the legal landscapes of adequate countries. The government recognises the balance of views, and assesses that, if used appropriately, ongoing monitoring can safeguard data subjects more effectively than intermittent review points. A well-functioning, rigorous and ongoing monitoring process removes the need for a formal review. The government therefore intends to proceed with relaxing the requirement to review adequacy regulations every 4 years.

Redress requirements (question 3.2.4)

The government proposed clarifying that when assessing another country for adequacy, it is acceptable for that country to provide either administrative or judicial redress for UK data subjects, as long as the redress mechanism is effective. Around half of respondents agreed with this proposal. The most common view was that the effectiveness of redress is more important than its form.

The government intends to proceed with this proposal. Under the reformed regime, the government will not specify the form in which redress should be provided. Instead, when conducting adequacy assessments, the government will consider the effectiveness of redress mechanisms available.

3.3 Alternative transfer mechanisms

Alternative transfer mechanisms provide a route for cross-border transfers of personal data to countries that are not subject to an adequacy decision. Many organisations send data all over the world and often have complex infrastructure to support such data sharing.

Proportionality of appropriate safeguards (questions 3.3.1, 3.3.2)

To facilitate safe and effective international data sharing, the government proposed changes to reinforce the importance of proportionality when assessing risk for alternative transfer mechanisms. The government called for views on support or guidance that could help organisations assess and mitigate risks in relation to international transfers of personal data when using alternative transfer mechanisms.

The majority of respondents agreed with this proposal, noting the challenges organisations have faced in assessing the risks of international transfers using alternative transfer mechanisms. Respondents who disagreed cited concerns around a perceived risk of degrading data protection standards. Respondents showed strong support for more clarity and guidance on the requirements for alternative transfer mechanisms.

The government will take forward reforms which ensure that data exporters can act pragmatically and proportionally when using alternative transfer mechanisms, whilst maintaining a high standard of protection for data subjects.

Reverse transfers (question 3.3.3)

The government proposed to remove 'reverse transfers' from the scope of the international transfer regime. There were mixed views regarding this proposal. Those in support agreed that it could reduce unnecessary and disproportionate burdens on organisations without corresponding risks to data protection.

However, there were mixed views on the extent of the positive impact anticipated by respondents. Those who disagreed with the proposed reform did so on the basis of the potential risk to data subject rights.

It was also noted that this reform will be complex and may not lead to a reduction in complexity for data controllers. The government agrees with this appraisal and therefore will not pursue legislative reform.

Adaptable transfer mechanisms (questions 3.3.4, 3.3.5, 3.3.6)

The government proposed allowing organisations to create or identify their own transfer mechanism. The majority of respondents disagreed with this proposal, on the grounds that this reform would be too difficult to use and may generate uncertainty about what is required for safeguarding transfers. Some expressed concern that the proposal may risk data protection standards. Respondents who supported the proposal believed it would help organisations overcome complex and specific transfer requirements in some situations.

Given the absence of clear use cases for this proposal, the government will not pursue this approach.

A power to create alternative transfer mechanisms (questions 3.3.7, 3.3.8)

The government proposed creating a new power for the DCMS Secretary of State to formally recognise new alternative transfer mechanisms, which would allow the Secretary of State to create new UK mechanisms for transferring data overseas or recognise in UK law other international data transfer mechanisms, if they achieve the outcomes required by UK law.

There were mixed views on this proposal, with support for the opportunities for interoperability and future-proofing, but some concern about the potential risk that new transfer mechanisms may not maintain data protection standards.

The government recognises the mixed views on this issue, but assesses that this reform will help to future-proof the UK's approach to international transfers by allowing the UK to respond rapidly to international developments. The government intends to take this reform forward and ensure that new mechanisms must meet the same high data protection standards as the other alternative transfer mechanisms.

3.4 UK certification schemes

Certification schemes are voluntary, market-driven frameworks of context-specific rules that, under the UK GDPR, can be used to demonstrate a high standard of compliance and to provide appropriate safeguards for international transfers. They are characteristically framed at the sectoral or industry level, defining data protection rules and practices covering specific products, processes and services within the context of that sector, industry or similar group.

However, certification schemes are complex measures that require significant time and resources to design, implement and maintain, and demonstrate accountability for. The government considered modifications to the framework for certification schemes, to provide for a more globally interoperable market-driven system that better supports the use of certifications as an alternative transfer mechanism.

Amending certification schemes to increase interoperability (questions 3.4.1, 3.4.2)

To facilitate compatibility with a wider range of personal data protection regimes, the government proposed two changes: firstly to allow certification to be provided for by different approaches to accountability, such as privacy management programmes; and secondly to clarify that certification bodies outside the UK can be accredited to run UK-approved international transfer schemes.

There were mixed views on both proposals. Respondents noted that the reforms could benefit UK businesses by facilitating easier personal data flows. Other respondents were less sure that these proposals would benefit them or their organisation directly.

Supporting interoperability is important for organisations. However, there remains potential within the current approach to use certifications more extensively. It is also unclear, at this time, whether the proposed reforms are the best way to deliver greater interoperability. The government will consider other approaches to meeting this goal.

3.5 Derogations

The consultation set out that the current overarching approach to the use of derogations will be maintained: they should be used only in situations where they are necessary and where neither adequacy nor other safeguards are appropriate. As outlined in this section of the consultation, technical changes may help to clarify the restrictions on using derogations.

Repetitive use of derogations (question 3.5.1)

The government proposed establishing a proportionate increase in flexibility for the use of derogations, by making explicit that repetitive use of derogations is permitted. There was some opposition to this proposal, with respondents expressing concerns that it may negatively impact data subject rights. There was minimal support, with respondents agreeing that it would represent a proportionate increase in flexibility for transfers. The government will not pursue this reform.

3.6 Further questions

At the end of the chapter, the government asked for views on whether any of the proposals would impact on anyone with protected characteristics. There were no specific concerns related to the impact any proposals would have on those with protected characteristics, nor were there significant issues raised by respondents in relation to the questions and topics in this chapter.

The consultation posed some open-ended questions at the end of this chapter for respondents to provide any other comments on the proposed reforms. Respondents highlighted the importance of protecting people's personal data when these reforms come into force, particularly those with protected characteristics. The protection of people's personal data is already at the heart of the UK's data regime and will continue to be as the government embarks on its reform agenda.

Annex A [to consultation response]: List of consultation proposals

Question	Proposal	Next steps
3.3.7	To reform the DCMS Secretary of State's adequacy making power.	A - The government plans to proceed with this proposal
3.2.2	Making adequacy regulations for groups of countries, regions and multilateral frameworks	B - The government will continue to consider this approach
3.2.3	To remove the requirement for the DCMS Secretary of State to conduct a review adequacy decisions every 4 years	A - The government plans to proceed with this proposal
3.3.7	Clarifying that either judicial or administrative redress is acceptable for international transfers	A - The government plans to proceed with this proposal
3.3.3	Exempt 'reverse transfers' from the scope of the UK ITR	C - The government does not plan to proceed with this proposal
3.3.4	Empowering organisations to create their own ATMs	C - The government does not plan to proceed with this proposal
3.3.1, 3.3.8	Creating a new power for the DCMS Secretary of State to formally recognise new ATMs	A - The government plans to proceed with this proposal
3.2.3	Reinforcing the importance of proportionality when using ATMs	A - The government plans to proceed with this proposal
3.4.1	Allowing certification for international transfers to be provided for by different approaches to accountability	C - The government does not plan to proceed with this proposal
3.4.1	Clarifying that prospective certification bodies outside the UK can be accredited to run UK-approved international transfer schemes	C - The government does not plan to proceed with this proposal

Data Protection and Digital Information Bill 2022

Bill 143 2022-23 (as introduced)

21 Transfers of personal data to third countries and international organisations

(1) Schedule 5 amends Chapter 5 of the UK GDPR (general processing and transfers of personal data to third countries and international organisations).

(2) Schedule 6 amends Chapter 5 of Part 3 of the 2018 Act (law enforcement processing and transfers of personal data to third countries and international organisations).

(3) Schedule 7 contains consequential and transitional provision.

SCHEDULE 5 Section 21

TRANSFERS OF PERSONAL DATA TO THIRD COUNTRIES ETC:
GENERAL PROCESSING

Introduction

1   Chapter 5 of the UK GDPR (transfers of personal data to third countries or international organisations) is amended as follows.

General principles for transfers

2   (1) Omit Article 44 (transfers of personal data to third countries etc: general principles for transfers).

(2) After that Article insert—

"Article 44A

General principles for transfers

1. A controller or processor may transfer personal data to a third country or an international organisation only if—

(a) the condition in paragraph 2 is met, and

(b) the transfer is carried out in compliance with the other provisions of this Regulation.

2. The condition is met if the transfer—

(a)   is approved by regulations under Article 45A that are in force at the time of the transfer,

(b)   is made subject to appropriate safeguards (see Article 46), or

(c)   is made in reliance on a derogation for special situations (see Article 49).

3. A transfer may not be made in reliance on paragraph 2(b) or (c) if, or to the extent that, it would breach a restriction in regulations under Article 49A."

Transfers approved by regulations

3   Omit Article 45 (transfers on the basis of an adequacy decision).

4   After that Article insert—

"Article 45A

Transfers approved by regulations

1. For the purposes of Article 44A, the Secretary of State may by regulations approve transfers of personal data to—

(a)   a third country, or

(b)   an international organisation.

2. The Secretary of State may only make regulations under this Article approving transfers to a third country or international organisation if the Secretary of State considers that the data protection test is met in relation to the transfers (see Article 45B).

3. In making regulations under this Article, the Secretary of State may have regard to any matter which the Secretary of State considers relevant, including the desirability of facilitating transfers of personal data to and from the United Kingdom.

4. Regulations under this Article may, among other things—

(a)   make provision in relation to a third country or international organisation specified in the regulations or a description of country or organisation;

(b)   approve all transfers of personal data to a third country or international organisation or only transfers specified or described in the regulations;

(c)   identify a transfer of personal data by any means, including by reference to—

(i)   a sector or geographic area within a third country,

(ii)   the controller or processor,

(iii) the recipient of the personal data,

(iv) the personal data transferred,

(v) the means by which the transfer is made, or

(vi) relevant legislation, schemes, lists or other arrangements or documents, as they have effect from time to time;

(d) confer a discretion on a person.

5. Regulations under this Article are subject to the negative resolution procedure.

Article 45B

The data protection test

1. For the purposes of Article 45A, the data protection test is met in relation to transfers of personal data to a third country or international organisation if the standard of the protection provided for data subjects with regard to general processing of personal data in the country or by the organisation is not materially lower than the standard of the protection provided for data subjects by or under—

(a) this Regulation,

(b) Part 2 of the 2018 Act, and

(c) Parts 5 to 7 of that Act, so far as relevant to general processing

2. In considering whether the data protection test is met in relation to transfers of personal data to a third country or international organisation, the Secretary of State must consider, among other things—

(a) respect for the rule of law and for human rights in the country or by the organisation,

(b) the existence, and powers, of an authority responsible for enforcing the protection of data subjects with regard to the processing of personal data in the country or by the organisation,

(c) arrangements for judicial or non-judicial redress for data subjects in connection with such processing,

(d) rules about the transfer of personal data from the country or by the organisation to other countries or international organisations,

(e) relevant international obligations of the country or organisation,

239

and

    (f)   the constitution, traditions and culture of the country or organisation.

3.   In paragraphs 1 and 2—

    (a)   the references to the protection provided for data subjects are to that protection taken as a whole,

    (b)   the references to general processing are to processing to which this Regulation applies or equivalent types of processing in the third country or by the international organisation (as appropriate), and

    (c)   the references to processing of personal data in the third country or by the international organisation are references only to the processing of personal data transferred from the United Kingdom.

4.   When the data protection test is applied only to certain transfers to a third country or international organisation that are specified or described, or to be specified or described, in regulations (in accordance with Article 45A(4)(b))—

    (a)   the references in paragraphs 1 to 3 to personal data are to be read as references only to personal data likely to be the subject of such transfers, and

    (b)   the reference in paragraph 2(d) to the transfer of personal data to other countries or international organisations is to be read as a including the transfer of personal data within the third country or international organisation."

Transfers approved by regulations: monitoring

5   After Article 45B (inserted by paragraph 4) insert—

"Article 45C

Transfers approved by regulations: monitoring

1. The Secretary of State must, on an ongoing basis, monitor developments in third countries and international organisations that could affect decisions to make regulations under Article 45A or to amend or revoke such regulations.

2. Where the Secretary of State becomes aware that the data protection test is no longer met in relation to transfers approved, or of a description approved, in regulations under Article 45A, the Secretary of State must, to the extent necessary, amend or revoke the regulations.

3. Where regulations under Article 45A are amended or revoked in accordance with paragraph 2, the Secretary of State must enter into consultations with the third country or international organisation concerned with a view to improving the protection provided to data subjects with regard to the processing of personal data in the country or by the organisation.

4. The Secretary of State must publish—

   (a) a list of the third countries and international organisations, and the descriptions of such countries and organisations, which are for the time being approved by regulations under Article 45A as places or persons to which personal data may be transferred, and

   (b) a list of the third countries and international organisations, and the descriptions of such countries and organisations, which have been but are no longer approved by such regulations.

5. In the case of regulations under Article 45A which approve only certain transfers to a third country or international organisation specified or described in the regulations (in accordance with Article 45A(4)(b)), the lists published under paragraph 4 must specify or describe the relevant transfers."

Transfers subject to appropriate safeguards

6 (1) Article 46 (transfers subject to appropriate safeguards) is amended as follows.

(2) Omit paragraph 1.

(3) After that paragraph insert—

   "1A. A transfer of personal data to a third country or an international organisation by a controller or processor is made subject to appropriate safeguards only—

   (a) in a case in which—

      (i) safeguards are provided in connection with the transfer as described in paragraph 2 or 3 or regulations made under Article 47A(4), and

      (ii) the controller or processor, acting reasonably and proportionately, considers that the data protection test is met in relation to the transfer or that type of transfer (see paragraph 6), or

   (b) in a case in which—

      (i) safeguards are provided in accordance with paragraph 2(a) by an instrument that is intended to be relied on in connection with the transfer or that type of transfer, and

        (ii)   each public body that is a party to the instrument, acting reasonably and proportionately, considers that the data protection test is met in relation to the transfers, or types of transfer, intended to be made in reliance on the instrument (see paragraph 6)."

(4)   In paragraph 2—

    (a)   in the words before point (a)—

        (i)   omit "appropriate", and

        (ii)   for "paragraph 1" substitute "paragraph 1A(a)",

    (b)   in point (a), for "public authorities or bodies" substitute "a public body and another relevant person or persons",

    (c)   in point (b), after "rules" insert "approved",

    (d)   in point (c), for "section 17C of the 2018 Act" substitute "Article 47A(1)",

    (e)   in point (e), for "appropriate safeguards" substitute "safeguards provided by the code", and

    (f)   in point (f), "appropriate safeguards" substitute "safeguards provided by the mechanism".

(5)   In paragraph 3, in the words before point (a)—

    (a)   omit "appropriate",

    (b)   for "paragraph 1" substitute "paragraph 1A(a)",

    (c)   omit ", in particular,", and

    (d)   in point (b), for "public authorities or bodies" substitute "a public body and another relevant person or persons".

(6)   At the end insert—

"6.   For the purposes of this Article, the data protection test is met in relation to a transfer, or a type of transfer, of personal data if, after the transfer, the standard of the protection provided for the data subject with regard to that personal data by the safeguards required under paragraph 1A, and (where relevant) by other means, would not be materially lower than the standard of the protection provided for the data subject with regard to the personal data by or under—

    (a)   this Regulation,

    (b)   Part 2 of the 2018 Act, and

    (c)   Parts 5 to 7 of that Act, so far as relevant to processing to which this Regulation applies.

7. For the purposes of paragraph 1A(a)(ii) and (b)(ii), what is reasonable and proportionate is to be determined by reference to all the circumstances, or likely circumstances, of the transfer or type of transfer, including the nature and volume of the personal data transferred.

8. In this Article—

   (a) references to the protection provided for the data subject are to that protection taken as a whole;

   (b) "relevant person" means a public body or another person exercising functions of a public nature."

7 In the heading of Article 47 (binding corporate rules) at the beginning insert

"Transfers subject to appropriate safeguards:".

8 After Article 47 insert—

"Article 47A

Transfers subject to appropriate safeguards: further provision

1. The Secretary of State may by regulations specify standard data protection clauses which the Secretary of State considers are capable of securing that the data protection test set out in Article 46 is met in relation to transfers of personal data generally or in relation to a type of transfer specified in the regulations.

2. The Secretary of State must keep under review the standard data protection clauses specified in regulations under paragraph 1 that are for the time being in force.

3. Regulations under paragraph 1 are subject to the negative resolution procedure.

4. The Secretary of State may by regulations make provision about further safeguards that may be relied on for the purposes of Article 46(1A)(a).

5. The Secretary of State may only make regulations under paragraph 4 if the Secretary of State considers that the further safeguards are capable of securing that the data protection test set out in Article 46 is met in relation to transfers of personal data generally or in relation to a type of transfer specified in the regulations.

6. Regulations under paragraph 4 may (among other things)—

   (a) make provision by adopting safeguards prepared or published by another person;

   (b) make provision about ways of providing safeguards which require authorisation from the Commissioner;

    (c)   amend Article 46 by—

        (i)   adding ways of providing safeguards, or

        (ii)   varying or omitting ways of providing safeguards which were added by regulations under this Article.

    7.   Regulations under paragraph 4 are subject to the affirmative resolution procedure."

Derogations for specific circumstances

9   (1)   Article 49 (derogations for specific situations) is amended as follows.

    (2)   In paragraph 1, in the first subparagraph—

        (a)   for "adequacy regulations under section 17A of the 2018 Act, or of appropriate safeguards pursuant to Article 46, including binding corporate rules" substitute "approval by regulations under Article 45A and of compliance with Article 46 (appropriate safeguards)",

      and

        (b)   in point (a), for "an adequacy decision" substitute "approval by regulations under Article 45A".

    (3)   In paragraph 1, in the second subparagraph, for "a provision in Article 45" substitute "Article 45A".

    (4)   In paragraph 4, for "section 18(1) of the 2018 Act" substitute "paragraph 4A".

    (5)   After paragraph 4 insert—

      "4A. The Secretary of State may by regulations specify for the purposes of point (d) of paragraph 1—

        (a)   circumstances in which a transfer of personal data to a third country or international organisation is to be taken to be necessary for important reasons of public interest, and

        (b)   circumstances in which a transfer of personal data to a third country or international organisation which is not required by an enactment is not to be taken to be necessary for important reasons of public interest."

    (6)   Omit paragraph 5A.

    (7)   After paragraph 6 insert—

      "7.   Regulations under this Article—

        (a)   are subject to the made affirmative resolution procedure where the Secretary of State has made an urgency statement in respect of them;

       (b)   otherwise, are subject to the affirmative resolution procedure.

8.   For the purposes of this Article, an urgency statement is a reasoned statement that the Secretary of State considers it desirable for the regulations to come into force without delay."

Public interest restrictions

10   After Article 49 insert—

"Article 49A

1.   The Secretary of State may by regulations restrict the transfer of a category of personal data to a third country or international organisation where—

    (a)   the transfer is not approved by regulations under Article 45A for the time being in force, and

    (b)   the Secretary of State considers the restriction to be necessary for important reasons of public interest.

2.   Regulations under this Article—

    (a)   are subject to the made affirmative resolution procedure where the Secretary of State has made an urgency statement in respect of them;

    (b)   otherwise, are subject to the affirmative resolution procedure.

3.   For the purposes of this Article, an urgency statement is a reasoned statement that the Secretary of State considers it desirable for the regulations to come into force without delay."

SCHEDULE 6

EU Adequacy Decision re UK Data Transfers

European Commission

Brussels, 28.6.2021

C(2021) 4800 final

COMMISSION IMPLEMENTING DECISION

of 28.6.2021

pursuant to Regulation (EU) 2016/679 of the European Parliament and of the Council on the adequate protection of personal data by the United Kingdom

(Text with EEA relevance)

COMMISSION IMPLEMENTING DECISION

of 28.6.2021

pursuant to Regulation (EU) 2016/679 of the European Parliament and of the Council on the adequate protection of personal data by the United Kingdom

(Text with EEA relevance)

Recitals (1) – (292) ………………..

HAS ADOPTED THIS DECISION:

Article 1

1. For the purposes of Article 45 of Regulation (EU) 2016/679, the United Kingdom ensures an adequate level of protection for personal data transferred within the scope of Regulation (EU) 2016/679 from the European Union to the United Kingdom.

2. This decision does not cover personal data that is transferred for purposes of United Kingdom immigration control or that otherwise falls within the scope of the exemption from certain data subject rights for purposes of the maintenance of effective immigration control pursuant to paragraph 4(1) of Schedule 2 to the DPA 2018

Article 2

Whenever the competent supervisory authorities in Member States, in order to protect individuals with regard to the processing of their personal data, exercise their powers pursuant to Article 58 of Regulation (EU) 2016/679 with respect to data transfers falling within the scope of application set out in Article 1, the Member State concerned shall inform the Commission without delay.

Article 3

1. The Commission shall continuously monitor the application of the legal framework upon which this Decision is based, including the conditions under which onward transfers are carried out, individual rights are exercised and United Kingdom public authorities have access to data transferred on the basis of this Decision, with a view to assessing whether the United Kingdom continues to ensure an adequate level of protection within the meaning of Article 1.

2. The Member States and the Commission shall inform each other of cases where the Information Commissioner, or any other competent United Kingdom authority, fails to ensure compliance with the legal framework upon which this Decision is based.

3. The Member States and the Commission shall inform each other of any indications that interferences by United Kingdom public authorities with the right of individuals to the protection of their personal data go beyond what is strictly necessary, or that there is no effective legal protection against such interferences.

4. Where the Commission has indications that an adequate level of protection is no longer ensured, the Commission shall inform the competent United Kingdom authorities and may suspend, repeal or amend this Decision.

5. The Commission may suspend, repeal or amend this Decision if the lack of cooperation of the United Kingdom government prevents the Commission from determining whether the finding in Article 1(1) is affected.

Article 4

This Decision shall expire on 27 June 2025, unless extended in accordance with the procedure referred to in Article 93(2) of Regulation (EU) 2016/679

Article 5

This Decision is addressed to the Member States.

Done at Brussels, 28.6.2021

For the Commission Didier REYNDERS Member of the Commission

EU Decision on Standard Contract Clauses between Controllers and Processors

COMMISSION IMPLEMENTING DECISION (EU) 2021/915

of 4 June 2021

on standard contractual clauses between controllers and processors under Article 28(7) of Regulation (EU) 2016/679 of the European Parliament and of the Council and Article 29(7) of Regulation (EU) 2018/1725 of the European Parliament and of the Council

(Text with EEA relevance)

THE EUROPEAN COMMISSION,

Having regard to the Treaty on the Functioning of the European Union,

Having regard to Regulation (EU) 2016/679 of the European Parliament and of the Council of 27 April 2016 on the protection of natural persons with regard to the processing of personal data and on the free movement of such data, and repealing Directive 95/46/EC (GDPR) (¹), and in particular Article 28(7) thereof,

Having regard to Regulation (EU) 2018/1725 of the European Parliament and of the Council of 23 October 2018 on the protection of natural persons with regard to the processing of personal data by the Union institutions, bodies, offices and agencies and on the free movement of such data, and repealing Regulation (EC) N 45/2001 and Decision No 1247/2002/EC (EUDPR) (²), and in particular Article 29(7) thereof,

Whereas:

Recitals (1) – (14) ....

HAS ADOPTED THIS DECISION:

Article 1

The standard contractual clauses as set out in the Annex fulfil the requirements for contracts between controllers and processors in Article 28(3) and (4) of

Regulation (EU) 2016/679 and of Article 29(3) and (4) of Regulation (EU) 2018/1725.

Article 2

The standard contractual clauses as set out in the Annex may be used in contracts between a controller and a processor who processes personal data on behalf of the controller.

Article 3

The Commission shall evaluate the practical application of the standard contractual clauses set out in the Annex on the basis of all available information as part of the periodic evaluation provided for in Article 97 of Regulation (EU) 2016/679.

Article 4

This Decision shall enter into force on the twentieth day following that of its publication in the Official Journal of the European Union.

Done at Brussels, 4 June 2021.

For the Commission

The President

Ursula VON DER LEYEN

....

ANNEX

STANDARD CONTRACTUAL CLAUSES

SECTION I

Clause 1

Purpose and scope

(a) The purpose of these Standard Contractual Clauses (the Clauses) is to ensure compliance with [choose relevant option: OPTION 1: Article 28(3) and (4) of Regulation (EU) 2016/679 of the European Parliament and of the Council of 27 April 2016 on the protection of natural persons with regard to the processing of personal data and on the free movement of such data, and repealing Directive 95/46/EC (General Data Protection Regulation)] / [OPTION 2: Article 29(3) and (4) of Regulation (EU) 2018/1725 of the European Parliament and of the Council of 23 October 2018 on the protection of natural persons with regard to the processing of personal data by the Union institutions, bodies, offices and agencies and on the free movement of such data, and repealing Regulation (EC) No 45/2001 and Decision No 1247/2002/EC].

(b) The controllers and processors listed in Annex I have agreed to these Clauses in order to ensure compliance with Article 28(3) and (4) of Regulation (EU) 2016/679 and/or Article 29(3) and (4) of Regulation (EU) 2018/1725.

(c) These Clauses apply to the processing of personal data as specified in Annex II.

(d) Annexes I to IV are an integral part of the Clauses.

(e) These Clauses are without prejudice to obligations to which the controller is subject by virtue of Regulation (EU) 2016/679 and/or Regulation (EU) 2018/1725.

(f) These Clauses do not by themselves ensure compliance with obligations related to international transfers in accordance with Chapter V of Regulation (EU) 2016/679 and/or Regulation (EU) 2018/1725.

Clause 2

Invariability of the Clauses

(a) The Parties undertake not to modify the Clauses, except for adding information to the Annexes or updating information in them.

(b) This does not prevent the Parties from including the standard contractual clauses laid down in these Clauses in a broader contract, or from adding other clauses or additional safeguards provided that they do not directly or indirectly contradict the Clauses or detract from the fundamental rights or freedoms of data subjects.

Clause 3

Interpretation

(a) Where these Clauses use the terms defined in Regulation (EU) 2016/679 or Regulation (EU) 2018/1725 respectively, those terms shall have the same meaning as in that Regulation.

(b) These Clauses shall be read and interpreted in the light of the provisions of Regulation (EU) 2016/679 or Regulation (EU) 2018/1725 respectively.

(c) These Clauses shall not be interpreted in a way that runs counter to the rights and obligations provided for in Regulation (EU) 2016/679 / Regulation (EU) 2018/1725 or in a way that prejudices the fundamental rights or freedoms of the data subjects.

Clause 4

Hierarchy

In the event of a contradiction between these Clauses and the provisions of related agreements between the Parties existing at the time when these Clauses are agreed or entered into thereafter, these Clauses shall prevail.

Clause 5 – Optional

Docking clause

(a) Any entity that is not a Party to these Clauses may, with the agreement of all the Parties, accede to these Clauses at any time as a controller or a processor by completing the Annexes and signing Annex I.

(b) Once the Annexes in (a) are completed and signed, the acceding entity shall be treated as a Party to these Clauses and have the rights and obligations of a controller or a processor, in accordance with its designation in Annex I.

(c) The acceding entity shall have no rights or obligations resulting from these Clauses from the period prior to becoming a Party.

SECTION II

OBLIGATIONS OF THE PARTIES

Clause 6

Description of processing(s)

The details of the processing operations, in particular the categories of personal data and the purposes of processing for which the personal data is processed on behalf of the controller, are specified in Annex II.

Clause 7

Obligations of the Parties

7.1. Instructions

(a) The processor shall process personal data only on documented instructions from the controller, unless required to do so by Union or Member State law to which the processor is subject. In this case, the processor shall inform the controller of that legal requirement before processing, unless the law prohibits this on important grounds of public interest. Subsequent instructions may also be given by the controller throughout the duration of the processing of personal data. These instructions shall always be documented.

(b) The processor shall immediately inform the controller if, in the processor's opinion, instructions given by the controller infringe Regulation (EU) 2016/679 / Regulation (EU) 2018/1725 or the applicable Union or Member State data protection provisions.

7.2. Purpose limitation

The processor shall process the personal data only for the specific purpose(s) of the processing, as set out in Annex II, unless it receives further instructions from the controller.

7.3. Duration of the processing of personal data

Processing by the processor shall only take place for the duration specified in Annex II.

7.4. Security of processing

(a) The processor shall at least implement the technical and organisational measures specified in Annex III to ensure the security of the personal data. This includes protecting the data against a breach of security leading to accidental or unlawful destruction, loss, alteration, unauthorised disclosure or access to the data (personal data breach). In assessing the appropriate level of security, the Parties shall take due account of the state of the art, the costs of implementation, the nature, scope, context and purposes of processing and the risks involved for the data subjects.

(b) The processor shall grant access to the personal data undergoing processing to members of its personnel only to the extent strictly necessary for implementing, managing and monitoring of the contract. The processor shall ensure that persons authorised to process the personal data received have committed themselves to confidentiality or are under an appropriate statutory obligation of confidentiality.

7.5. Sensitive data

If the processing involves personal data revealing racial or ethnic origin, political opinions, religious or philosophical beliefs, or trade union membership, genetic data or biometric data for the purpose of uniquely identifying a natural person, data concerning health or a person's sex life or sexual orientation, or data relating to criminal convictions and offences ("sensitive data"), the processor shall apply specific restrictions and/or additional safeguards.

7.6. Documentation and compliance

(a) The Parties shall be able to demonstrate compliance with these Clauses.

(b) The processor shall deal promptly and adequately with inquiries from the controller about the processing of data in accordance with these Clauses.

(c) The processor shall make available to the controller all information necessary to demonstrate compliance with the obligations that are set out in these Clauses and stem directly from Regulation (EU) 2016/679 and/or Regulation (EU) 2018/1725. At the controller's request, the processor shall also permit and contribute to audits of the processing activities covered by these Clauses, at reasonable intervals or if there are indications of non-compliance. In deciding on a review or an audit, the controller may take into account relevant certifications held by the processor.

(d) The controller may choose to conduct the audit by itself or mandate an independent auditor. Audits may also include inspections at the premises or physical facilities of the processor and shall, where appropriate, be carried out with reasonable notice.

(e) The Parties shall make the information referred to in this Clause, including the results of any audits, available to the competent supervisory authority/ies on request.

7.7. Use of sub-processors

(a) OPTION 1: PRIOR SPECIFIC AUTHORISATION: The processor shall not subcontract any of its processing operations performed on behalf of the controller in accordance with these Clauses to a sub-processor, without the controller's prior specific written authorisation. The processor shall submit the request for specific authorisation at least [SPECIFY TIME PERIOD] prior to the engagement of the sub-processor in question, together with the information necessary to enable the controller to decide on the authorisation. The list of sub-processors authorised by the controller can be found in Annex IV. The Parties shall keep Annex IV up to date.

OPTION 2: GENERAL WRITTEN AUTHORISATION: The processor has the controller's general authorisation for the engagement of sub-processors from an agreed list. The processor shall specifically inform in writing the controller of any intended changes of that list through the addition or replacement of sub-processors at least [SPECIFY TIME PERIOD] in advance, thereby giving the controller sufficient time to be able to object to such changes prior to the engagement of the concerned sub-processor(s). The processor shall provide the controller with the information necessary to enable the controller to exercise the right to object.

(b) Where the processor engages a sub-processor for carrying out specific processing activities (on behalf of the controller), it shall do so by way of a contract which imposes on the sub-processor, in substance, the same data protection obligations as the ones imposed on the data processor in accordance with these Clauses. The processor shall ensure that the sub-processor complies with the obligations to which the processor is subject pursuant to these Clauses and to Regulation (EU) 2016/679 and/or Regulation (EU) 2018/1725.

(c) At the controller's request, the processor shall provide a copy of such a sub-processor agreement and any subsequent amendments to the controller. To the extent necessary to protect business secret or other confidential information, including personal data, the processor may redact the text of the agreement prior to sharing the copy.

(d) The processor shall remain fully responsible to the controller for the performance of the sub-processor's obligations in accordance with its contract with the processor. The processor shall notify the controller of any failure by the sub-processor to fulfil its contractual obligations.

(e) The processor shall agree a third party beneficiary clause with the sub-processor whereby – in the event the processor has factually disappeared, ceased to exist in law or has become insolvent – the controller shall have the right to terminate the sub-processor contract and to instruct the sub-processor to erase or return the personal data.

7.8. International transfers

(a) Any transfer of data to a third country or an international organisation by the processor shall be done only on the basis of documented instructions from the controller or in order to fulfil a specific requirement under Union or Member State law to which the processor is subject and shall take place in compliance with Chapter V of Regulation (EU) 2016/679 or Regulation (EU) 2018/1725.

(b) The controller agrees that where the processor engages a sub-processor in accordance with Clause 7.7. for carrying out specific processing activities (on behalf of the controller) and those processing activities involve a transfer of personal data within the meaning of Chapter V of Regulation (EU) 2016/679, the processor and the sub-processor can ensure compliance with Chapter V of Regulation (EU) 2016/679 by using standard contractual clauses adopted by the Commission in accordance with of Article 46(2) of Regulation (EU) 2016/679, provided the conditions for the use of those standard contractual clauses are met.

Clause 8

Assistance to the controller

(a) The processor shall promptly notify the controller of any request it has received from the data subject. It shall not respond to the request itself, unless authorised to do so by the controller.

(b) The processor shall assist the controller in fulfilling its obligations to respond to data subjects' requests to exercise their rights, taking into account the nature of the processing. In fulfilling its obligations in accordance with (a) and (b), the processor shall comply with the controller's instructions

(c) In addition to the processor's obligation to assist the controller pursuant to Clause 8(b), the processor shall furthermore assist the controller in ensuring compliance with the following obligations, taking into account the nature of the data processing and the information available to the processor:

   (1) the obligation to carry out an assessment of the impact of the envisaged processing operations on the protection of personal data (a 'data protection impact assessment') where a type of processing is likely to result in a high risk to the rights and freedoms of natural persons;

   (2) the obligation to consult the competent supervisory authority/ies prior to processing where a data protection impact assessment indicates that the processing would result in a high risk in the absence of measures taken by the controller to mitigate the risk;

   (3) the obligation to ensure that personal data is accurate and up to date, by informing the controller without delay if the processor becomes aware that the personal data it is processing is inaccurate or has become outdated;

   (4) the obligations in [OPTION 1] Article 32 of Regulation (EU) 2016/679/ [OPTION 2] Articles 33 and 36 to 38 of Regulation (EU) 2018/1725.

(d) The Parties shall set out in Annex III the appropriate technical and organisational measures by which the processor is required to assist the controller in the application of this Clause as well as the scope and the extent of the assistance required.

Clause 9

Notification of personal data breach

In the event of a personal data breach, the processor shall cooperate with and assist the controller for the controller to comply with its obligations under Articles 33 and 34 of Regulation (EU) 2016/679 or under Articles 34 and 35 of Regulation (EU) 2018/1725, where applicable, taking into account the nature of processing and the information available to the processor.

9.1 Data breach concerning data processed by the controller

In the event of a personal data breach concerning data processed by the controller, the processor shall assist the controller:

(a) in notifying the personal data breach to the competent supervisory authority/ies, without undue delay after the controller has become aware of it, where relevant/(unless the personal data breach is unlikely to result in a risk to the rights and freedoms of natural persons);

(b) in obtaining the following information which, pursuant to [OPTION 1] Article 33(3) of Regulation (EU) 2016/679/ [OPTION 2] Article 34(3) of Regulation (EU) 2018/1725, shall be stated in the controller's notification, and must at least include:

  (1) the nature of the personal data including where possible, the categories and approximate number of data subjects concerned and the categories and approximate number of personal data records concerned;

  (2) the likely consequences of the personal data breach;

  (3) the measures taken or proposed to be taken by the controller to address the personal data breach, including, where appropriate, measures to mitigate its possible adverse effects.

  Where, and insofar as, it is not possible to provide all this information at the same time, the initial notification shall contain the information then available and further information shall, as it becomes available, subsequently be provided without undue delay.

(c) in complying, pursuant to [OPTION 1] Article 34 of Regulation (EU) 2016/679 / [OPTION 2] Article 35 of Regulation (EU) 2018/1725, with the obligation to communicate without undue delay the personal data breach to the data subject, when the personal data breach is likely to result in a high risk to the rights and freedoms of natural persons.

9.2 Data breach concerning data processed by the processor

In the event of a personal data breach concerning data processed by the processor, the processor shall notify the controller without undue delay after the processor having become aware of the breach. Such notification shall contain, at least:

(a)   a description of the nature of the breach (including, where possible, the categories and approximate number of data subjects and data records concerned);

(b)   the details of a contact point where more information concerning the personal data breach can be obtained;

(c)   its likely consequences and the measures taken or proposed to be taken to address the breach, including to mitigate its possible adverse effects.

Where, and insofar as, it is not possible to provide all this information at the same time, the initial notification shall contain the information then available and further information shall, as it becomes available, subsequently be provided without undue delay.

The Parties shall set out in Annex III all other elements to be provided by the processor when assisting the controller in the compliance with the controller's obligations under [OPTION 1] Articles 33 and 34 of Regulation (EU) 2016/679 / [OPTION 2] Articles 34 and 35 of Regulation (EU) 2018/1725.

SECTION III
FINAL PROVISIONS

Clause 10

Non-compliance with the Clauses and termination

(a) Without prejudice to any provisions of Regulation (EU) 2016/679 and/or Regulation (EU) 2018/1725, in the event that the processor is in breach of its obligations under these Clauses, the controller may instruct the processor to suspend the processing of personal data until the latter complies with these Clauses or the contract is terminated. The processor shall promptly inform the controller in case it is unable to comply with these Clauses, for whatever reason.

(b) The controller shall be entitled to terminate the contract insofar as it concerns processing of personal data in accordance with these Clauses if:

(1) the processing of personal data by the processor has been suspended by the controller pursuant to point (a) and if compliance with these Clauses is not restored within a reasonable time and in any event within one month following suspension;

(2) the processor is in substantial or persistent breach of these Clauses or its obligations under Regulation (EU) 2016/679 and/or Regulation (EU) 2018/1725;

(3) the processor fails to comply with a binding decision of a competent court or the competent supervisory authority/ies regarding its obligations pursuant to these Clauses or to Regulation (EU) 2016/679 and/or Regulation (EU) 2018/1725.

(c) The processor shall be entitled to terminate the contract insofar as it concerns processing of personal data under these Clauses where, after having informed the controller that its instructions infringe applicable legal requirements in accordance with Clause 7.1 (b), the controller insists on compliance with the instructions.

(d) Following termination of the contract, the processor shall, at the choice of the controller, delete all personal data processed on behalf of the controller and certify to the controller that it has done so, or, return all the personal data to the controller and delete existing copies unless Union or Member State law requires storage of the personal data. Until the data is deleted or returned, the processor shall continue to ensure compliance with these Clauses.

ANNEX I

LIST OF PARTIES

Controller(s): [*Identity and contact details of the controller(s), and, where applicable, of the controller's data protection officer*]

1. Name: ...

    Address: ...

    Contact person's name, position and contact details: ...

    Signature and accession date: ...

2. ...

Processor(s): [*Identity and contact details of the processor(s) and, where applicable, of the processor's data protection officer*]

1. Name: ...

    Address: ...

    Contact person's name, position and contact details: ...

    Signature and accession date: ...

2. ...

ANNEX II

DESCRIPTION OF THE PROCESSING

Categories of data subjects whose personal data is processed

...

Categories of personal data processed

....

Sensitive data processed (if applicable) and applied restrictions or safeguards that fully take into consideration the nature of the data and the risks involved, such as for instance strict purpose limitation, access restrictions (including access only for staff having followed specialised training), keeping a record of access to the data, restrictions for onward transfers or additional security measures.

...

Nature of the processing

....

Purpose(s) for which the personal data is processed on behalf of the controller

...

Duration of the processing

...

...

For processing by (sub-) processors, also specify subject matter, nature and duration of the processing

ANNEX III

TECHNICAL AND ORGANISATIONAL MEASURES INCLUDING TECHNICAL AND ORGANISATIONAL MEASURES TO ENSURE THE SECURITY OF THE DATA

EXPLANATORY NOTE:

The technical and organisational measures need to be described concretely and not in a generic manner.

Description of the technical and organisational security measures implemented by the processor(s) (including any relevant certifications) to ensure an appropriate level of security, taking into account the nature, scope, context and purpose of the processing, as well as the risks for the rights and freedoms of natural persons. Examples of possible measures:

Measures of pseudonymisation and encryption of personal data

Measures for ensuring ongoing confidentiality, integrity, availability and resilience of processing systems and services

Measures for ensuring the ability to restore the availability and access to personal data in a timely manner in the event of a physical or technical incident

Processes for regularly testing, assessing and evaluating the effectiveness of technical and organisational measures in order to ensure the security of the processing

Measures for user identification and authorisation

Measures for the protection of data during transmission

Measures for the protection of data during storage

261

Measures for ensuring physical security of locations at which personal data are processed

Measures for ensuring events logging

Measures for ensuring system configuration, including default configuration

Measures for internal IT and IT security governance and management

Measures for certification/assurance of processes and products

Measures for ensuring data minimisation

Measures for ensuring data quality

Measures for ensuring limited data retention

Measures for ensuring accountability

Measures for allowing data portability and ensuring erasure]

For transfers to (sub-) processors, also describe the specific technical and organisational measures to be taken by the (sub-) processor to be able to provide assistance to the controller

Description of the specific technical and organisational measures to be taken by the processor to be able to provide assistance to the controller.

ANNEX IV

LIST OF SUB-PROCESSORS

EXPLANATORY NOTE:

This Annex needs to be completed in case of specific authorisation of sub-processors (Clause 7.7(a), Option 1).

The controller has authorised the use of the following sub-processors:

1. Name: ...

    Address: ...

    Contact person's name, position and contact details: ...

    Description of the processing (including a clear delimitation of responsibilities in case several sub-processors are authorised): ...

2. ...

SCHEDULE 8

EU Decision on Standard Contract Clauses to Third Countries

COMMISSION IMPLEMENTING DECISION (EU) 2021/914

of 4 June 2021

on standard contractual clauses for the transfer of personal data to third countries pursuant to Regulation (EU) 2016/679 of the European Parliament and of the Council

(Text with EEA relevance)

THE EUROPEAN COMMISSION,

Having regard to the Treaty on the Functioning of the European Union,

Having regard to Regulation (EU) 2016/679 of the European Parliament and of the Council of 27 April 2016 on the protection of natural persons with regard to the processing of personal data and on the free movement of such data, and repealing Directive 95/46/EC (General Data Protection Regulation) (¹), and in particular Article 28(7) and Article 46(2)(c) thereof,

Whereas:

Recitals (1) – (26)

HAS ADOPTED THIS DECISION:

Article 1

1. The standard contractual clauses set out in the Annex are considered to provide appropriate safeguards within the meaning of Article 46(1) and (2) (c) of Regulation (EU) 2016/679 for the transfer by a controller or processor of personal data processed subject to that Regulation (data exporter) to a controller or (sub-)processor whose processing of the data is not subject to that Regulation (data importer).

2. The standard contractual clauses also set out the rights and obligations of controllers and processors with respect to the matters referred to in Article 28(3) and (4) of Regulation (EU) 2016/679, as regards the transfer of personal data from a controller to a processor, or from a processor to a sub-processor.

Article 2

Where the competent Member State authorities exercise corrective powers pursuant to Article 58 of Regulation (EU) 2016/679 in response to the data importer being or becoming subject to laws or practices in the third country of destination that prevent it from complying with the standard contractual clauses set out in the Annex, leading to the suspension or ban of data transfers to third countries, the Member State concerned shall, without delay, inform the Commission, which will forward the information to the other Member States.

Article 3

The Commission shall evaluate the practical application of the standard contractual clauses set out in the Annex on the basis of all available information, as part of the periodic evaluation required by Article 97 of Regulation (EU) 2016/679.

Article 4

1. This Decision shall enter into force on the twentieth day following that of its publication in the *Official Journal of the European Union*.

2. Decision 2001/497/EC is repealed with effect from 27 September 2021.

3. Decision 2010/87/EU is repealed with effect from 27 September 2021.

4. Contracts concluded before 27 September 2021 on the basis of Decision 2001/497/EC or Decision 2010/87/EU shall be deemed to provide appropriate safeguards within the meaning of Article 46(1) of Regulation (EU) 2016/679 until 27 December 2022, provided the processing operations that are the subject matter of the contract remain unchanged and that reliance on those clauses ensures that the transfer of personal data is subject to appropriate safeguards.

Done at Brussels, 4 June 2021.

For the Commission

The President

Ursula VON DER LEYEN

ANNEX

STANDARD CONTRACTUAL CLAUSES

SECTION I

Clause 1

Purpose and scope

(a) The purpose of these standard contractual clauses is to ensure compliance with the requirements of Regulation (EU) 2016/679 of the European Parliament and of the Council of 27 April 2016 on the protection of natural persons with regard to the processing of personal data and on the free movement of such data (General Data Protection Regulation) (^{1}) for the transfer of personal data to a third country.

(b) The Parties:

   (i)   the natural or legal person(s), public authority/ies, agency/ies or other body/ies (hereinafter 'entity/ies') transferring the personal data, as listed in Annex I.A (hereinafter each 'data exporter'), and

   (ii) the entity/ies in a third country receiving the personal data from the data exporter, directly or indirectly via another entity also Party to these Clauses, as listed in Annex I.A (hereinafter each 'data importer')

   have agreed to these standard contractual clauses (hereinafter: 'Clauses').

(c) These Clauses apply with respect to the transfer of personal data as specified in Annex I.B.

(d) The Appendix to these Clauses containing the Annexes referred to therein forms an integral part of these Clauses.

Clause 2

Effect and invariability of the Clauses

(a) These Clauses set out appropriate safeguards, including enforceable data subject rights and effective legal remedies, pursuant to Article 46(1) and Article 46(2)(c) of Regulation (EU) 2016/679 and, with respect to data transfers from controllers to processors and/or processors to processors, standard contractual clauses pursuant to Article 28(7) of Regulation (EU) 2016/679, provided they are not modified, except to select the appropriate Module(s) or to add or update information in the Appendix. This does not prevent the Parties from including the standard contractual clauses laid down in these Clauses in a wider contract and/or to add other clauses or additional safeguards, provided that they do not contradict, directly or indirectly, these Clauses or prejudice the fundamental rights or freedoms of data subjects.

(b) These Clauses are without prejudice to obligations to which the data exporter is subject by virtue of Regulation (EU) 2016/679.

Clause 3

Third-party beneficiaries

(a) Data subjects may invoke and enforce these Clauses, as third-party beneficiaries, against the data exporter and/or data importer, with the following exceptions:

    (i) Clause 1, Clause 2, Clause 3, Clause 6, Clause 7;

    (ii) Clause 8 – Module One: Clause 8.5 (e) and Clause 8.9(b); Module Two: Clause 8.1(b), 8.9(a), (c), (d) and (e); Module Three: Clause 8.1(a), (c) and (d) and Clause 8.9(a), (c), (d), (e), (f) and (g); Module Four: Clause 8.1 (b) and Clause 8.3(b);

    (iii) Clause 9 – Module Two: Clause 9(a), (c), (d) and (e); Module Three: Clause 9(a), (c), (d) and (e);

    (iv) Clause 12 – Module One: Clause 12(a) and (d); Modules Two and Three: Clause 12(a), (d) and (f);

    (v) Clause 13;

    (vi) Clause 15.1(c), (d) and (e);

    (vii) Clause 16(e);

    (viii) Clause 18 – Modules One, Two and Three: Clause 18(a) and (b); Module Four: Clause 18.

(b) Paragraph (a) is without prejudice to rights of data subjects under Regulation (EU) 2016/679.

Clause 4

Interpretation

(a) Where these Clauses use terms that are defined in Regulation (EU) 2016/679, those terms shall have the same meaning as in that Regulation.

(b) These Clauses shall be read and interpreted in the light of the provisions of Regulation (EU) 2016/679.

(c) These Clauses shall not be interpreted in a way that conflicts with rights and obligations provided for in Regulation (EU) 2016/679.

Clause 5

Hierarchy

In the event of a contradiction between these Clauses and the provisions of related agreements between the Parties, existing at the time these Clauses are agreed or entered into thereafter, these Clauses shall prevail.

Clause 6

Description of the transfer(s)

The details of the transfer(s), and in particular the categories of personal data that are transferred and the purpose(s) for which they are transferred, are specified in Annex I.B.

Clause 7 – Optional

Docking clause

(a) An entity that is not a Party to these Clauses may, with the agreement of the Parties, accede to these Clauses at any time, either as a data exporter or as a data importer, by completing the Appendix and signing Annex I.A.

(b) Once it has completed the Appendix and signed Annex I.A, the acceding entity shall become a Party to these Clauses and have the rights and obligations of a data exporter or data importer in accordance with its designation in Annex I.A.

(c) The acceding entity shall have no rights or obligations arising under these Clauses from the period prior to becoming a Party.

SECTION II – OBLIGATIONS OF THE PARTIES

Clause 8

Data protection safeguards

The data exporter warrants that it has used reasonable efforts to determine that the data importer is able, through the implementation of appropriate technical and organisational measures, to satisfy its obligations under these Clauses.

MODULE ONE: Transfer controller to controller

8.1 Purpose limitation

The data importer shall process the personal data only for the specific purpose(s) of the transfer, as set out in Annex I.B. It may only process the personal data for another purpose:

(i) where it has obtained the data subject's prior consent;

(ii) where necessary for the establishment, exercise or defence of legal claims in the context of specific administrative, regulatory or judicial proceedings; or

(iii) where necessary in order to protect the vital interests of the data subject or of another natural person.

8.2 Transparency

(a) In order to enable data subjects to effectively exercise their rights pursuant to Clause 10, the data importer shall inform them, either directly or through the data exporter:

    (i) of its identity and contact details;

    (ii) of the categories of personal data processed;

    (iii) of the right to obtain a copy of these Clauses;

    (iv) where it intends to onward transfer the personal data to any third party/ies, of the recipient or categories of recipients (as appropriate with a view to providing meaningful information), the purpose of such onward transfer and the ground therefore pursuant to Clause 8.7.

(b) Paragraph (a) shall not apply where the data subject already has the information, including when such information has already been provided by the data exporter, or providing the information proves impossible or would involve a disproportionate effort for the data importer. In the latter case, the data importer shall, to the extent possible, make the information publicly available.

(c) On request, the Parties shall make a copy of these Clauses, including the Appendix as completed by them, available to the data subject free of charge. To the extent necessary to protect business secrets or other confidential information, including personal data, the Parties may redact part of the text of the Appendix prior to sharing a copy, but shall provide a meaningful summary where the data subject would otherwise not be able to understand its content or exercise his/her rights. On request, the Parties shall provide the data subject with the reasons for the redactions, to the extent possible without revealing the redacted information.

(d) Paragraphs (a) to (c) are without prejudice to the obligations of the data exporter under Articles 13 and 14 of Regulation (EU) 2016/679.

8.3 Accuracy and data minimisation

(a) Each Party shall ensure that the personal data is accurate and, where necessary, kept up to date. The data importer shall take every reasonable step to ensure that personal data that is inaccurate, having regard to the purpose(s) of processing, is erased or rectified without delay.

(b) If one of the Parties becomes aware that the personal data it has transferred or received is inaccurate, or has become outdated, it shall inform the other Party without undue delay.

(c) The data importer shall ensure that the personal data is adequate, relevant and limited to what is necessary in relation to the purpose(s) of processing.

8.4 Storage limitation

The data importer shall retain the personal data for no longer than necessary for the purpose(s) for which it is processed. It shall put in place appropriate technical or organisational measures to ensure compliance with this obligation, including erasure or anonymisation (^{2}) of the data and all back-ups at the end of the retention period.

8.5 Security of processing

(a) The data importer and, during transmission, also the data exporter shall implement appropriate technical and organisational measures to ensure the security of the personal data, including protection against a breach of security leading to accidental or unlawful destruction, loss, alteration, unauthorised disclosure or access (hereinafter 'personal data breach'). In assessing the appropriate level of security, they shall take due account of the state of the art, the costs of implementation, the nature, scope, context and purpose(s) of processing and the risks involved in the processing for the data subject. The Parties shall in particular consider having recourse to encryption or pseudonymisation, including during transmission, where the purpose of processing can be fulfilled in that manner.

(b) The Parties have agreed on the technical and organisational measures set out in Annex II. The data importer shall carry out regular checks to ensure that these measures continue to provide an appropriate level of security.

(c) The data importer shall ensure that persons authorised to process the personal data have committed themselves to confidentiality or are under an appropriate statutory obligation of confidentiality.

(d) In the event of a personal data breach concerning personal data processed by the data importer under these Clauses, the data importer shall take appropriate measures to address the personal data breach, including measures to mitigate its possible adverse effects.

(e) In case of a personal data breach that is likely to result in a risk to the rights and freedoms of natural persons, the data importer shall without undue delay notify both the data exporter and the competent supervisory authority pursuant to Clause 13. Such notification shall contain i) a description of the nature of the breach (including, where possible, categories and approximate number of data subjects and personal data records concerned), ii) its likely consequences, iii) the measures taken or proposed to address the breach, and iv) the details of a contact point from whom more information can be obtained. To the extent it is not possible for the data importer to provide all the information at the same time, it may do so in phases without undue further delay.

(f) In case of a personal data breach that is likely to result in a high risk to the rights and freedoms of natural persons, the data importer shall also notify without undue delay the data subjects concerned of the personal data breach and its nature, if necessary in cooperation with the data exporter, together with the information referred to in paragraph (e), points ii) to iv), unless the data importer has implemented measures to significantly reduce the risk to the rights or freedoms of natural persons, or notification would involve disproportionate efforts. In the latter case, the data importer shall instead

269

issue a public communication or take a similar measure to inform the public of the personal data breach.

(g) The data importer shall document all relevant facts relating to the personal data breach, including its effects and any remedial action taken, and keep a record thereof.

8.6 Sensitive data

Where the transfer involves personal data revealing racial or ethnic origin, political opinions, religious or philosophical beliefs, or trade union membership, genetic data, or biometric data for the purpose of uniquely identifying a natural person, data concerning health or a person's sex life or sexual orientation, or data relating to criminal convictions or offences (hereinafter 'sensitive data'), the data importer shall apply specific restrictions and/or additional safeguards adapted to the specific nature of the data and the risks involved. This may include restricting the personnel permitted to access the personal data, additional security measures (such as pseudonymisation) and/or additional restrictions with respect to further disclosure.

8.7 Onward transfers

The data importer shall not disclose the personal data to a third party located outside the European Union (^{3}) (in the same country as the data importer or in another third country, hereinafter 'onward transfer') unless the third party is or agrees to be bound by these Clauses, under the appropriate Module. Otherwise, an onward transfer by the data importer may only take place if:

(i) it is to a country benefitting from an adequacy decision pursuant to Article 45 of Regulation (EU) 2016/679 that covers the onward transfer;

(ii) the third party otherwise ensures appropriate safeguards pursuant to Articles 46 or 47 of Regulation (EU) 2016/679 with respect to the processing in question;

(iii) the third party enters into a binding instrument with the data importer ensuring the same level of data protection as under these Clauses, and the data importer provides a copy of these safeguards to the data exporter;

(iv) it is necessary for the establishment, exercise or defence of legal claims in the context of specific administrative, regulatory or judicial proceedings;

(v) it is necessary in order to protect the vital interests of the data subject or of another natural person; or

(vi) where none of the other conditions apply, the data importer has obtained the explicit consent of the data subject for an onward transfer in a specific situation, after having informed him/her of its purpose(s), the identity of the recipient and the possible risks of such transfer to him/her due to the lack of appropriate data protection safeguards. In this case, the data importer shall inform the data exporter and, at the request of the latter, shall transmit to it a copy of the information provided to the data subject.

Any onward transfer is subject to compliance by the data importer with all the other safeguards under these Clauses, in particular purpose limitation.

8.8 Processing under the authority of the data importer

The data importer shall ensure that any person acting under its authority, including a processor, processes the data only on its instructions.

8.9 Documentation and compliance

(a) Each Party shall be able to demonstrate compliance with its obligations under these Clauses. In particular, the data importer shall keep appropriate documentation of the processing activities carried out under its responsibility.

(b) The data importer shall make such documentation available to the competent supervisory authority on request.

MODULE TWO: Transfer controller to processor

8.1 Instructions

(a) The data importer shall process the personal data only on documented instructions from the data exporter. The data exporter may give such instructions throughout the duration of the contract.

(b) The data importer shall immediately inform the data exporter if it is unable to follow those instructions.

8.2 Purpose limitation

The data importer shall process the personal data only for the specific purpose(s) of the transfer, as set out in Annex I.B, unless on further instructions from the data exporter.

8.3 Transparency

On request, the data exporter shall make a copy of these Clauses, including the Appendix as completed by the Parties, available to the data subject free of charge. To the extent necessary to protect business secrets or other confidential information, including the measures described in Annex II and personal data, the data exporter may redact part of the text of the Appendix to these Clauses prior to sharing a copy, but shall provide a meaningful summary where the data subject would otherwise not be able to understand the its content or exercise his/her rights. On request, the Parties shall provide the data subject with the reasons for the redactions, to the extent possible without revealing the redacted information. This Clause is without prejudice to the obligations of the data exporter under Articles 13 and 14 of Regulation (EU) 2016/679.

8.4   Accuracy

If the data importer becomes aware that the personal data it has received is inaccurate, or has become outdated, it shall inform the data exporter without undue delay. In this case, the data importer shall cooperate with the data exporter to erase or rectify the data.

8.5   Duration of processing and erasure or return of data

Processing by the data importer shall only take place for the duration specified in Annex I.B. After the end of the provision of the processing services, the data importer shall, at the choice of the data exporter, delete all personal data processed on behalf of the data exporter and certify to the data exporter that it has done so, or return to the data exporter all personal data processed on its behalf and delete existing copies. Until the data is deleted or returned, the data importer shall continue to ensure compliance with these Clauses. In case of local laws applicable to the data importer that prohibit return or deletion of the personal data, the data importer warrants that it will continue to ensure compliance with these Clauses and will only process it to the extent and for as long as required under that local law. This is without prejudice to Clause 14, in particular the requirement for the data importer under Clause 14(e) to notify the data exporter throughout the duration of the contract if it has reason to believe that it is or has become subject to laws or practices not in line with the requirements under Clause 14(a).

8.6   Security of processing

(a)   The data importer and, during transmission, also the data exporter shall implement appropriate technical and organisational measures to ensure the security of the data, including protection against a breach of security leading to accidental or unlawful destruction, loss, alteration, unauthorised disclosure or access to that data (hereinafter 'personal data breach'). In assessing the appropriate level of security, the Parties shall take due account of the state of the art, the costs of implementation, the nature, scope, context and purpose(s) of processing and the risks involved in the processing for the data subjects. The Parties shall in particular consider having recourse to encryption or pseudonymisation, including during transmission, where the purpose of processing can be fulfilled in that manner. In case of pseudonymisation, the additional information for attributing the personal data to a specific data subject shall, where possible, remain under the exclusive control of the data exporter. In complying with its obligations under this paragraph, the data importer shall at least implement the technical and organisational measures specified in Annex II. The data importer shall carry out regular checks to ensure that these measures continue to provide an appropriate level of security.

(b)   The data importer shall grant access to the personal data to members of its personnel only to the extent strictly necessary for the implementation, management and monitoring of the contract. It shall ensure that persons authorised to process the personal data have committed themselves to confidentiality or are under an appropriate statutory obligation of confidentiality.

(c) In the event of a personal data breach concerning personal data processed by the data importer under these Clauses, the data importer shall take appropriate measures to address the breach, including measures to mitigate its adverse effects. The data importer shall also notify the data exporter without undue delay after having become aware of the breach. Such notification shall contain the details of a contact point where more information can be obtained, a description of the nature of the breach (including, where possible, categories and approximate number of data subjects and personal data records concerned), its likely consequences and the measures taken or proposed to address the breach including, where appropriate, measures to mitigate its possible adverse effects. Where, and in so far as, it is not possible to provide all information at the same time, the initial notification shall contain the information then available and further information shall, as it becomes available, subsequently be provided without undue delay.

(d) The data importer shall cooperate with and assist the data exporter to enable the data exporter to comply with its obligations under Regulation (EU) 2016/679, in particular to notify the competent supervisory authority and the affected data subjects, taking into account the nature of processing and the information available to the data importer.

8.7 Sensitive data

Where the transfer involves personal data revealing racial or ethnic origin, political opinions, religious or philosophical beliefs, or trade union membership, genetic data, or biometric data for the purpose of uniquely identifying a natural person, data concerning health or a person's sex life or sexual orientation, or data relating to criminal convictions and offences (hereinafter 'sensitive data'), the data importer shall apply the specific restrictions and/or additional safeguards described in Annex I.B.

8.8 Onward transfers

The data importer shall only disclose the personal data to a third party on documented instructions from the data exporter. In addition, the data may only be disclosed to a third party located outside the European Union ([4]) (in the same country as the data importer or in another third country, hereinafter 'onward transfer') if the third party is or agrees to be bound by these Clauses, under the appropriate Module, or if:

(i) the onward transfer is to a country benefitting from an adequacy decision pursuant to Article 45 of Regulation (EU) 2016/679 that covers the onward transfer;

(ii) the third party otherwise ensures appropriate safeguards pursuant to Articles 46 or 47 Regulation of (EU) 2016/679 with respect to the processing in question;

(iii) the onward transfer is necessary for the establishment, exercise or defence of legal claims in the context of specific administrative, regulatory or judicial proceedings; or

(iv) the onward transfer is necessary in order to protect the vital interests of the data subject or of another natural person.

Any onward transfer is subject to compliance by the data importer with all the other safeguards under these Clauses, in particular purpose limitation.

8.9 Documentation and compliance

(a) The data importer shall promptly and adequately deal with enquiries from the data exporter that relate to the processing under these Clauses.

(b) The Parties shall be able to demonstrate compliance with these Clauses. In particular, the data importer shall keep appropriate documentation on the processing activities carried out on behalf of the data exporter.

(c) The data importer shall make available to the data exporter all information necessary to demonstrate compliance with the obligations set out in these Clauses and at the data exporter's request, allow for and contribute to audits of the processing activities covered by these Clauses, at reasonable intervals or if there are indications of non-compliance. In deciding on a review or audit, the data exporter may take into account relevant certifications held by the data importer.

(d) The data exporter may choose to conduct the audit by itself or mandate an independent auditor. Audits may include inspections at the premises or physical facilities of the data importer and shall, where appropriate, be carried out with reasonable notice.

(e) The Parties shall make the information referred to in paragraphs (b) and (c), including the results of any audits, available to the competent supervisory authority on request.

MODULE THREE: Transfer processor to processor

8.1 Instructions

(a) The data exporter has informed the data importer that it acts as processor under the instructions of its controller(s), which the data exporter shall make available to the data importer prior to processing.

(b) The data importer shall process the personal data only on documented instructions from the controller, as communicated to the data importer by the data exporter, and any additional documented instructions from the data exporter. Such additional instructions shall not conflict with the instructions from the controller. The controller or data exporter may give further documented instructions regarding the data processing throughout the duration of the contract.

(c)   The data importer shall immediately inform the data exporter if it is unable to follow those instructions. Where the data importer is unable to follow the instructions from the controller, the data exporter shall immediately notify the controller.

(d)   The data exporter warrants that it has imposed the same data protection obligations on the data importer as set out in the contract or other legal act under Union or Member State law between the controller and the data exporter (⁵).

8.2   Purpose limitation

The data importer shall process the personal data only for the specific purpose(s) of the transfer, as set out in Annex I.B., unless on further instructions from the controller, as communicated to the data importer by the data exporter, or from the data exporter.

8.3   Transparency

On request, the data exporter shall make a copy of these Clauses, including the Appendix as completed by the Parties, available to the data subject free of charge. To the extent necessary to protect business secrets or other confidential information, including personal data, the data exporter may redact part of the text of the Appendix prior to sharing a copy, but shall provide a meaningful summary where the data subject would otherwise not be able to understand its content or exercise his/her rights. On request, the Parties shall provide the data subject with the reasons for the redactions, to the extent possible without revealing the redacted information.

8.4   Accuracy

If the data importer becomes aware that the personal data it has received is inaccurate, or has become outdated, it shall inform the data exporter without undue delay. In this case, the data importer shall cooperate with the data exporter to rectify or erase the data.

8.5   Duration of processing and erasure or return of data

Processing by the data importer shall only take place for the duration specified in Annex I.B. After the end of the provision of the processing services, the data importer shall, at the choice of the data exporter, delete all personal data processed on behalf of the controller and certify to the data exporter that it has done so, or return to the data exporter all personal data processed on its behalf and delete existing copies. Until the data is deleted or returned, the data importer shall continue to ensure compliance with these Clauses. In case of local laws applicable to the data importer that prohibit return or deletion of the personal data, the data importer warrants that it will continue to ensure compliance with these Clauses and will only process it to the extent and for as long as required under that local law. This is without prejudice to Clause 14, in particular the requirement for the data importer under Clause 14(e) to notify the data exporter throughout the duration of the contract if it has reason to believe that it is or has become subject to laws or practices not in line with the requirements under Clause 14(a).

8.6 Security of processing

(a) The data importer and, during transmission, also the data exporter shall implement appropriate technical and organisational measures to ensure the security of the data, including protection against a breach of security leading to accidental or unlawful destruction, loss, alteration, unauthorised disclosure or access to that data (hereinafter 'personal data breach'). In assessing the appropriate level of security, they shall take due account of the state of the art, the costs of implementation, the nature, scope, context and purpose(s) of processing and the risks involved in the processing for the data subject. The Parties shall in particular consider having recourse to encryption or pseudonymisation, including during transmission, where the purpose of processing can be fulfilled in that manner. In case of pseudonymisation, the additional information for attributing the personal data to a specific data subject shall, where possible, remain under the exclusive control of the data exporter or the controller. In complying with its obligations under this paragraph, the data importer shall at least implement the technical and organisational measures specified in Annex II. The data importer shall carry out regular checks to ensure that these measures continue to provide an appropriate level of security.

(b) The data importer shall grant access to the data to members of its personnel only to the extent strictly necessary for the implementation, management and monitoring of the contract. It shall ensure that persons authorised to process the personal data have committed themselves to confidentiality or are under an appropriate statutory obligation of confidentiality.

(c) In the event of a personal data breach concerning personal data processed by the data importer under these Clauses, the data importer shall take appropriate measures to address the breach, including measures to mitigate its adverse effects. The data importer shall also notify, without undue delay, the data exporter and, where appropriate and feasible, the controller after having become aware of the breach. Such notification shall contain the details of a contact point where more information can be obtained, a description of the nature of the breach (including, where possible, categories and approximate number of data subjects and personal data records concerned), its likely consequences and the measures taken or proposed to address the data breach, including measures to mitigate its possible adverse effects. Where, and in so far as, it is not possible to provide all information at the same time, the initial notification shall contain the information then available and further information shall, as it becomes available, subsequently be provided without undue delay.

(d)   The data importer shall cooperate with and assist the data exporter to enable the data exporter to comply with its obligations under Regulation (EU) 2016/679, in particular to notify its controller so that the latter may in turn notify the competent supervisory authority and the affected data subjects, taking into account the nature of processing and the information available to the data importer.

8.7   Sensitive data

Where the transfer involves personal data revealing racial or ethnic origin, political opinions, religious or philosophical beliefs, or trade union membership, genetic data, or biometric data for the purpose of uniquely identifying a natural person, data concerning health or a person's sex life or sexual orientation, or data relating to criminal convictions and offences (hereinafter 'sensitive data'), the data importer shall apply the specific restrictions and/or additional safeguards set out in Annex I.B.

8.8   Onward transfers

The data importer shall only disclose the personal data to a third party on documented instructions from the controller, as communicated to the data importer by the data exporter. In addition, the data may only be disclosed to a third party located outside the European Union ([6]) (in the same country as the data importer or in another third country, hereinafter 'onward transfer') if the third party is or agrees to be bound by these Clauses, under the appropriate Module, or if:

(i)   the onward transfer is to a country benefitting from an adequacy decision pursuant to Article 45 of Regulation (EU) 2016/679 that covers the onward transfer;

(ii)   the third party otherwise ensures appropriate safeguards pursuant to Articles 46 or 47 of Regulation (EU) 2016/679;

(iii)   the onward transfer is necessary for the establishment, exercise or defence of legal claims in the context of specific administrative, regulatory or judicial proceedings; or

(iv)   the onward transfer is necessary in order to protect the vital interests of the data subject or of another natural person.

Any onward transfer is subject to compliance by the data importer with all the other safeguards under these Clauses, in particular purpose limitation.

8.9   Documentation and compliance

(a)   The data importer shall promptly and adequately deal with enquiries from the data exporter or the controller that relate to the processing under these Clauses.

(b) The Parties shall be able to demonstrate compliance with these Clauses. In particular, the data importer shall keep appropriate documentation on the processing activities carried out on behalf of the controller.

(c) The data importer shall make all information necessary to demonstrate compliance with the obligations set out in these Clauses available to the data exporter, which shall provide it to the controller.

(d) The data importer shall allow for and contribute to audits by the data exporter of the processing activities covered by these Clauses, at reasonable intervals or if there are indications of non-compliance. The same shall apply where the data exporter requests an audit on instructions of the controller. In deciding on an audit, the data exporter may take into account relevant certifications held by the data importer.

(e) Where the audit is carried out on the instructions of the controller, the data exporter shall make the results available to the controller.

(f) The data exporter may choose to conduct the audit by itself or mandate an independent auditor. Audits may include inspections at the premises or physical facilities of the data importer and shall, where appropriate, be carried out with reasonable notice.

(g) The Parties shall make the information referred to in paragraphs (b) and (c), including the results of any audits, available to the competent supervisory authority on request.

MODULE FOUR: Transfer processor to controller

8.1 Instructions

(a) The data exporter shall process the personal data only on documented instructions from the data importer acting as its controller.

(b) The data exporter shall immediately inform the data importer if it is unable to follow those instructions, including if such instructions infringe Regulation (EU) 2016/679 or other Union or Member State data protection law.

(c) The data importer shall refrain from any action that would prevent the data exporter from fulfilling its obligations under Regulation (EU) 2016/679, including in the context of sub-processing or as regards cooperation with competent supervisory authorities.

(d) After the end of the provision of the processing services, the data exporter shall, at the choice of the data importer, delete all personal data processed on behalf of the data importer and certify to the data importer that it has done so, or return to the data importer all personal data processed on its behalf and delete existing copies.

8.2 Security of processing

(a) The Parties shall implement appropriate technical and organisational measures to ensure the security of the data, including during transmission, and protection against a breach of security leading to accidental or unlawful destruction, loss, alteration, unauthorised disclosure or access (hereinafter 'personal data breach'). In assessing the appropriate level of security, they shall take due account of the state of the art, the costs of implementation, the nature of the personal data ([7]), the nature, scope, context and purpose(s) of processing and the risks involved in the processing for the data subjects, and in particular consider having recourse to encryption or pseudonymisation, including during transmission, where the purpose of processing can be fulfilled in that manner.

(b) The data exporter shall assist the data importer in ensuring appropriate security of the data in accordance with paragraph (a). In case of a personal data breach concerning the personal data processed by the data exporter under these Clauses, the data exporter shall notify the data importer without undue delay after becoming aware of it and assist the data importer in addressing the breach.

(c) The data exporter shall ensure that persons authorised to process the personal data have committed themselves to confidentiality or are under an appropriate statutory obligation of confidentiality.

8.3 Documentation and compliance

(a) The Parties shall be able to demonstrate compliance with these Clauses.

(b) The data exporter shall make available to the data importer all information necessary to demonstrate compliance with its obligations under these Clauses and allow for and contribute to audits.

Clause 9

Use of sub-processors

MODULE TWO: Transfer controller to processor

(a) OPTION 1: SPECIFIC PRIOR AUTHORISATION The data importer shall not sub-contract any of its processing activities performed on behalf of the data exporter under these Clauses to a sub-processor without the data exporter's prior specific written authorisation. The data importer shall submit the request for specific authorisation at least [*Specify time period*] prior to the engagement of the sub-processor, together with the information necessary to enable the data exporter to decide on the authorisation. The list of sub-processors already authorised by the data exporter can be found in Annex III. The Parties shall keep Annex III up to date.

OPTION 2: GENERAL WRITTEN AUTHORISATION The data importer has the data exporter's general authorisation for the engagement of sub-processor(s) from an agreed list. The data importer shall specifically inform the data exporter in writing of any intended changes to that list through the addition or replacement of sub-processors at least [*Specify time period*] in advance, thereby giving the data exporter sufficient time to be able to object

279

to such changes prior to the engagement of the sub-processor(s). The data importer shall provide the data exporter with the information necessary to enable the data exporter to exercise its right to object.

(b) Where the data importer engages a sub-processor to carry out specific processing activities (on behalf of the data exporter), it shall do so by way of a written contract that provides for, in substance, the same data protection obligations as those binding the data importer under these Clauses, including in terms of third-party beneficiary rights for data subjects. (^{8}) The Parties agree that, by complying with this Clause, the data importer fulfils its obligations under Clause 8.8. The data importer shall ensure that the sub-processor complies with the obligations to which the data importer is subject pursuant to these Clauses.

(c) The data importer shall provide, at the data exporter's request, a copy of such a sub-processor agreement and any subsequent amendments to the data exporter. To the extent necessary to protect business secrets or other confidential information, including personal data, the data importer may redact the text of the agreement prior to sharing a copy.

(d) The data importer shall remain fully responsible to the data exporter for the performance of the sub-processor's obligations under its contract with the data importer. The data importer shall notify the data exporter of any failure by the sub-processor to fulfil its obligations under that contract.

(e) The data importer shall agree a third-party beneficiary clause with the sub-processor whereby – in the event the data importer has factually disappeared, ceased to exist in law or has become insolvent – the data exporter shall have the right to terminate the sub-processor contract and to instruct the sub-processor to erase or return the personal data.

MODULE THREE: Transfer processor to processor

(a) OPTION 1: SPECIFIC PRIOR AUTHORISATION The data importer shall not sub-contract any of its processing activities performed on behalf of the data exporter under these Clauses to a sub-processor without the prior specific written authorisation of the controller. The data importer shall submit the request for specific authorisation at least [*Specify time period*] prior to the engagement of the sub-processor, together with the information necessary to enable the controller to decide on the authorisation. It shall inform the data exporter of such engagement. The list of sub-processors already authorised by the controller can be found in Annex III. The Parties shall keep Annex III up to date.

OPTION 2: GENERAL WRITTEN AUTHORISATION The data importer has the controller's general authorisation for the engagement of sub-processor(s) from an agreed list. The data importer shall specifically inform the controller in writing of any intended changes to that list through the addition or replacement of sub-processors at least [*Specify time period*] in advance, thereby giving the controller sufficient time to be able to object to such changes prior to the engagement of the sub-processor(s). The data importer shall provide the controller with the information necessary to enable the controller to exercise its right to object. The data importer shall inform the data exporter of the engagement of the sub-processor(s).

(b) Where the data importer engages a sub-processor to carry out specific processing activities (on behalf of the controller), it shall do so by way of a written contract that provides for, in substance, the same data protection obligations as those binding the data importer under these Clauses, including in terms of third-party beneficiary rights for data subjects. (⁹) The Parties agree that, by complying with this Clause, the data importer fulfils its obligations under Clause 8.8. The data importer shall ensure that the sub-processor complies with the obligations to which the data importer is subject pursuant to these Clauses.

(c) The data importer shall provide, at the data exporter's or controller's request, a copy of such a sub-processor agreement and any subsequent amendments. To the extent necessary to protect business secrets or other confidential information, including personal data, the data importer may redact the text of the agreement prior to sharing a copy.

(d) The data importer shall remain fully responsible to the data exporter for the performance of the sub-processor's obligations under its contract with the data importer. The data importer shall notify the data exporter of any failure by the sub-processor to fulfil its obligations under that contract.

(e) The data importer shall agree a third-party beneficiary clause with the sub-processor whereby – in the event the data importer has factually disappeared, ceased to exist in law or has become insolvent – the data exporter shall have the right to terminate the sub-processor contract and to instruct the sub-processor to erase or return the personal data.

Clause 10

Data subject rights

MODULE ONE: Transfer controller to controller

(a) The data importer, where relevant with the assistance of the data exporter, shall deal with any enquiries and requests it receives from a data subject relating to the processing of his/her personal data and the exercise of his/her rights under these Clauses without undue delay and at the latest within one month of the receipt of the enquiry or request. (¹⁰) The data importer shall take appropriate measures to facilitate such enquiries, requests and the exercise of data subject rights. Any information provided to the data subject shall be in an intelligible and easily accessible form, using clear and plain language.

(b) In particular, upon request by the data subject the data importer shall, free of charge:

    (i) provide confirmation to the data subject as to whether personal data concerning him/her is being processed and, where this is the case, a copy of the data relating to him/her and the information in Annex I; if personal data has been or will be onward transferred, provide information on recipients or categories of recipients (as appropriate with a view to providing meaningful information) to which the personal data has been or will be onward transferred, the purpose of such onward transfers and their ground pursuant to Clause 8.7; and provide information on the right to lodge a complaint with a supervisory authority in accordance with Clause 12(c)(i);

(ii)　rectify inaccurate or incomplete data concerning the data subject;

(iii)　erase personal data concerning the data subject if such data is being or has been processed in violation of any of these Clauses ensuring third-party beneficiary rights, or if the data subject withdraws the consent on which the processing is based.

(c)　Where the data importer processes the personal data for direct marketing purposes, it shall cease processing for such purposes if the data subject objects to it.

(d)　The data importer shall not make a decision based solely on the automated processing of the personal data transferred (hereinafter 'automated decision'), which would produce legal effects concerning the data subject or similarly significantly affect him/her, unless with the explicit consent of the data subject or if authorised to do so under the laws of the country of destination, provided that such laws lays down suitable measures to safeguard the data subject's rights and legitimate interests. In this case, the data importer shall, where necessary in cooperation with the data exporter:

(i)　inform the data subject about the envisaged automated decision, the envisaged consequences and the logic involved; and

(ii)　implement suitable safeguards, at least by enabling the data subject to contest the decision, express his/her point of view and obtain review by a human being.

(e)　Where requests from a data subject are excessive, in particular because of their repetitive character, the data importer may either charge a reasonable fee taking into account the administrative costs of granting the request or refuse to act on the request.

(f)　The data importer may refuse a data subject's request if such refusal is allowed under the laws of the country of destination and is necessary and proportionate in a democratic society to protect one of the objectives listed in Article 23(1) of Regulation (EU) 2016/679.

(g)　If the data importer intends to refuse a data subject's request, it shall inform the data subject of the reasons for the refusal and the possibility of lodging a complaint with the competent supervisory authority and/or seeking judicial redress.

MODULE TWO: Transfer controller to processor

(a) The data importer shall promptly notify the data exporter of any request it has received from a data subject. It shall not respond to that request itself unless it has been authorised to do so by the data exporter.

(b) The data importer shall assist the data exporter in fulfilling its obligations to respond to data subjects' requests for the exercise of their rights under Regulation (EU) 2016/679. In this regard, the Parties shall set out in Annex II the appropriate technical and organisational measures, taking into account the nature of the processing, by which the assistance shall be provided, as well as the scope and the extent of the assistance required.

(c) In fulfilling its obligations under paragraphs (a) and (b), the data importer shall comply with the instructions from the data exporter.

MODULE THREE: Transfer processor to processor

(a) The data importer shall promptly notify the data exporter and, where appropriate, the controller of any request it has received from a data subject, without responding to that request unless it has been authorised to do so by the controller.

(b) The data importer shall assist, where appropriate in cooperation with the data exporter, the controller in fulfilling its obligations to respond to data subjects' requests for the exercise of their rights under Regulation (EU) 2016/679 or Regulation (EU) 2018/1725, as applicable. In this regard, the Parties shall set out in Annex II the appropriate technical and organisational measures, taking into account the nature of the processing, by which the assistance shall be provided, as well as the scope and the extent of the assistance required.

(c) In fulfilling its obligations under paragraphs (a) and (b), the data importer shall comply with the instructions from the controller, as communicated by the data exporter.

MODULE FOUR: Transfer processor to controller

The Parties shall assist each other in responding to enquiries and requests made by data subjects under the local law applicable to the data importer or, for data processing by the data exporter in the EU, under Regulation (EU) 2016/679.

Clause 11

Redress

(a) The data importer shall inform data subjects in a transparent and easily accessible format, through individual notice or on its website, of a contact point authorised to handle complaints. It shall deal promptly with any complaints it receives from a data subject.

[OPTION: The data importer agrees that data subjects may also lodge a complaint with an independent dispute resolution body ([11]) at no cost to the data subject. It shall inform the data subjects, in the manner set out in paragraph (a), of such redress mechanism and that they are not required to use it, or follow a particular sequence in seeking redress.]

MODULE ONE: Transfer controller to controller

MODULE TWO: Transfer controller to processor

MODULE THREE: Transfer processor to processor

(b) In case of a dispute between a data subject and one of the Parties as regards compliance with these Clauses, that Party shall use its best efforts to resolve the issue amicably in a timely fashion. The Parties shall keep each other informed about such disputes and, where appropriate, cooperate in resolving them.

(c) Where the data subject invokes a third-party beneficiary right pursuant to Clause 3, the data importer shall accept the decision of the data subject to:

   (i) lodge a complaint with the supervisory authority in the Member State of his/her habitual residence or place of work, or the competent supervisory authority pursuant to Clause 13;

   (ii) refer the dispute to the competent courts within the meaning of Clause 18.

(d) The Parties accept that the data subject may be represented by a not-for-profit body, organisation or association under the conditions set out in Article 80(1) of Regulation (EU) 2016/679.

(e) The data importer shall abide by a decision that is binding under the applicable EU or Member State law.

(f) The data importer agrees that the choice made by the data subject will not prejudice his/her substantive and procedural rights to seek remedies in accordance with applicable laws.

Clause 12

Liability

MODULE ONE: Transfer controller to controller

MODULE FOUR: Transfer processor to controller

(a) Each Party shall be liable to the other Party/ies for any damages it causes the other Party/ies by any breach of these Clauses.

(b) Each Party shall be liable to the data subject, and the data subject shall be entitled to receive compensation, for any material or non-material damages that the Party causes the data subject by breaching the third-party beneficiary rights under these Clauses. This is without prejudice to the liability of the data exporter under Regulation (EU) 2016/679.

(c) Where more than one Party is responsible for any damage caused to the data subject as a result of a breach of these Clauses, all responsible Parties shall be jointly and severally liable and the data subject is entitled to bring an action in court against any of these Parties.

(d) The Parties agree that if one Party is held liable under paragraph (c), it shall be entitled to claim back from the other Party/ies that part of the compensation corresponding to its/their responsibility for the damage.

(e) The data importer may not invoke the conduct of a processor or sub-processor to avoid its own liability.

MODULE TWO: Transfer controller to processor

MODULE THREE: Transfer processor to processor

(a) Each Party shall be liable to the other Party/ies for any damages it causes the other Party/ies by any breach of these Clauses.

(b) The data importer shall be liable to the data subject, and the data subject shall be entitled to receive compensation, for any material or non-material damages the data importer or its sub-processor causes the data subject by breaching the third-party beneficiary rights under these Clauses.

(c) Notwithstanding paragraph (b), the data exporter shall be liable to the data subject, and the data subject shall be entitled to receive compensation, for any material or non-material damages the data exporter or the data importer (or its sub-processor) causes the data subject by breaching the third-party beneficiary rights under these Clauses. This is without prejudice to the liability of the data exporter and, where the data exporter is a processor acting on behalf of a controller, to the liability of the controller under Regulation (EU) 2016/679 or Regulation (EU) 2018/1725, as applicable.

(d) The Parties agree that if the data exporter is held liable under paragraph (c) for damages caused by the data importer (or its sub-processor), it shall be entitled to claim back from the data importer that part of the compensation corresponding to the data importer's responsibility for the damage.

(e) Where more than one Party is responsible for any damage caused to the data subject as a result of a breach of these Clauses, all responsible Parties shall be jointly and severally liable and the data subject is entitled to bring an action in court against any of these Parties.

(f) The Parties agree that if one Party is held liable under paragraph (e), it shall be entitled to claim back from the other Party/ies that part of the compensation corresponding to its/their responsibility for the damage.

(g) The data importer may not invoke the conduct of a sub-processor to avoid its own liability.

285

Clause 13

Supervision

MODULE ONE: Transfer controller to controller

MODULE TWO: Transfer controller to processor

MODULE THREE: Transfer processor to processor

(a) [Where the data exporter is established in an EU Member State:] The supervisory authority with responsibility for ensuring compliance by the data exporter with Regulation (EU) 2016/679 as regards the data transfer, as indicated in Annex I.C, shall act as competent supervisory authority.

[Where the data exporter is not established in an EU Member State, but falls within the territorial scope of application of Regulation (EU) 2016/679 in accordance with its Article 3(2) and has appointed a representative pursuant to Article 27(1) of Regulation (EU) 2016/679:] The supervisory authority of the Member State in which the representative within the meaning of Article 27(1) of Regulation (EU) 2016/679 is established, as indicated in Annex I.C, shall act as competent supervisory authority.

[Where the data exporter is not established in an EU Member State, but falls within the territorial scope of application of Regulation (EU) 2016/679 in accordance with its Article 3(2) without however having to appoint a representative pursuant to Article 27(2) of Regulation (EU) 2016/679:] The supervisory authority of one of the Member States in which the data subjects whose personal data is transferred under these Clauses in relation to the offering of goods or services to them, or whose behaviour is monitored, are located, as indicated in Annex I.C, shall act as competent supervisory authority.

(b) The data importer agrees to submit itself to the jurisdiction of and cooperate with the competent supervisory authority in any procedures aimed at ensuring compliance with these Clauses. In particular, the data importer agrees to respond to enquiries, submit to audits and comply with the measures adopted by the supervisory authority, including remedial and compensatory measures. It shall provide the supervisory authority with written confirmation that the necessary actions have been taken.

SECTION III – LOCAL LAWS AND OBLIGATIONS IN CASE OF ACCESS BY PUBLIC AUTHORITIES

Clause 14

Local laws and practices affecting compliance with the Clauses

MODULE ONE: Transfer controller to controller

MODULE TWO: Transfer controller to processor

MODULE THREE: Transfer processor to processor

MODULE FOUR: Transfer processor to controller

(where the EU processor combines the personal data received from the third country-controller with personal data collected by the processor in the EU)

(a) The Parties warrant that they have no reason to believe that the laws and practices in the third country of destination applicable to the processing of the personal data by the data importer, including any requirements to disclose personal data or measures authorising access by public authorities, prevent the data importer from fulfilling its obligations under these Clauses. This is based on the understanding that laws and practices that respect the essence of the fundamental rights and freedoms and do not exceed what is necessary and proportionate in a democratic society to safeguard one of the objectives listed in Article 23(1) of Regulation (EU) 2016/679, are not in contradiction with these Clauses.

(b) The Parties declare that in providing the warranty in paragraph (a), they have taken due account in particular of the following elements:

(i) the specific circumstances of the transfer, including the length of the processing chain, the number of actors involved and the transmission channels used; intended onward transfers; the type of recipient; the purpose of processing; the categories and format of the transferred personal data; the economic sector in which the transfer occurs; the storage location of the data transferred;

(ii) the laws and practices of the third country of destination– including those requiring the disclosure of data to public authorities or authorising access by such authorities – relevant in light of the specific circumstances of the transfer, and the applicable limitations and safeguards ([12]);

(iii) any relevant contractual, technical or organisational safeguards put in place to supplement the safeguards under these Clauses, including measures applied during transmission and to the processing of the personal data in the country of destination.

(c) The data importer warrants that, in carrying out the assessment under paragraph (b), it has made its best efforts to provide the data exporter with relevant information and agrees that it will continue to cooperate with the data exporter in ensuring compliance with these Clauses.

(d) The Parties agree to document the assessment under paragraph (b) and make it available to the competent supervisory authority on request.

(e) The data importer agrees to notify the data exporter promptly if, after having agreed to these Clauses and for the duration of the contract, it has reason to believe that it is or has become subject to laws or practices not in line with the requirements under paragraph (a), including following a change in the laws of the third country or a measure (such as a disclosure request) indicating an application of such laws in practice that is not in line with the requirements in paragraph (a). [For Module Three: The data exporter shall forward the notification to the controller.]

(f) Following a notification pursuant to paragraph (e), or if the data exporter otherwise has reason to believe that the data importer can no longer fulfil its obligations under these Clauses, the data exporter shall promptly identify appropriate measures (e.g. technical or organisational measures to ensure security and confidentiality) to be adopted by the data exporter and/or data importer to address the situation [for Module Three:, if appropriate in consultation with the controller]. The data exporter shall suspend the data transfer if it considers that no appropriate safeguards for such transfer can be ensured, or if instructed by [for Module Three: the controller or] the competent supervisory authority to do so. In this case, the data exporter shall be entitled to terminate the contract, insofar as it concerns the processing of personal data under these Clauses. If the contract involves more than two Parties, the data exporter may exercise this right to termination only with respect to the relevant Party, unless the Parties have agreed otherwise. Where the contract is terminated pursuant to this Clause, Clause 16(d) and (e) shall apply.

Clause 15
Obligations of the data importer in case of access by public authorities

MODULE ONE: Transfer controller to controller

MODULE TWO: Transfer controller to processor

MODULE THREE: Transfer processor to processor

MODULE FOUR: Transfer processor to controller

(where the EU processor combines the personal data received from the third country-controller with personal data collected by the processor in the EU)

15.1 Notification

(a) The data importer agrees to notify the data exporter and, where possible, the data subject promptly (if necessary with the help of the data exporter) if it:

   (i) receives a legally binding request from a public authority, including judicial authorities, under the laws of the country of destination for the disclosure of personal data transferred pursuant to these Clauses; such notification shall include information about the personal data requested, the requesting authority, the legal basis for the request and the response provided; or

   (ii) becomes aware of any direct access by public authorities to personal data transferred pursuant to these Clauses in accordance with the laws of the country of destination; such notification shall include all information available to the importer.

[For Module Three: The data exporter shall forward the notification to the controller.]

(b) If the data importer is prohibited from notifying the data exporter and/ or the data subject under the laws of the country of destination, the data importer agrees to use its best efforts to obtain a waiver of the prohibition, with a view to communicating as much information as possible, as soon as possible. The data importer agrees to document its best efforts in order to be able to demonstrate them on request of the data exporter.

(c) Where permissible under the laws of the country of destination, the data importer agrees to provide the data exporter, at regular intervals for the duration of the contract, with as much relevant information as possible on the requests received (in particular, number of requests, type of data requested, requesting authority/ies, whether requests have been challenged and the outcome of such challenges, etc.). [For Module Three: The data exporter shall forward the information to the controller.]

(d) The data importer agrees to preserve the information pursuant to paragraphs (a) to (c) for the duration of the contract and make it available to the competent supervisory authority on request.

(e) Paragraphs (a) to (c) are without prejudice to the obligation of the data importer pursuant to Clause 14(e) and Clause 16 to inform the data exporter promptly where it is unable to comply with these Clauses.

15.2 Review of legality and data minimisation

(a) The data importer agrees to review the legality of the request for disclosure, in particular whether it remains within the powers granted to the requesting public authority, and to challenge the request if, after careful assessment, it concludes that there are reasonable grounds to consider that the request is unlawful under the laws of the country of destination, applicable obligations under international law and principles of international comity. The data importer shall, under the same conditions, pursue possibilities of appeal. When challenging a request, the data importer shall seek interim measures with a view to suspending the effects of the request until the competent judicial authority has decided on its merits. It shall not disclose the personal data requested until required to do so under the applicable procedural rules. These requirements are without prejudice to the obligations of the data importer under Clause 14(e).

(b) The data importer agrees to document its legal assessment and any challenge to the request for disclosure and, to the extent permissible under the laws of the country of destination, make the documentation available to the data exporter. It shall also make it available to the competent supervisory authority on request. [For Module Three: The data exporter shall make the assessment available to the controller.]

(c) The data importer agrees to provide the minimum amount of information permissible when responding to a request for disclosure, based on a reasonable interpretation of the request.

SECTION IV – FINAL PROVISIONS

Clause 16
Non-compliance with the Clauses and termination

(a) The data importer shall promptly inform the data exporter if it is unable to comply with these Clauses, for whatever reason.

(b) In the event that the data importer is in breach of these Clauses or unable to comply with these Clauses, the data exporter shall suspend the transfer of personal data to the data importer until compliance is again ensured or the contract is terminated. This is without prejudice to Clause 14(f).

(c) The data exporter shall be entitled to terminate the contract, insofar as it concerns the processing of personal data under these Clauses, where:

    (i) the data exporter has suspended the transfer of personal data to the data importer pursuant to paragraph (b) and compliance with these Clauses is not restored within a reasonable time and in any event within one month of suspension;

    (ii) the data importer is in substantial or persistent breach of these Clauses; or

    (iii) the data importer fails to comply with a binding decision of a competent court or supervisory authority regarding its obligations under these Clauses.

In these cases, it shall inform the competent supervisory authority [for Module Three: and the controller] of such non-compliance. Where the contract involves more than two Parties, the data exporter may exercise this right to termination only with respect to the relevant Party, unless the Parties have agreed otherwise.

(d) [For Modules One, Two and Three: Personal data that has been transferred prior to the termination of the contract pursuant to paragraph (c) shall at the choice of the data exporter immediately be returned to the data exporter or deleted in its entirety. The same shall apply to any copies of the data.] [For Module Four: Personal data collected by the data exporter in the EU that has been transferred prior to the termination of the contract pursuant to paragraph (c) shall immediately be deleted in its entirety, including any copy thereof.] The data importer shall certify the deletion of the data to the data exporter. Until the data is deleted or returned, the data importer shall continue to ensure compliance with these Clauses. In case of local laws applicable to the data importer that prohibit the return or deletion of the transferred personal data, the data importer warrants that it will continue to ensure compliance with these Clauses and will only process the data to the extent and for as long as required under that local law.

(e) Either Party may revoke its agreement to be bound by these Clauses where (i) the European Commission adopts a decision pursuant to Article 45(3) of Regulation (EU) 2016/679 that covers the transfer of personal data to which these Clauses apply; or (ii) Regulation (EU) 2016/679 becomes part of the legal framework of the country to which the personal data is transferred. This is without prejudice to other obligations applying to the processing in question under Regulation (EU) 2016/679.

Clause 17
Governing law

MODULE ONE: Transfer controller to controller

MODULE TWO: Transfer controller to processor

MODULE THREE: Transfer processor to processor

[OPTION 1: These Clauses shall be governed by the law of one of the EU Member States, provided such law allows for third-party beneficiary rights. The Parties agree that this shall be the law of _____ (*specify Member State*).]

[OPTION 2 (for Modules Two and Three): These Clauses shall be governed by the law of the EU Member State in which the data exporter is established. Where such law does not allow for third-party beneficiary rights, they shall be governed by the law of another EU Member State that does allow for third-party beneficiary rights. The Parties agree that this shall be the law of _____ (*specify Member State*).]

MODULE FOUR: Transfer processor to controller

These Clauses shall be governed by the law of a country allowing for third-party beneficiary rights. The Parties agree that this shall be the law of _____ (*specify country*).

Clause 18
Choice of forum and jurisdiction

MODULE ONE: Transfer controller to controller

MODULE TWO: Transfer controller to processor

MODULE THREE: Transfer processor to processor

(a) Any dispute arising from these Clauses shall be resolved by the courts of an EU Member State.

(b) The Parties agree that those shall be the courts of _____ (*specify Member State*).

(c) A data subject may also bring legal proceedings against the data exporter and/or data importer before the courts of the Member State in which he/she has his/her habitual residence.

(d) The Parties agree to submit themselves to the jurisdiction of such courts.

MODULE FOUR: Transfer processor to controller

Any dispute arising from these Clauses shall be resolved by the courts of _____ (*specify country*).

....

ANNEX I

A. LIST OF PARTIES

MODULE ONE: Transfer controller to controller

MODULE TWO: Transfer controller to processor

MODULE THREE: Transfer processor to processor

MODULE FOUR: Transfer processor to controller

Data exporter(s): [*Identity and contact details of the data exporter(s) and, where applicable, of its/their data protection officer and/or representative in the European Union*]

1. Name: ...

    Address: ...

    Contact person's name, position and contact details: ...

    Activities relevant to the data transferred under these Clauses: ...

    Signature and date: ...

    Role (controller/processor): ...

2. ...

Data importer(s): [*Identity and contact details of the data importer(s), including any contact person with responsibility for data protection*]

1. Name: ...

    Address: ...

    Contact person's name, position and contact details: ...

    Activities relevant to the data transferred under these Clauses: ...

    Signature and date: ...

    Role (controller/processor): ...

2. ...

B. DESCRIPTION OF TRANSFER

MODULE ONE: Transfer controller to controller

MODULE TWO: Transfer controller to processor

MODULE THREE: Transfer processor to processor

MODULE FOUR: Transfer processor to controller

Categories of data subjects whose personal data is transferred

…

Categories of personal data transferred

…

Sensitive data transferred (if applicable) and applied restrictions or safeguards that fully take into consideration the nature of the data and the risks involved, such as for instance strict purpose limitation, access restrictions (including access only for staff having followed specialised training), keeping a record of access to the data, restrictions for onward transfers or additional security measures.

…

The frequency of the transfer (e.g. whether the data is transferred on a one-off or continuous basis).

…

Nature of the processing

…

Purpose(s) of the data transfer and further processing

…

The period for which the personal data will be retained, or, if that is not possible, the criteria used to determine that period

…

For transfers to (sub-) processors, also specify subject matter, nature and duration of the processing

…

C. COMPETENT SUPERVISORY AUTHORITY

MODULE ONE: Transfer controller to controller

MODULE TWO: Transfer controller to processor

MODULE THREE: Transfer processor to processor

Identify the competent supervisory authority/ies in accordance with Clause 13

...

ANNEX II

TECHNICAL AND ORGANISATIONAL MEASURES INCLUDING
TECHNICAL AND ORGANISATIONAL MEASURES TO ENSURE THE
SECURITY OF THE DATA

MODULE ONE: Transfer controller to controller

MODULE TWO: Transfer controller to processor

MODULE THREE: Transfer processor to processor

EXPLANATORY NOTE:

The technical and organisational measures must be described in specific (and not generic) terms. See also the general comment on the first page of the Appendix, in particular on the need to clearly indicate which measures apply to each transfer/ set of transfers.

Description of the technical and organisational measures implemented by the data importer(s) (including any relevant certifications) to ensure an appropriate level of security, taking into account the nature, scope, context and purpose of the processing, and the risks for the rights and freedoms of natural persons.

[Examples of possible measures:

Measures of pseudonymisation and encryption of personal data

Measures for ensuring ongoing confidentiality, integrity, availability and resilience of processing systems and services

Measures for ensuring the ability to restore the availability and access to personal data in a timely manner in the event of a physical or technical incident

Processes for regularly testing, assessing and evaluating the effectiveness of technical and organisational measures in order to ensure the security of the processing

Measures for user identification and authorisation

Measures for the protection of data during transmission

Measures for the protection of data during storage

Measures for ensuring physical security of locations at which personal data are processed

Measures for ensuring events logging

Measures for ensuring system configuration, including default configuration

Measures for internal IT and IT security governance and management

Measures for certification/assurance of processes and products

Measures for ensuring data minimisation

Measures for ensuring data quality

Measures for ensuring limited data retention

Measures for ensuring accountability

Measures for allowing data portability and ensuring erasure]

For transfers to (sub-) processors, also describe the specific technical and organisational measures to be taken by the (sub-) processor to be able to provide assistance to the controller and, for transfers from a processor to a sub-processor, to the data exporter

ANNEX III

LIST OF SUB-PROCESSORS

MODULE TWO: Transfer controller to processor

MODULE THREE: Transfer processor to processor

EXPLANATORY NOTE:

This Annex must be completed for Modules Two and Three, in case of the specific authorisation of sub-processors (Clause 9(a), Option 1).

The controller has authorised the use of the following sub-processors:

1. Name: ...

    Address: ...

    Contact person's name, position and contact details: ...

    Description of processing (including a clear delimitation of responsibilities in case several sub-processors are authorised): ...

2. ...

SCHEDULE 9

EU-US Transfers: Trans-Atlantic Data Privacy Framework (replacing Privacy Shield)

EU COMMISSION STATEMENT 2022

The European Commission and the United States reached an agreement in principle for a Trans-Atlantic Data Privacy Framework.

Key principles

- Based on the new framework, data will be able to flow freely and safely between the EU and participating U.S. companies

- A new set of rules and binding safeguards to limit access to data by U.S. intelligence authorities to what is necessary and proportionate to protect national security; U.S. intelligence agencies will adopt procedures to ensure effective oversight of new privacy and civil liberties standards

- A new two-tier redress system to investigate and resolve complaints of Europeans on access of data by U.S. Intelligence authorities, which includes a Data Protection Review

Court

- Strong obligations for companies processing data transferred from the EU, which will continue to include the requirement to self-certify their adherence to the Principles through the U.S. Department of Commerce

- Specific monitoring and review mechanisms

Benefits of the deal

- Adequate protection of Europeans' data transferred to the US, addressing the ruling of the European Court of Justice (Schrems II)

- Safe and secure data flows

- Durable and reliable legal basis

- Competitive digital economy and economic cooperation

- Continued data flows underpinning €900 billion in cross-border commerce every year

Next steps: The agreement in principle will now be translated into legal documents. The U.S. commitments will be included in an Executive Order that will form the basis of a draft adequacy decision by the Commission to put in place the new Trans-Atlantic Data Privacy Framework.

US Order: Executive Order on Enhancing Safeguards for United States Signals Intelligence Activities

By the authority vested in me as President by the Constitution and the laws of the United States of America, it is hereby ordered as follows:

SECTION 1. PURPOSE.

The United States collects signals intelligence so that its national security decisionmakers have access to the timely, accurate, and insightful information necessary to advance the national security interests of the United States and to protect its citizens and the citizens of its allies and partners from harm. Signals intelligence capabilities are a major reason we have been able to adapt to a dynamic and challenging security environment, and the United States must preserve and continue to develop robust and technologically advanced signals intelligence capabilities to protect our security and that of our allies and partners. At the same time, the United States recognizes that signals intelligence activities must take into account that all persons should be treated with dignity and respect, regardless of their nationality or wherever they might reside, and that all persons have legitimate privacy interests in the handling of their personal information. Therefore, this order establishes safeguards for such signals intelligence activities.

SEC. 2. SIGNALS INTELLIGENCE ACTIVITIES.

(a) Principles. Signals intelligence activities shall be authorized and conducted consistent with the following principles:

    (i) Signals intelligence activities shall be authorized by statute or by Executive Order, proclamation, or other Presidential directive and undertaken in accordance with the Constitution and with applicable statutes and Executive Orders, proclamations, and other Presidential directives.

    (ii) Signals intelligence activities shall be subject to appropriate safeguards, which shall ensure that privacy and civil liberties are integral considerations in the planning and implementation of such activities so that:

        (A) signals intelligence activities shall be conducted only following a determination, based on a reasonable assessment of all relevant factors, that the activities are necessary to advance a validated intelligence priority, although signals intelligence does not have to be the sole means available or used for advancing aspects of the validated intelligence priority; and

(B) signals intelligence activities shall be conducted only to the extent and in a manner that is proportionate to the validated intelligence priority for which they have been authorized, with the aim of achieving a proper balance between the importance of the validated intelligence priority being advanced and the impact on the privacy and civil liberties of all persons, regardless of their nationality or wherever they might reside.

(iii) Signals intelligence activities shall be subjected to rigorous oversight in order to ensure that they comport with the principles identified above.

(b) Objectives. Signals intelligence collection activities shall be conducted in pursuit of legitimate objectives.

(i) Legitimate objectives.

(A) Signals intelligence collection activities shall be conducted only in pursuit of one or more of the following objectives:

(1) understanding or assessing the capabilities, intentions, or activities of a foreign government, a foreign military, a faction of a foreign nation, a foreign-based political organization, or an entity acting on behalf of or controlled by any such foreign government, military, faction, or political organization, in order to protect the national security of the United States and of its allies and partners;

(2) understanding or assessing the capabilities, intentions, or activities of foreign organizations, including international terrorist organizations, that pose a current or potential threat to the national security of the United States or of its allies or partners;

(3) understanding or assessing transnational threats that impact global security, including climate and other ecological change, public health risks, humanitarian threats, political instability, and geographic rivalry;

(4) protecting against foreign military capabilities and activities;

(5) protecting against terrorism, the taking of hostages, and the holding of individuals captive (including the identification, location, and rescue of hostages and captives) conducted by or on behalf of a foreign government, foreign organization, or foreign person;

(6) protecting against espionage, sabotage, assassination, or other intelligence activities conducted by, on behalf of, or with the assistance of a foreign government, foreign organization, or foreign person;

(7) protecting against threats from the development, possession, or proliferation of weapons of mass destruction or related technologies and threats conducted by, on behalf of, or with the assistance of a foreign government, foreign organization, or foreign person;

(8) protecting against cybersecurity threats created or exploited by, or malicious cyber activities conducted by or on behalf of, a foreign government, foreign organization, or foreign person;

(9) protecting against threats to the personnel of the United States or of its allies or partners;

(10) protecting against transnational criminal threats, including illicit finance and sanctions evasion related to one or more of the other objectives identified in subsection (b)(i) of this section;

(11) protecting the integrity of elections and political processes, government property, and United States infrastructure (both physical and electronic) from activities conducted by, on behalf of, or with the assistance of a foreign government, foreign organization, or foreign person; and

(12) advancing collection or operational capabilities or activities in order to further a legitimate objective identified in subsection (b)(i) of this section.

(B) The President may authorize updates to the list of objectives in light of new national security imperatives, such as new or heightened threats to the national security of the United States, for which the President determines that signals intelligence collection activities may be used. The Director of National Intelligence (Director) shall publicly release any updates to the list of objectives authorized by the President, unless the President determines that doing so would pose a risk to the national security of the United States.

(ii) Prohibited objectives.

(A) Signals intelligence collection activities shall not be conducted for the purpose of:

(1) suppressing or burdening criticism, dissent, or the free expression of ideas or political opinions by individuals or the press;

      (2)   suppressing or restricting legitimate privacy interests;

      (3)   suppressing or restricting a right to legal counsel; or

      (4)   disadvantaging persons based on their ethnicity, race, gender, gender identity, sexual orientation, or religion.

(B)   It is not a legitimate objective to collect foreign private commercial information or trade secrets to afford a competitive advantage to United States companies and United States business sectors commercially. The collection of such information is authorized only to protect the national security of the United States or of its allies or partners.

(iii)   Validation of signals intelligence collection priorities.

(A)   Under section 102A of the National Security Act of 1947, as amended (50 U.S.C. 3024), the Director must establish priorities for the Intelligence Community to ensure the timely and effective collection of national intelligence, including national intelligence collected through signals intelligence. The Director does this through the National Intelligence Priorities Framework (NIPF), which the Director maintains and presents to the President, through the Assistant to the President for National Security Affairs, on a regular basis. In order to ensure that signals intelligence collection activities are undertaken to advance legitimate objectives, before presenting the NIPF or any successor framework that identifies intelligence priorities to the President, the Director shall obtain from the Civil Liberties Protection Officer of the Office of the Director of National Intelligence (CLPO) an assessment as to whether, with regard to anticipated signals intelligence collection activities, each of the intelligence priorities identified in the NIPF or successor framework:

      (1)   advances one or more of the legitimate objectives set forth in subsection (b)(i) of this section;

      (2)   neither was designed nor is anticipated to result in signals intelligence collection in contravention of the prohibited objectives set forth in subsection (b)(ii) of this section; and

      (3)   was established after appropriate consideration for the privacy and civil liberties of all persons, regardless of their nationality or wherever they might reside.

(B)   If the Director disagrees with any aspect of the CLPO's assessment with respect to any of the intelligence priorities identified in the NIPF or successor framework, the Director shall include the CLPO's assessment and the Director's views when presenting the NIPF to the President.

(c)   Privacy and civil liberties safeguards. The following safeguards shall fulfill the principles contained in subsections (a)(ii) and (a)(iii) of this section.

(i)   Collection of signals intelligence.

   (A) The United States shall conduct signals intelligence collection
        activities only following a determination that a specific signals
        intelligence collection activity, based on a reasonable assessment
        of all relevant factors, is necessary to advance a validated
        intelligence priority, although signals intelligence does not have
        to be the sole means available or used for advancing aspects of
        the validated intelligence priority; it could be used, for example,
        to ensure alternative pathways for validation or for maintaining
        reliable access to the same information. In determining whether
        to collect signals intelligence consistent with this principle,
        the United States — through an element of the Intelligence
        Community or through an interagency committee consisting
        in whole or in part of the heads of elements of the Intelligence
        Community, the heads of departments containing such elements,
        or their designees — shall consider the availability, feasibility,
        and appropriateness of other less intrusive sources and methods
        for collecting the information necessary to advance a validated
        intelligence priority, including from diplomatic and public
        sources, and shall prioritize such available, feasible, and
        appropriate alternatives to signals intelligence.

   (B) Signals intelligence collection activities shall be as tailored as
        feasible to advance a validated intelligence priority and, taking
        due account of relevant factors, not disproportionately impact
        privacy and civil liberties. Such factors may include, depending
        on the circumstances, the nature of the pursued objective; the
        feasible steps taken to limit the scope of the collection to the
        authorized purpose; the intrusiveness of the collection activity,
        including its duration; the probable contribution of the collection
        to the objective pursued; the reasonably foreseeable consequences
        to individuals, including unintended third parties; the nature and
        sensitivity of the data to be collected; and the safeguards afforded
        to the information collected.

   (C) For purposes of subsection (c)(i) of this section, the scope of a
        specific signals intelligence collection activity may include, for
        example, a specific line of effort or target, as appropriate.

(ii)   Bulk collection of signals intelligence.

   (A) Targeted collection shall be prioritized. The bulk collection
        of signals intelligence shall be authorized only based on a
        determination — by an element of the Intelligence Community
        or through an interagency committee consisting in whole or in
        part of the heads of elements of the Intelligence Community,
        the heads of departments containing such elements, or their
        designees — that the information necessary to advance a
        validated intelligence priority cannot reasonably be obtained

303

by targeted collection. When it is determined to be necessary to engage in bulk collection in order to advance a validated intelligence priority, the element of the Intelligence Community shall apply reasonable methods and technical measures in order to limit the data collected to only what is necessary to advance a validated intelligence priority, while minimizing the collection of non-pertinent information.

(B) Each element of the Intelligence Community that collects signals intelligence through bulk collection shall use such information only in pursuit of one or more of the following objectives:

(1) protecting against terrorism, the taking of hostages, and the holding of individuals captive (including the identification, location, and rescue of hostages and captives) conducted by or on behalf of a foreign government, foreign organization, or foreign person;

(2) protecting against espionage, sabotage, assassination, or other intelligence activities conducted by, on behalf of, or with the assistance of a foreign government, foreign organization, or foreign person;

(3) protecting against threats from the development, possession, or proliferation of weapons of mass destruction or related technologies and threats conducted by, on behalf of, or with the assistance of a foreign government, foreign organization, or foreign person;

(4) protecting against cybersecurity threats created or exploited by, or malicious cyber activities conducted by or on behalf of, a foreign government, foreign organization, or foreign person;

(5) protecting against threats to the personnel of the United States or of its allies or partners; and

(6) protecting against transnational criminal threats, including illicit finance and sanctions evasion related to one or more of the other objectives identified in subsection (c)(ii) of this section.

(C) The President may authorize updates to the list of objectives in light of new national security imperatives, such as new or heightened threats to the national security of the United States, for which the President determines that bulk collection may be used. The Director shall publicly release any updates to the list of objectives authorized by the President, unless the President determines that doing so would pose a risk to the national security of the United States.

(D) In order to minimize any impact on privacy and civil liberties, a targeted signals intelligence collection activity that temporarily uses data acquired without discriminants (for example, without specific identifiers or selection terms) shall be subject to the safeguards described in this subsection, unless such data is:

   (1) used only to support the initial technical phase of the targeted signals intelligence collection activity;

   (2) retained for only the short period of time required to complete this phase; and

   (3) thereafter deleted.

(iii) Handling of personal information collected through signals intelligence.

   (A) Minimization. Each element of the Intelligence Community that handles personal information collected through signals intelligence shall establish and apply policies and procedures designed to minimize the dissemination and retention of personal information collected through signals intelligence.

      (1) Dissemination. Each element of the Intelligence Community that handles personal information collected through signals intelligence:

         (a) shall disseminate non-United States persons' personal information collected through signals intelligence only if it involves one or more of the comparable types of information that section 2.3 of Executive Order 12333 of December 4, 1981 (United States Intelligence Activities), as amended, states may be disseminated in the case of information concerning United States persons;

         (b) shall not disseminate personal information collected through signals intelligence solely because of a person's nationality or country of residence;

         (c) shall disseminate within the United States Government personal information collected through signals intelligence only if an authorized and appropriately trained individual has a reasonable belief that the personal information will be appropriately protected and that the recipient has a need to know the information;

         (d) shall take due account of the purpose of the dissemination, the nature and extent of the personal information being disseminated, and the potential for harmful impact on the person or persons concerned before disseminating personal information collected through signals intelligence to recipients outside the United States Government, including to a foreign government or international organization; and

(e) shall not disseminate personal information collected through signals intelligence for the purpose of circumventing the provisions of this order.

(2) Retention. Each element of the Intelligence Community that handles personal information collected through signals intelligence:

(a) shall retain non-United States persons' personal information collected through signals intelligence only if the retention of comparable information concerning United States persons would be permitted under applicable law and shall subject such information to the same retention periods that would apply to comparable information concerning United States persons;

(b) shall subject non-United States persons' personal information collected through signals intelligence for which no final retention determination has been made to the same temporary retention periods that would apply to comparable information concerning United States persons; and

(c) shall delete non-United States persons' personal information collected through signals intelligence that may no longer be retained in the same manner that comparable information concerning United States persons would be deleted.

(B) Data security and access. Each element of the Intelligence Community that handles personal information collected through signals intelligence:

(1) shall process and store personal information collected through signals intelligence under conditions that provide appropriate protection and prevent access by unauthorized persons, consistent with the applicable safeguards for sensitive information contained in relevant Executive Orders, proclamations, other Presidential directives, Intelligence Community directives, and associated policies;

(2) shall limit access to such personal information to authorized personnel who have a need to know the information to perform their mission and have received appropriate training on the requirements of applicable United States law, as described in policies and procedures issued under subsection (c)(iv) of this section; and

(3) shall ensure that personal information collected through signals intelligence for which no final retention determination has been made is accessed only in order to make or support such a determination or to conduct authorized administrative, testing, development, security, or oversight functions.

(C) Data quality. Each element of the Intelligence Community that handles personal information collected through signals intelligence shall include such personal information in intelligence products only as consistent with applicable Intelligence Community standards for accuracy and objectivity, with a focus on applying standards relating to the quality and reliability of the information, consideration of alternative sources of information and interpretations of data, and objectivity in performing analysis.

(D) Queries of bulk collection. Each element of the Intelligence Community that conducts queries of unminimized signals intelligence obtained by bulk collection shall do so consistent with the permissible uses of signals intelligence obtained by bulk collection identified in subsection (c)(ii)(B) of this section and according to policies and procedures issued under subsection (c)(iv) of this section, which shall appropriately take into account the impact on the privacy and civil liberties of all persons, regardless of their nationality or wherever they might reside.

(E) Documentation. In order to facilitate the oversight processes set forth in subsection (d) of this section and the redress mechanism set forth in section 3 of this order, each element of the Intelligence Community that engages in signals intelligence collection activities shall maintain documentation to the extent reasonable in light of the nature and type of collection at issue and the context in which it is collected. The content of any such documentation may vary based on the circumstances but shall, to the extent reasonable, provide the factual basis pursuant to which the element of the Intelligence Community, based on a reasonable assessment of all relevant factors, assesses that the signals intelligence collection activity is necessary to advance a validated intelligence priority.

(iv) Update and publication of policies and procedures. The head of each element of the Intelligence Community:

(A) shall continue to use the policies and procedures issued pursuant to Presidential Policy Directive 28 of January 17, 2014 (Signals Intelligence Activities) (PPD-28), until they are updated pursuant to subsection (c)(iv)(B) of this section;

(B) shall, within 1 year of the date of this order, in consultation with the Attorney General, the CLPO, and the Privacy and Civil Liberties Oversight Board (PCLOB), update those policies and

307

procedures as necessary to implement the privacy and civil liberties safeguards in this order; and

(C) shall, within 1 year of the date of this order, release these policies and procedures publicly to the maximum extent possible, consistent with the protection of intelligence sources and methods, in order to enhance the public's understanding of, and to promote public trust in, the safeguards pursuant to which the United States conducts signals intelligence activities.

(v) Review by the PCLOB.

(A) Nature of review. Consistent with applicable law, the PCLOB is encouraged to conduct a review of the updated policies and procedures described in subsection (c)(iv)(B) of this section once they have been issued to ensure that they are consistent with the enhanced safeguards contained in this order.

(B) Consideration of review. Within 180 days of completion of any review by the PCLOB described in subsection (c)(v)(A) of this section, the head of each element of the Intelligence Community shall carefully consider and shall implement or otherwise address all recommendations contained in such review, consistent with applicable law.

(d) Subjecting signals intelligence activities to rigorous oversight. The actions directed in this subsection are designed to build on the oversight mechanisms that elements of the Intelligence Community already have in place, in order to further ensure that signals intelligence activities are subjected to rigorous oversight.

(i) Legal, oversight, and compliance officials. Each element of the Intelligence Community that collects signals intelligence:

(A) shall have in place senior-level legal, oversight, and compliance officials who conduct periodic oversight of signals intelligence activities, including an Inspector General, a Privacy and Civil Liberties Officer, and an officer or officers in a designated compliance role with the authority to conduct oversight of and ensure compliance with applicable United States law;

(B) shall provide such legal, oversight, and compliance officials access to all information pertinent to carrying out their oversight responsibilities under this subsection, consistent with the protection of intelligence sources or methods, including their oversight responsibilities to ensure that any appropriate actions are taken to remediate an incident of non-compliance with applicable United States law; and

(C) shall not take any actions designed to impede or improperly influence such legal, oversight, and compliance officials in carrying out their oversight responsibilities under this subsection.

(ii) Training. Each element of the Intelligence Community shall maintain appropriate training requirements to ensure that all employees with access to signals intelligence know and understand the requirements of this order and the policies and procedures for reporting and remediating incidents of non-compliance with applicable United States law.

(iii) Significant incidents of non-compliance.

(A) Each element of the Intelligence Community shall ensure that, if a legal, oversight, or compliance official, as described in subsection (d)(i) of this section, or any other employee, identifies a significant incident of non-compliance with applicable United States law, the incident is reported promptly to the head of the element of the Intelligence Community, the head of the executive department or agency (agency) containing the element of the Intelligence Community (to the extent relevant), and the Director.

(B) Upon receipt of such report, the head of the element of the Intelligence Community, the head of the agency containing the element of the Intelligence Community (to the extent relevant), and the Director shall ensure that any necessary actions are taken to remediate and prevent the recurrence of the significant incident of non-compliance.

(e) Savings clause. Provided the signals intelligence collection is conducted consistent with and in the manner prescribed by this section of this order, this order does not limit any signals intelligence collection technique authorized under the National Security Act of 1947, as amended (50 U.S.C. 3001 et seq.), the Foreign Intelligence Surveillance Act of 1978, as amended (50 U.S.C. 1801 et seq.) (FISA), Executive Order 12333, or other applicable law or Presidential directive.

SEC. 3. SIGNALS INTELLIGENCE REDRESS MECHANISM.

(a) Purpose. This section establishes a redress mechanism to review qualifying complaints transmitted by the appropriate public authority in a qualifying state concerning United States signals intelligence activities for any covered violation of United States law and, if necessary, appropriate remediation.

(b) Process for submission of qualifying complaints. Within 60 days of the date of this order, the Director, in consultation with the Attorney General and the heads of elements of the Intelligence Community that collect or handle personal information collected through signals intelligence, shall establish a process for the submission of qualifying complaints transmitted by the appropriate public authority in a qualifying state.

(c) Initial investigation of qualifying complaints by the CLPO.

(i) Establishment. The Director, in consultation with the Attorney General, shall establish a process that authorizes the CLPO to investigate, review, and, as necessary, order appropriate remediation

309

for qualifying complaints. This process shall govern how the CLPO will review qualifying complaints in a manner that protects classified or otherwise privileged or protected information and shall ensure, at a minimum, that for each qualifying complaint the CLPO shall:

(A) review information necessary to investigate the qualifying complaint;

(B) exercise its statutory and delegated authority to determine whether there was a covered violation by:

    (i) taking into account both relevant national security interests and applicable privacy protections;

    (ii) giving appropriate deference to any relevant determinations made by national security officials; and

    (iii) applying the law impartially;

(C) determine the appropriate remediation for any covered violation;

(D) provide a classified report on information indicating a violation of any authority subject to the oversight of the Foreign Intelligence Surveillance Court (FISC) to the Assistant Attorney General for National Security, who shall report violations to the FISC in accordance with its rules of procedure;

(E) after the review is completed, inform the complainant, through the appropriate public authority in a qualifying state and without confirming or denying that the complainant was subject to United States signals intelligence activities, that:

    (1) 'the review either did not identify any covered violations or the Civil Liberties Protection Officer of the Office of the Director of National Intelligence issued a determination requiring appropriate remediation';

    (2) the complainant or an element of the Intelligence Community may, as prescribed in the regulations issued by the Attorney General pursuant to section 3(d)(i) of this order, apply for review of the CLPO's determinations by the Data Protection Review Court described in subsection (d) of this section; and

    (3) if either the complainant or an element of the Intelligence Community applies for review by the Data Protection Review Court, a special advocate will be selected by the Data Protection Review Court to advocate regarding the complainant's interest in the matter;

(F) maintain appropriate documentation of its review of the qualifying complaint and produce a classified decision explaining the basis for its factual findings, determination with respect to whether a covered violation occurred, and determination of the appropriate

310

remediation in the event there was such a violation, consistent with its statutory and delegated authority;

(G) prepare a classified ex parte record of review, which shall consist of the appropriate documentation of its review of the qualifying complaint and the classified decision described in subsection (c) (i)(F) of this section; and

(H) provide any necessary support to the Data Protection Review Court.

(ii) Binding effect. Each element of the Intelligence Community, and each agency containing an element of the Intelligence Community, shall comply with any determination by the CLPO to undertake appropriate remediation pursuant to subsection (c)(i)(C) of this section, subject to any contrary determination by the Data Protection Review Court.

(iii) Assistance. Each element of the Intelligence Community shall provide the CLPO with access to information necessary to conduct the reviews described in subsection (c)(i) of this section, consistent with the protection of intelligence sources and methods, and shall not take any actions designed to impede or improperly influence the CLPO's reviews. Privacy and civil liberties officials within elements of the Intelligence Community shall also support the CLPO as it performs the reviews described in subsection (c)(i) of this section.

(iv) Independence. The Director shall not interfere with a review by the CLPO of a qualifying complaint under subsection (c)(i) of this section; nor shall the Director remove the CLPO for any actions taken pursuant to this order, except for instances of misconduct, malfeasance, breach of security, neglect of duty, or incapacity.

(d) Data Protection Review Court.

(i) Establishment. The Attorney General is authorized to and shall establish a process to review determinations made by the CLPO under subsection (c)(i) of this section. In exercising that authority, the Attorney General shall, within 60 days of the date of this order, promulgate regulations establishing a Data Protection Review Court to exercise the Attorney General's authority to review such determinations. These regulations shall, at a minimum, provide that:

(A) The Attorney General, in consultation with the Secretary of Commerce, the Director, and the PCLOB, shall appoint individuals to serve as judges on the Data Protection Review Court, who shall be legal practitioners with appropriate experience in the fields of data privacy and national security law, giving weight to individuals with prior judicial experience, and who shall not be, at the time of their initial appointment, employees of the United States Government. During their term of appointment on the Data Protection Review Court, such judges shall not have any official duties or employment within

311

the United States Government other than their official duties and employment as judges on the Data Protection Review Court.

(B) Upon receipt of an application for review filed by the complainant or an element of the Intelligence Community of a determination made by the CLPO under subsection (c) of this section, a three-judge panel of the Data Protection Review Court shall be convened to review the application. Service on the Data Protection Review Court panel shall require that the judge hold the requisite security clearances to access classified national security information.

(C) Upon being convened, the Data Protection Review Court panel shall select a special advocate through procedures prescribed in the Attorney General's regulations. The special advocate shall assist the panel in its consideration of the application for review, including by advocating regarding the complainant's interest in the matter and ensuring that the Data Protection Review Court panel is well informed of the issues and the law with respect to the matter. Service as a special advocate shall require that the special advocate hold the requisite security clearances to access classified national security information and to adhere to restrictions prescribed in the Attorney General's regulations on communications with the complainant to ensure the protection of classified or otherwise privileged or protected information.

(D) The Data Protection Review Court panel shall impartially review the determinations made by the CLPO with respect to whether a covered violation occurred and the appropriate remediation in the event there was such a violation. The review shall be based at a minimum on the classified ex parte record of review described in subsection (c)(i)(F) of this section and information or submissions provided by the complainant, the special advocate, or an element of the Intelligence Community. In reviewing determinations made by the CLPO, the Data Protection Review Court panel shall be guided by relevant decisions of the United States Supreme Court in the same way as are courts established under Article III of the United States Constitution, including those decisions regarding appropriate deference to relevant determinations of national security officials.

(E) In the event that the Data Protection Review Court panel disagrees with any of the CLPO's determinations with respect to whether a covered violation occurred or the appropriate remediation in the event there was such a violation, the panel shall issue its own determinations.

(F) The Data Protection Review Court panel shall provide a classified report on information indicating a violation of any authority subject to the oversight of the FISC to the Assistant Attorney

General for National Security, who shall report violations to the FISC in accordance with its rules of procedure.

(G) After the review is completed, the CLPO shall be informed of the Data Protection Review Court panel's determinations through procedures prescribed by the Attorney General's regulations.

(H) After a review is completed in response to a complainant's application for review, the Data Protection Review Court, through procedures prescribed by the Attorney General's regulations, shall inform the complainant, through the appropriate public authority in a qualifying state and without confirming or denying that the complainant was subject to United States signals intelligence activities, that 'the review either did not identify any covered violations or the Data Protection Review Court issued a determination requiring appropriate remediation.'

(ii) Binding effect. Each element of the Intelligence Community, and each agency containing an element of the Intelligence Community, shall comply with any determination by a Data Protection Review Court panel to undertake appropriate remediation.

(iii) Assistance. Each element of the Intelligence Community shall provide the CLPO with access to information necessary to conduct the review described in subsection (d)(i) of this section, consistent with the protection of intelligence sources and methods, that a Data Protection Review Court panel requests from the CLPO and shall not take any actions for the purpose of impeding or improperly influencing a panel's review.

(iv) Independence. The Attorney General shall not interfere with a review by a Data Protection Review Court panel of a determination the CLPO made regarding a qualifying complaint under subsection (c)(i) of this section; nor shall the Attorney General remove any judges appointed as provided in subsection (d)(i)(A) of this section, or remove any judge from service on a Data Protection Review Court panel, except for instances of misconduct, malfeasance, breach of security, neglect of duty, or incapacity, after taking due account of the standards in the Rules for Judicial-Conduct and Judicial-Disability Proceedings promulgated by the Judicial Conference of the United States pursuant to the Judicial Conduct and Disability Act (28 U.S.C. 351 et seq.).

(v) Record of determinations. For each qualifying complaint transmitted by the appropriate public authority in a qualifying state, the Secretary of Commerce shall:

(A) maintain a record of the complainant who submitted such complaint;

(B) not later than 5 years after the date of this order and no less than every 5 years thereafter, contact the relevant element or elements of the Intelligence Community regarding whether information pertaining to the review of such complaint by the CLPO has been declassified and whether information pertaining to the review of any application for review submitted to the Data Protection Review Court has been declassified, including whether an element of the Intelligence Community filed an application for review with the Data Protection Review Court; and

(C) if informed that such information has been declassified, notify the complainant, through the appropriate public authority in a qualifying state, that information pertaining to the review of their complaint by the CLPO or to the review of any application for review submitted to the Data Protection Review Court may be available under applicable law.

(e) Annual review by PCLOB of redress process.

(i) Nature of review. Consistent with applicable law, the PCLOB is encouraged to conduct an annual review of the processing of qualifying complaints by the redress mechanism established by section 3 of this order, including whether the CLPO and the Data Protection Review Court processed qualifying complaints in a timely manner; whether the CLPO and the Data Protection Review Court are obtaining full access to necessary information; whether the CLPO and the Data Protection Review Court are operating consistent with this order; whether the safeguards established by section 2 of this order are properly considered in the processes of the CLPO and the Data Protection Review Court; and whether the elements of the Intelligence Community have fully complied with determinations made by the CLPO and the Data Protection Review Court.

(ii) Assistance. The Attorney General, the CLPO, and the elements of the Intelligence Community shall provide the PCLOB with access to information necessary to conduct the review described in subsection (e)(i) of this section, consistent with the protection of intelligence sources and methods.

(iii) Report and certification. Within 30 days of completing any review described in subsection (e)(i) of this section, the PCLOB is encouraged to:

(A) provide the President, the Attorney General, the Director, the heads of elements of the Intelligence Community, the CLPO, and the congressional intelligence committees with a classified report detailing the results of its review;

(B) release to the public an unclassified version of the report; and

(C) make an annual public certification as to whether the redress mechanism established pursuant to section 3 of this order is processing complaints consistent with this order.

(iv) Consideration of review. Within 180 days of receipt of any report by the PCLOB described in subsection (e)(iii)(A) of this section, the Attorney General, the Director, the heads of elements of the Intelligence Community, and the CLPO shall carefully consider and shall implement or otherwise address all recommendations contained in such report, consistent with applicable law.

(f) Designation of qualifying state.

    (i) To implement the redress mechanism established by section 3 of this order, the Attorney General is authorized to designate a country or regional economic integration organization as a qualifying state for purposes of the redress mechanism established pursuant to section 3 of this order, effective immediately or on a date specified by the Attorney General, if the Attorney General determines, in consultation with the Secretary of State, the Secretary of Commerce, and the Director, that:

        (A) the laws of the country, the regional economic integration organization, or the regional economic integration organization's member countries require appropriate safeguards in the conduct of signals intelligence activities for United States persons' personal information that is transferred from the United States to the territory of the country or a member country of the regional economic integration organization;

        (B) the country, the regional economic integration organization, or the regional economic integration organization's member countries of the regional economic integration organization permit, or are anticipated to permit, the transfer of personal information for commercial purposes between the territory of that country or those member countries and the territory of the United States; and

        (C) such designation would advance the national interests of the United States.

    (ii) The Attorney General may revoke or amend such a designation, effective immediately or on a date specified by the Attorney General, if the Attorney General determines, in consultation with the Secretary of State, the Secretary of Commerce, and the Director, that:

        (A) the country, the regional economic integration organization, or the regional economic integration organization's member countries do not provide appropriate safeguards in the conduct of signals intelligence activities for United States persons' personal information that is transferred from the United States to the territory of the country or to a member country of the regional economic integration organization;

        (B) the country, the regional economic integration organization, or the regional economic integration organization's member countries do not permit the transfer of personal information for

> commercial purposes between the territory of that country or those member countries and the territory of the United States; or
>
> (C) such designation is not in the national interests of the United States.

SEC. 4. DEFINITIONS. FOR PURPOSES OF THIS ORDER:

(a) 'Appropriate remediation' means lawful measures designed to fully redress an identified covered violation regarding a specific complainant and limited to measures designed to address that specific complainant's complaint, taking into account the ways that a violation of the kind identified have customarily been addressed. Such measures may include, depending on the specific covered violation at issue, curing through administrative measures violations found to have been procedural or technical errors relating to otherwise lawful access to or handling of data, terminating acquisition of data where collection is not lawfully authorized, deleting data that had been acquired without lawful authorization, deleting the results of inappropriately conducted queries of otherwise lawfully collected data, restricting access to lawfully collected data to those appropriately trained, or recalling intelligence reports containing data acquired without lawful authorization or that were otherwise disseminated in a manner inconsistent with United States law. Appropriate remediation shall be narrowly tailored to redress the covered violation and to minimize adverse impacts on the operations of the Intelligence Community and the national security of the United States.

(b) 'Bulk collection' means the authorized collection of large quantities of signals intelligence data that, due to technical or operational considerations, is acquired without the use of discriminants (for example, without the use of specific identifiers or selection terms).

(c) 'Counterintelligence' shall have the same meaning as it has in Executive Order 12333.

(d) 'Covered violation' means a violation that:

    (i) arises from signals intelligence activities conducted after the date of this order regarding data transferred to the United States from a qualifying state after the effective date of the Attorney General's designation for such state, as provided in section 3(f)(i) of this order;

    (ii) adversely affects the complainant's individual privacy and civil liberties interests; and

    (iii) violates one or more of the following:

        (A) the United States Constitution;

        (B) the applicable sections of FISA or any applicable FISC-approved procedures;

(C) Executive Order 12333 or any applicable agency procedures pursuant to Executive Order 12333;

(D) this order or any applicable agency policies and procedures issued or updated pursuant to this order (or the policies and procedures identified in section 2(c)(iv)(A) of this order before they are updated pursuant to section 2(c)(iv)(B) of this order);

(E) any successor statute, order, policies, or procedures to those identified in section 4(d)(iii)(B)-(D) of this order; or

(F) any other statute, order, policies, or procedures adopted after the date of this order that provides privacy and civil liberties safeguards with respect to United States signals intelligence activities within the scope of this order, as identified in a list published and updated by the Attorney General, in consultation with the Director of National Intelligence.

(e) 'Foreign intelligence' shall have the same meaning as it has in Executive Order 12333.

(f) 'Intelligence' shall have the same meaning as it has in Executive Order 12333.

(g) 'Intelligence Community' and 'elements of the Intelligence Community' shall have the same meaning as they have in Executive Order 12333.

(h) 'National security' shall have the same meaning as it has in Executive Order 13526 of December 29, 2009 (Classified National Security Information).

(i) 'Non-United States person' means a person who is not a United States person.

(j) 'Personnel of the United States or of its allies or partners' means any current or former member of the Armed Forces of the United States, any current or former official of the United States Government, and any other person currently or formerly employed by or working on behalf of the United States Government, as well as any current or former member of the military, current or former official, or other person currently or formerly employed by or working on behalf of an ally or partner.

(k) 'Qualifying complaint' means a complaint, submitted in writing, that:

(i) alleges a covered violation has occurred that pertains to personal information of or about the complainant, a natural person, reasonably believed to have been transferred to the United States from a qualifying state after the effective date of the Attorney General's designation for such state, as provided in section 3(f)(i) of this order;

(ii) includes the following basic information to enable a review: information that forms the basis for alleging that a covered violation has occurred, which need not demonstrate that the complainant's data has in fact been subject to United States signals intelligence activities; the nature of the relief sought; the specific means by which personal

317

information of or about the complainant was believed to have been transmitted to the United States; the identities of the United States Government entities believed to be involved in the alleged violation (if known); and any other measures the complainant pursued to obtain the relief requested and the response received through those other measures;

(iii) is not frivolous, vexatious, or made in bad faith;

(iv) is brought on behalf of the complainant, acting on that person's own behalf, and not as a representative of a governmental, nongovernmental, or intergovernmental organization; and

(v) is transmitted by the appropriate public authority in a qualifying state, after it has verified the identity of the complainant and that the complaint satisfies the conditions of section 5(k)(i)-(iv) of this order.

(l) 'Significant incident of non-compliance' shall mean a systemic or intentional failure to comply with a principle, policy, or procedure of applicable United States law that could impugn the reputation or integrity of an element of the Intelligence Community or otherwise call into question the propriety of an Intelligence Community activity, including in light of any significant impact on the privacy and civil liberties interests of the person or persons concerned.

(m) 'United States person' shall have the same meaning as it has in Executive Order 12333.

(n) 'Validated intelligence priority' shall mean, for most United States signals intelligence collection activities, a priority validated under the process described in section 2(b)(iii) of this order; or, in narrow circumstances (for example, when such process cannot be carried out because of a need to address a new or evolving intelligence requirement), shall mean a priority set by the President or the head of an element of the Intelligence Community in accordance with the criteria described in section 2(b)(iii)(A)(1)-(3) of this order to the extent feasible.

(o) 'Weapons of mass destruction' shall have the same meaning as it has in Executive Order 13526.

SEC. 5. GENERAL PROVISIONS.

(a) Nothing in this order shall be construed to impair or otherwise affect:

(i) the authority granted by law to an executive department, agency, or the head thereof; or

(ii) the functions of the Director of the Office of Management and Budget relating to budgetary, administrative, or legislative proposals.

(b) This order shall be implemented consistent with applicable law, including orders of and procedures approved by the FISC, and subject to the availability of appropriations.

(c) Nothing in this order precludes the application of more privacy-protective safeguards for United States signals intelligence activities that would apply in the absence of this order. In the case of any conflict between this order and other applicable law, the more privacy-protective safeguards shall govern the conduct of signals intelligence activities, to the maximum extent allowed by law.

(d) Nothing in this order prohibits elements of the Intelligence Community from disseminating information relating to a crime for law enforcement purposes; disseminating warnings of threats of killing, serious bodily injury, or kidnapping; disseminating cyber threat, incident, or intrusion response information; notifying victims or warning potential victims of crime; or complying with dissemination obligations required by statute, treaty, or court order, including orders of and procedures approved by the FISC or other court orders.

(e) The collection, retention, and dissemination of information concerning United States persons is governed by multiple legal and policy requirements, such as those required by FISA and Executive Order 12333. This order is not intended to alter the rules applicable to United States persons adopted pursuant to FISA, Executive Order 12333, or other applicable law.

(f) This order shall apply to signals intelligence activities consistent with the scope of PPD-28's application to such activities prior to PPD-28's partial revocation by the national security memorandum issued concurrently with this order. To implement this subsection, the head of each agency containing an element of the Intelligence Community, in consultation with the Attorney General and the Director, is hereby delegated the authority to issue guidance, which may be classified, as appropriate, as to the scope of application of this order with respect to the element or elements of the Intelligence Community within their agency. The CLPO and the Data Protection Review Court, in carrying out the functions assigned to it under this order, shall treat such guidance as authoritative and binding.

(g) Nothing in this order confers authority to declassify or disclose classified national security information except as authorized pursuant to Executive Order 13526 or any successor order. Consistent with the requirements of Executive Order 13526, the CLPO, the Data Protection Review Court, and the special advocates shall not have authority to declassify classified national security information, nor shall they disclose any classified or otherwise privileged or protected information except to authorized and appropriately cleared individuals who have a need to know the information.

(h) This order creates an entitlement to submit qualifying complaints to the CLPO and to obtain review of the CLPO's decisions by the Data Protection Review Court in accordance with the redress mechanism established in section 3 of this order. This order is not intended to, and does not, create any other entitlement, right, or benefit, substantive or procedural, enforceable at law or in equity by any party against the United States, its departments, agencies, or entities, its officers, employees, or agents, or any other person.

This order is not intended to, and does not, modify the availability or scope of any judicial review of the decisions rendered through the redress mechanism, which is governed by existing law.

JOSEPH R. BIDEN JR.

THE WHITE HOUSE,

October 7, 2022.

Index

[all references are to paragraph number]